THE TROJANS AND
THEIR NEIGHBOURS

In *The Trojans and their Neighbours* the secrets of Troy – one of the most iconic cities in ancient history – are unearthed. Once the lost site of the mythological battle which unfolded in Homer's *Iliad*, the discovery of ancient Troy at Hislarlık has revealed a living, breathing city with a history spanning 4,000 years.

Starting with an account of Troy's part in the *Iliad* and the question of the historicity of the Trojan War, Trevor Bryce shows how the recently discovered Hittite texts illuminate the question that has fascinated scholars and travellers since the Renaissance.

For the first time, Troy's neighbouring communities and allies, for example the Lycians, are brought into the analysis and given equal weight. Encompassing the very latest research, the city and its inhabitants are placed in historical context with their neighbours and contemporaries to form a complete and vivid view of life within the Trojan walls and beyond, from its beginning in *c*.3000 BC to its decline and obscurity in the Byzantine period. Documented here are the archaeological watershed discoveries from the Victorian era to the present that reveal, through Troy's nine levels, the story of a metropolis punctuated by signs of economic prosperity, natural disaster and war.

Trevor Bryce is an Honorary Research Consultant at the University of Queensland and Fellow of the Australian Academy of the Humanities. He is the author of numerous works on the ancient Near East. His most recent publications are *The Kingdom of the Hittites* (1998), *Life and Society in the Hittite World* (2002) and *Letters of the Great Kings of the Ancient Near East* (Routledge, 2003).

THE TROJANS
AND THEIR
NEIGHBOURS

Trevor Bryce

Routledge
Taylor & Francis Group

LONDON AND NEW YORK

First published 2006
by Routledge
2 Park Square, Milton Park, Abingdon, Oxon OX14 4RN

Simultaneously published in the USA and Canada
by Routledge
270 Madison Ave, New York, NY 10016

Routledge is an imprint of the Taylor & Francis Group

Typeset in Garamond 3 by
Florence Production Ltd, Stoodleigh, Devon
Printed and bound in Great Britain by
TJ International Ltd, Padstow, Cornwall

British Library Cataloguing in Publication Data
A catalogue record for this book is available from the British Library

Library of Congress Cataloging in Publication Data
Bryce, Trevor, 1940–
The Trojans and their neighbours: an introduction/Trevor Bryce.
p. cm.
Includes bibliographical references and index.
1. Troy (Extinct city) – History.   2. Middle East –
History – To 622.   I. Title.
DF221.T8B79 2005
939′.21–dc22   2005003604

ISBN10: 0–415–34959–1 (hbk)
ISBN10: 0–415–34955–9 (pbk)
ISBN13: 9–78–0–415–34959–8 (hbk)
ISBN13: 9–78–0–415–34955–0 (pbk)

CONTENTS

114777

MAPS AND FIGURES

MAPS

FIGURES

TIME LINE	TROY	ANATOLIA	MESOPOTAMIA	EGYPT	GREECE	ROME
3000	I (3000–2500)	Early Bronze Age communities	Sumerian civilisation (2900–2334)	Early Dynastic period	Early Helladic settlements (to 2300)	
2500	II (2500–2300)	Early Bronze Age kingdoms	Akkadian Empire (2334–2193)	Old Kingdom (2686–2125)		
2000	III–IV (2300–1700)	Assyrian Colony Period (20th–18th centuries)	Ur III Dynasty (2112–2004) Assyrian Old Kingdom (20th–18th centuries)		Arrival of proto-Greeks (c. 2100)	
			Babylonian Old Kingdom (1750–1595)	Middle Kingdom (2055–1650)	Middle Helladic (1900–c. 1600)	
1500	VI (1700–1280)	Hittite Kingdom (1680–1180)	Kassite Babylonia (16th–12th		Mycenean period	

Frontispiece Comparative chronologies (most dates are approximate)

VIIa (1260–1180) VIIb (1180–1050)	Phrygian Kingdom → 8th century	Kingdom (14th–11th centuries)	(1550–1069)?	Migrations to Anatolia	Rome founded (753) Kings
			Third Intermediate and Late period (1069–323)	Archaic period (8th–6th centuries)	
VIII (700–85)	Lydian Kingdom 7th–mid-6th centuries	Assyrian New Kingdom (911–630)			Republican period (c. 509–27)
		Chaldean Empire (630–540)		Classical period (479–323)	
	Persian domination (540–334)	Persian domination (540–334)			
	Alexander and Heirs (334–190)	Alexander and Heirs (334–129)	Ptolemaic period (323–31)	Hellenistic period (323–31)	
IX (85 BC–5th century AD)	Roman domination (190 BC–4th century AD)	Parthian domination (129 BC–2nd century AD)			Imperial period (27 BC–4th century AD →)
	Byzantine period (4th century AD →)	Byzantine period (4th century AD →)	Byzantine period (4th century AD →)	Byzantine period (4th century AD →)	Byzantine period (4th century AD →)

1000

500

0

ACKNOWLEDGEMENTS

τῷ Ὁμήρῳ τῷ ἀρίστῳ καὶ θειοτάτῳ τῶν ποιητῶν

My sincere thanks are due to Dr Michael Apthorp for his advice and comments on a number of Homeric matters; to Dr Chris Mee for his advice on Aegean matters; to Professor David Hawkins, for his photograph of the Karabel monument and permission to use his reproductions of several hieroglyphic inscriptions; to Dr Geoff Tully for his artwork; to the Troja Projekt, University of Tübingen, for permission to use its photograph of the seal found at Hisarlık; and to the School of History, Philosophy, Religion and Classics, University of Queensland, for its most valuable support during the book's preparation.

INTRODUCTION

It is hardly coincidence that the release of the Hollywood blockbuster *Troy* has been followed by a fresh crop of television programmes, books and articles on the Trojan War. Yet there is no need of a Brad Pitt to rekindle interest in one of the greatest stories ever told. Indeed, ever since Homer first recited his poem about Troy's fall, almost 3,000 years ago, there has seldom been a time when the poem's characters and events have not captured popular imagination and given rise to a multitude of spin-offs in art, literature and theatrical productions and, more recently on cinema and television screens.

But the focus of these treatments has been almost invariably a very narrow one. Troy was the city[1] of King Priam and his son Hector.[2] Troy was the city of the so-called Trojan horse (though the horse plays no part in Homer's *Iliad*), the city besieged by an alliance of Greek forces who were led by Agamemnon and whose star performer was Achilles. The war between the Greeks and the Trojans was fought over the abduction or seduction of the Spartan queen Helen by the Trojan prince Paris. Greek tradition assigned a period of ten years to the war. The *Iliad* encompasses only a few weeks of it near its end, and Hollywood reduces the entire conflict to a few days. Yet even if we allow that the war did last for ten years — and it has to be said that Hollywood's drastic reduction of the time frame is much more historically plausible than Greek tradition — this represents only a small fraction of the relevant phase of Troy's history. Scholars now generally agree that Troy Level VI most closely represents the city of the Trojan War. Given that this city lasted more than 400 years, the period dealt with in Greek tradition occupies less than 10 per cent – very likely a great deal less – of its entire lifespan.

But the sixth city is only one of nine major phases in the history of the site. The first phase began around 3000 BC, the ninth ended around the middle of the first millennium AD. Even after this, Troy, now called Ilium, did not entirely disappear, and as late as the tenth century it *may* have been the seat of a bishopric. That is to say, the history of the site extends over 4,000 years. Yet in popular thought Troy will forever be the city of the Trojan War. Understandably so, for the war is quite simply the site's meal ticket. As in ancient Greek and Roman times, Troy continues to attract large numbers of visitors – as well, today, as substantial funding for its ongoing excavations. Yet it is an unprepossessing site, surprisingly small in the eyes of many first-time visitors who, on paying their entrance fee find themselves confronted with a confusing jumble of walls, fragmentary building foundations and broken pavements, all within an area little bigger than a football field. Deprive it of its legendary associations and it would very likely lose its financial backers and warrant barely a single star in a tourist guidebook.

But there really is much more to Troy than a war which for all its renown may never have taken place. And one of the main purposes of this book is to give a brief survey of the city's history from its first to its last days. There is another purpose as well. When Routledge's editor Richard Stoneman invited me to write a book about Troy, he suggested that the emphasis should be as much on Troy's neighbours as on the Trojans themselves. Hence the title. At that time we both expressed surprise at the dearth of recent books on Troy. Since then I became aware that Professor Latacz's *Troia und Homer* was soon to appear in a revised English version, and I have subsequently heard of several other books on Troy that are currently in preparation. To the best of my knowledge, the focus of all these publications will be on Troy in the Late Bronze Age.

This period also figures fairly prominently in the pages that follow, though the book's overall scope and approach is rather different. Taking on board Richard Stoneman's suggestion, I have given almost as much emphasis to Troy's neighbours as to the Trojans themselves. The word 'neighbours' I have defined in a chronological as well as in a geographical sense. Thus, at any particular stage in Troy's history, I will refer not only to Troy's geographically proximate neighbours, but also to its contemporaries and near contemporaries further afield – as far afield as Egypt and Mesopotamia. Of course, within the book's 70,000 word limit, it will be impossible to give more than outline surveys of other peoples and places. But brief though these surveys must be, they will, I hope, provide sufficient context for us to address several important questions about Troy: How did Troy compare with its neighbours – culturally, commercially, politically and militarily? What relations did it have with other parts of the contemporary Aegean and Near Eastern worlds? Where did it rank within the hierarchy of the cities and kingdoms of these worlds? Legendary tradition gives the impression that the Trojan War was something like a superhuman clash between Titans. Hollywood represents the war as a conflict between the two mightiest nations on earth. How far does the real Troy measure up to or fall short of these legendary and screen images? To judge from reports of the most recent excavations at Troy, we now have a much better picture of the size and nature of the site as a whole, and can thus make more informed comparisons with other cities and kingdoms that existed during Troy's various ages.

There is a further question. Who *were* the Trojans? We can give a simple response. The Trojans were whoever happened to be living in Troy at any given time. It really depends on what period we're talking about. One could give the same response to the question, Who were the inhabitants of Byzantium/Constantinople/Istanbul? But even if we were to specify a particular period of time for our question, we would still find that cities like Troy and Constantinople had a broad mix of ethnic groups in their populations. There was no such thing as a typical Trojan, or a typical Constantinopolitan. This adds a further dimension to our question. In attempting to identify who the Trojans were, we have to consider which groups of people were likely to have been living in the city at any stated time in its history. There may well have been a predominant ethnic group and a predominant language spoken in the city at a particular time – perhaps Luwian in the Late Bronze Age and Greek in the first millennium BC. But Troy's culture and civilization were almost certainly a blend of a number of different elements, some filtering down from earlier phases in its existence, some the result of cultural and commercial contacts with the wider world, some the result of the intermixture of the various ethnic groups that made up its population. We cannot provide even a tentative answer to our question without considering the whole spectrum of Trojan history and the wider context of the world to which Troy belonged.

There is another reason for writing this book. Scholarly and popular fascination with Homer's tale has generated a plethora of theories on just about anything and everything to do with Troy and the Trojan War. Many of the theories are ingenious and eloquently argued and have done much to enliven and maintain interest in the topic. Many have been proposed by very reputable scholars, and may well be right. But it is often difficult, particularly for the general reader, to distinguish where hard fact and attractive but unprovable theory part company. Repeat an unsubstantiated theory often enough and persuasively enough, and it will eventually acquire the status of 'established fact'. But for the purposes of serious study, it is important to identify quite clearly what we know about Troy as a matter of fact, what is probable but lacks conclusive proof, and what is pure speculation. There has been a tendency in recent scholarship to drift increasingly into the realms of the last of these. A sober re-evaluation of what our evidence actually tells us will not be untimely.

One final comment. It has become almost de rigueur for books on Troy to have at least a chapter or two devoted to the question of whether or not there really was a Trojan War. The new publications will no doubt engage in fresh attempts to answer this question. Indeed it would be perverse to write a book about Troy and refuse to address it. Clearly that is what the reader expects, no matter how many times the question has been dealt with in the past. In concluding my account with my own reflections on the matter, I have acknowledged this expectation. But I do believe we have reached the stage where nothing more can usefully be said about a possible historical basis for Homer's tale – at least until fresh evidence comes to light. Perhaps we can revisit the whole question if and when archaeologists do succeed in unearthing on the site of Troy proof positive of a war such as Homer describes. But one would be well advised not to hold one's breath.

Trevor Bryce
November, 2004

1

THE POET AND THE TRADITION

IN THE BEGINNING

The trouble all began with a wedding. Thetis, a sea nymph, had rejected the amorous advances of Zeus and, as punishment, the father of the gods condemned her to marry a mere mortal, a prince called Peleus from the island of Aegina. To show himself worthy of his divine bride, Peleus had first to defeat her in a wrestling contest, a task which she made more difficult by changing into different shapes during the contest, including fire, water, wind, a lion, a tiger, a snake and various other members of the animal kingdom. Peleus eventually triumphed, plans for the wedding proceeded, and invitations were sent out. It was a distinguished guest list, headed by the gods themselves. Unfortunately the goddess Eris, a name meaning 'Strife', was also present at the celebrations. According to a late tradition, she was not an invited guest but a gatecrasher, and either out of pique at being left off the official guest list, or simply because it was her nature to behave in this way, she sought to disrupt the festivities. With the object of provoking a squabble amongst the female guests, she threw into their midst a golden apple inscribed 'To the Fairest'. Immediately, three goddesses stepped forward to claim the prize: Hera, wife of Zeus; Athena, goddess of war and wisdom (amongst other things); and Aphrodite, goddess of love.

To their credit, none of the trio wished to spoil the happy couple's special day. They agreed to resolve the matter with a beauty contest – but at another time and in another place. Mount Ida in north-western Anatolia and not far from Troy was chosen as the venue for the contest, and Alexander Paris, second son of the Trojan king

Priam was appointed as its judge. Sadly, notions of fair play were not conspicuous amongst the goddesses' qualities and, prior to the judging, each of them secretly approached Paris and attempted to suborn him: Hera promised him rule over all Asia and great wealth if he awarded the contest to her; Athena declared she would endow him with great wisdom and military prowess; Aphrodite offered him the most beautiful woman in the world as his wife. Paris found the third of these offers by far the most appealing (a typical example, some later Greek commentators would say, of Trojan decadence), and so he declared Aphrodite the winner.

The problem with Aphrodite's offer was that the world's most beautiful woman, Helen, was already married – to Menelaus, King of Sparta. But this, the goddess assured Paris, was a mere technicality and would prove no major obstacle. With her help and guidance, the Trojan prince secured an invitation to Sparta where he was regally entertained by Menelaus, and then repaid his host's hospitality by seducing his wife and persuading her to elope with him back to Troy. That created a furore in the Greek world. Prior to her marriage, Helen had been courted by a number of royal suitors, including Menelaus' brother Agamemnon. The suitors made a pact that irrespective of where Helen's choice finally settled, the others would protect her for the rest of their lives. They were now honour-bound to seek her out and restore her to her home in Sparta, whether or not she had left it willingly in the first place. (There was a later tradition that she had been raped and forcibly abducted by Paris.) Hence the genesis of the Greek expedition against Troy.

Agamemnon, King of Mycenae and indisputably the most powerful Greek ruler of the time, sent out a call for support through the whole of Greece. Some 164 kingdoms and communities responded, and an armada of 1,186 ships was mustered under Agamemnon's overall command. The assembly point for this vast fleet was the harbour of Aulis on the coast of Boeotia. But right from the outset there was a problem, for Agamemnon had provoked the wrath of the goddess Artemis, who becalmed the fleet and refused winds to take it to Troy until its commander had sacrificed his daughter Iphigeneia. The sacrifice was duly carried out, and fresh winds carried the fleet across the wine-dark sea to Troy on Anatolia's north-west coast. For Agamemnon there would be a day of reckoning for the killing of his daughter. But that was some years in the future.

The Greeks anchored their fleet in a large bay and set up their camp on the edge of the plain outside Troy's massively fortified citadel. Thereupon began a ten-year investment of the city. It was punctuated by many sorties of Trojan warriors against the Greek besiegers and much waxing and waning of the military fortunes of both sides in the contests fought by the heroes on Troy's increasingly blood-drenched plain. The Greeks' repeated attempts to breach the city's defences ended in failure until finally one of them, Odysseus, hit upon the ruse of the wooden horse, which he persuaded his comrades-in-arms to build. Upon completing it, they tricked the Trojans into thinking that they were abandoning the siege and returning to their own lands. The massive equine edifice which they were leaving behind was, they claimed, intended to expiate a crime they had committed in removing a sacred statue called the Palladium from the citadel of Troy. But instead of returning home, the Greeks merely withdrew their fleet to the nearby island of Tenedos, anchoring well out of sight of Troy.

The Trojans streamed forth onto the plain, and by one means or another were induced to drag the horse up into their citadel as a thank-offering to Athena, breaking down part of the fortifications to do so. Then they abandoned themselves to drunken revelry to celebrate their apparent victory. In the midst of the festivities, the Greeks who had been concealed in the horse's belly quietly let themselves out through a trapdoor and lit pre-arranged signal fires to summon back the fleet. This was the last act in the saga. The Greek forces poured through the breach in the fortifications and created mayhem in the now defenceless city. All its inhabitants were slaughtered or taken prisoner for selling into slavery, and the city itself was plundered and put to the torch.

THE STORY OF THE *ILIAD*

So much for the tale of Troy, a tale forever associated with the name of one man above all others – an epic poet called Homer who lived on or close by Anatolia's western coast, in the region called Ionia in the first millennium BC. The poetic narrative, which he composed and which we know as the *Iliad*, was first recited to audiences at the very dawn of Greek literature, probably in the second half of the eighth century BC. The *Iliad* is in fact our chief source for the most widely known narrative tradition in the whole of Western literature. From the time of its composition, it has served as a major source of inspiration for successive generations of artists, poets, playwrights, composers of operas and novelists, to say nothing of an ever-increasing cohort of film producers for both television and cinema.

Yet how much of all this can we really attribute to Homer? A great deal of the story we have outlined above makes no appearance at all in the *Iliad*, or at best is referred to only in passing. And far from covering the entire ten-year period of the war, the *Iliad* extends over no more than a few weeks – fifty-one days to be precise – at the very end of the war. Indeed, most of the account, from Books 2 to 22, is confined to just six days (four days of fighting separated by two days of truce). Occasionally the poet inserts references to earlier episodes, as far back as the seduction which sparked the whole thing off (though he mentions this only obliquely), and subsequently the mustering of the Greek fleet in preparation for the assault upon the seducer's homeland. But these are mere passing reminders of the overall context in which the *Iliad* is set. What is more, Homer's story stops short of the climactic event, the actual sack of Troy. To be sure, there are a number of times throughout the poem, especially as it approaches its end, when Troy's destruction is clearly foreshadowed. We are left in no doubt that the city's fate is irrevocably sealed. But the *Iliad* itself is not about the fall of Troy. And for that matter there is not even one mention, in almost 16,000 lines of verse, of what has long and widely been regarded as the war's defining symbol – the Trojan horse.

The narrative of the poem arises out of a dispute that erupted between Agamemnon, Commander-in-Chief of the Greek forces, and Achilles, son of Peleus and Thetis. Of all the Greek heroes at Troy, Achilles is by far the most accomplished and the most feared by the Trojans. The cause of his dispute with Agamemnon seems on the surface a trivial one. During a raiding expedition, the Greeks have seized Chryseis, daughter of a priest of Apollo called Chryses, and have presented her to Agamemnon as his share of the spoils brought back from the raid. When Chryses approaches Agamemnon to buy back his daughter, the Greek commander rudely rejects him. Apollo is outraged and responds by inflicting a devastating plague upon the Greek camp. The plague rages unabated until the prophet

Calchas informs an assembly of the Greek forces summoned by Achilles that the god's anger will only be appeased if Agamemnon gives up his prize.

Grudgingly Agamemnon agrees and demands that Achilles' favourite slave-girl Briseis, awarded to Achilles as a booty-prize, be surrendered to him by way of compensation. Achilles has no option but to hand her over, but he is furious at losing her to Agamemnon and promptly withdraws his services from the Greek forces, retires into his tent and refuses to take any further part in the action until his honour is satisfied. He also begs his mother Thetis to persuade Zeus (who owes her a favour) to turn the conflict the Trojans' way so that his fellow Greeks will realize how essential he is to their victory and will make every effort to give him the satisfaction he demands. Zeus does as he is asked. Things go very badly for the Greeks. Under the leadership of King Priam's eldest son, Hector, the Trojans drive the enemy back to their beached ships, repeatedly inflicting heavy casualties upon them. Desperate attempts are made to bring Achilles back into the battle line. To no avail. Agamemnon's offers of rich gifts and even the offer of the hand of

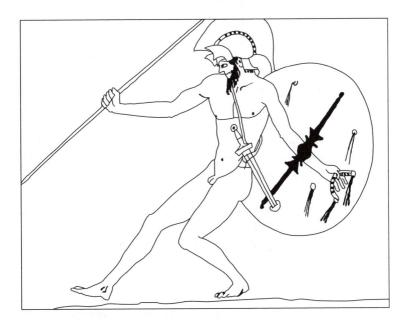

Figure 1.1 Hector, son of Priam.

his daughter in marriage are spurned by the sulking hero. Patroclus too, Achilles' closest and dearest companion, fails to make any significant impact on his friend, though Achilles relents so far as to allow Patroclus to lead his troops and wear his armour into battle.

Ironically and tragically, this provides the catalyst for the return of Achilles. After inflicting much devastation on the Trojan ranks, Patroclus is finally brought down by Hector, with the assistance of Apollo, and killed and stripped of Achilles' armour. In his grief and with his fury now directed against Hector, Achilles is reconciled with Agamemnon and returns to the fray, wearing a new set of armour wrought by the god Hephaestus. Many Trojans fall victim to Achilles, before the Greek superwarrior finally comes face to face with his arch-enemy Hector. Fate has decreed that Hector should die at Achilles' hands, and so it comes to pass. After slaughtering the Trojan prince, Achilles ties his body to his chariot and drags it to his tent. He then turns his attention to the burial of his beloved Patroclus and organizes funeral games in his honour. Following these games, Achilles receives a visit from King Priam who begs for the return of his son's body. Realizing that he himself must soon die and conscious that he too will leave behind a father who will grieve for him, Achilles takes pity on his aged adversary and hands back to him his son's body. With the burial of Hector, the *Iliad* comes to an end. The fall of Troy is imminent. But it has yet to occur.

As the *Iliad*'s opening words make clear, the Wrath of Achilles is Homer's major theme: 'Sing, o goddess, of the wrath of Achilles, Peleus' son'. Given the poem's monumental length and relatively narrow compass, its author has much scope for presenting detailed pictures of the chief participants in the conflict; on the Greek side: Achilles, Agamemnon, Patroclus, the two Ajaxes, Diomedes; on the Trojan side: Hector, Priam, Paris, Aeneas, Sarpedon; as well as brief sketches of a host of minor participants. There is a particular focus on heroic behaviour in the face of death, on the question of how the hero so passionately devoted to life reacts to the certainty and often the imminence of his own death. This is a prospect of which Achilles is particularly conscious, given the sure knowledge that his life will, of his own choosing, be a short and glorious rather than a long and undistinguished one.

An eighth-century poet could draw on a vast store of oral tradition in composing an account of the Trojan War, and there must have been many bards in the Greek world at this time who preserved, presented and handed on stories that had arisen out of the tradition. Homer himself consciously sought to avoid yet another retelling of already widely known tales. The brief allusions he makes to the events that preceded and followed his narrative make quite clear that the prequels and sequels to his tale were firmly established in the repertoire of stories sung and recited to audiences in the early centuries of the first millennium.

THE EPIC CYCLE

Traces of this repertoire are preserved in fragmentary remains of a group of poems which post-date the *Iliad*'s composition (though some of them are mistakenly attributed to Homer in ancient sources) but are probably no later than the seventh or early sixth century. The group belonged to what is commonly referred to as the epic cycle, which dealt with the legendary wars fought against both Thebes and Troy. Those dealing with the former (considered the earlier) are now completely lost. Fragments of the latter have, however, survived, and include:

(a) the *Cypria*, a poem originally in eleven books, that begins with the lead-up to the war – including the wedding of Peleus and Thetis, the beauty contest judged by Paris and the seduction of Helen – and then narrates the first part of the war, perhaps up to the point where the *Iliad* begins;

(b) the *Little Iliad*, which tells the story of the Trojan horse and the breach of Troy's defences by the Greeks;

(c) the *Iliu Persis* ('Sack of Troy') which tells of the Trojan priest Laocoon's unheeded warnings to his fellow Trojans about the horse, and then describes the sack of the city by the Greeks and their departure after Troy's fall;

(d) the *Nostoi* ('Homecomings') which narrates the journeys home by several of the Greek leaders, including Agamemnon and Menelaus, and what happens when they arrive there.

The various poems making up the epic cycle were eventually organized into a continuous narrative of myth and legend, seasoned here and there with a dash of genuine history, from the world's beginning to the end of the heroic age. Undoubtedly they reflect surviving elements of the large body of folk tradition and oral narrative poetry in circulation in Homer's own time and probably for many generations before it. From the remains of the epic cycle as well as from the Homeric compositions and other sources, we can reconstruct more or less completely the Trojan War tradition as represented in Greek and Roman art and literature from its alleged first causes, through the various stages of the conflict itself, to the subsequent travels and homecomings of several of its main participants. The post-war adventures of the Greek hero Odysseus as told in the *Odyssey*, the second great epic attributed to Homer, belong to this last category. So too does the homecoming of the ill-fated Agamemnon, whose assassination by his wife Clytemnestra and her lover Aegisthus furnished Greek art and literature with one of its favourite themes.

All this serves to emphasize how highly selective Homer was in his treatment of the tradition. One might have supposed that in limiting his narrative to the very last days of an alleged ten-year conflict, the Greek poet's intention was to focus specifically on the conflict's final stage – the triumph of the Greek forces and the destruction of Troy. After all, was not Homer a Greek poet singing his tale to a Greek audience, whose ancestors were the sworn enemies of Troy? For such an audience would not the destruction of Troy have been a fitting climax to the poet's story? Yet Homer stops short of the expected climax. Though Achilles has triumphed over his arch-enemy, and Troy's fall is now imminent, the poem does not describe its fall. In fact it ends on a sad and solemn note. After venting his rage for a time on Hector's corpse, Achilles' wrath fades. Aware that he too must soon die, aware that his father, like Hector's father, will be consumed with grief at his death, his wrath gives way to pity for the aged Priam who has come to him to beg for the return of Hector's body. Achilles agrees, and with this gesture the poem draws to a close: 'Thus they went about the burial of Hector, tamer of horses.' Artistically, this is an appropriate ending. We have come full circle. The poem begins with an act of pitilessness: a king, Agamemnon, rejects the plea of an old man, Chryses, for the return of his daughter. It is this which sets in motion the sequence of events that leads ultimately to the final contest between the story's protagonists: Greek Achilles and Trojan Hector. The poem ends with an act of pity: the victor, Achilles, accedes to the plea of an old man, Priam, for the return of his son, in this case for burial.

Was this really the ending that the poet's audience would have expected, or appreciated? That raises the question of who Homer's audience was. Which also raises the question of who Homer himself was.

THE COMPOSER AND THE COMPOSITION

To deal with the second question first, the most widely held view is that our poet lived in the eighth or early seventh century, on or near Asia Minor's western coast in the region first settled by Ionian Greek colonists in the twelfth and eleventh centuries BC. The island of Chios and the city of Smyrna (modern Izmir) are favoured locations for his birthplace. (They are in fact only two of the seven places proposed by the ancient Greeks themselves.[1]) But scholarly conclusions about this are purely assumption and inference, based on a range of climatological, topographical, linguistic and chronological considerations. The oft-quoted Homeric simile that refers to storm winds blowing in a southerly and easterly direction across the Aegean Sea from Thrace, the poet's apparently first-hand knowledge of western Anatolia's coastal fringe, especially around Miletus and the Troad region in the north-west, and the predominantly Ionic dialect of the epic compositions are held to be significant pointers to Homer's place of origin. Further, what appear to be contemporary allusions within the poems suggest a date of composition no earlier than the second half of the eighth century and no later than the first decades of the seventh.[2]

But none of this tells us anything about the poet himself. There is just one possible piece of personal information about him: he was allegedly blind. This long and widely held belief is based primarily on a reference to the poet's affliction in the well-known *Hymn to Apollo*,[3] a poem once wrongly attributed to Homer himself. However, blindness seems to have been a disability suffered by a number of early Greek poets. Which is cause for some suspicion. There is something strangely appealing about the notion of a blind bard – to the point, perhaps, where the disability came to be regarded as a kind of generic affliction once suffered by practitioners of the bardic arts in general.[4] But there is no reason to believe that it was a *genuine* occupational hazard of the profession! We should be wary about giving too much weight to the one single scrap of personal information we have about Homer.

Indeed the poet's very existence has been called into question by a number of scholars, who regard the 'blind' Ionian as a process rather than a person. 'It seems fairly clear', comments Professor Vermeule, 'that no one used the name "Homer" to refer to an individual person until, c. 500 B.C., Xenophanes and Heraclitus created him to find fault with him.'[5] In fact our earliest reference to Homer occurs already in the seventh century, when the elegiac poet Callinus wrongly attributed to him authorship of the *Thebaid*, the lost epic on the legendary war against Thebes. But even if we are confident that there really was an eighth-century bard called Homer, are we justified in crediting him with the composition of the *Iliad* in the form in which we know it today? Or was this composition very largely the product of a group of poets or editors who patched together various individual lays and folk tales about the Trojan War to form a single connected narrative? That view was already expressed in the first century AD by the Jewish author Josephus, who claimed that the epics were not written down by Homer but were creations of a later period, put together from Homer's orally transmitted poems.[6] So too many scholars, the so-called 'Analysts', have argued in more recent times, taking their lead from an eighteenth- to nineteenth-century German scholar called Friedrich Wolf.

One of the factors which long influenced this line of thinking was the sheer size of the epic poems: 15,693 lines of verse for the *Iliad* and some 12,000 lines for the *Odyssey*. The belief that the epics originated as oral compositions was, and still is, widely held. But without the aid of writing, was any human being capable of such a monumental achievement of composition, particularly given the strict demands of the Greek epic metre? This was the hexameter, described by Tennyson in 'To Virgil' as 'the stateliest measure ever moulded by the lips of man', in which the poet could choose between only two possibilities, a spondee (two long syllables) and a dactyl (a long followed by two short syllables), for each of its six feet. In fact, Professor Latacz and others believe that the hexameter was a metre used in Greek oral poetry by the fifteenth century at the latest.[7] Researches into oral poetry, like those conducted by Milman

Figure 1.2 Homer, the 'blind' bard, second century BC, sculptor unknown, in the National Museum of Archaeology, Naples.

Parry and his assistant Albert Lord in the southern Balkans, have demonstrated that such a feat is indeed possible, that illiterate tellers of tales (like the *guslari* who performed for Parry and Lord) are indeed capable of what to us are prodigious feats of memory, reciting epic sagas for many hours, perhaps over several days – and often doing so within the confines of strict metrical patterns.

Of course the use of verse as a narrative medium greatly facilitates the process of memorizing a long tale or series of tales – just as a child, before learning to read and write, has little trouble in committing to memory a large repertoire of nursery rhymes. The process of oral composition is greatly assisted when the poet has at his disposal a stock of formulaic phrases and passages, already packaged in the appropriate metrical form, which he can insert at suitable places within his poem. Undoubtedly the composer of the Homeric epics drew heavily upon a wide range of formulaic expressions and stock epithets that he had inherited from a bardic tradition extending back many generations before his own time. Indeed, some scholars have gone so far as to suggest that almost 90 per cent of the material in the *Iliad* and the *Odyssey* consists of formulaic elements taken over from earlier oral tradition. That would of course substantially detract from the epics' standing as works of great creative genius.

Certainly lines and groups of lines are frequently repeated throughout the epics (one line in eight is repeated at least once), and stock epithets, phrases and sentences occur in virtually every passage. As often as not, the formulaic expressions appear to have little function beyond helping to complete a particular line or passage with a ready-made metrical unit, which in terms of its content has no particular relevance to the passage itself. The labels regularly attached to the names of the heroes serve to illustrate this. From the wide range of epithets associated (for example) with the Greek heroes Odysseus and Achilles, the one which the poet uses on each occasion is generally determined not by what the hero is actually doing at the time but by what best fulfils the requirements of the metre at that point in the poem. Thus Odysseus is called 'much-enduring' or 'a man of many counsels' in contexts where neither of these qualities is on display or called for, and Achilles is labelled 'fleet of foot' even when he is doing nothing more than sulking in his tent after having totally withdrawn from any further participation in the war.[8] But that is all part and parcel of the venerable oral tradition of which the Homeric epics represent an end product. At least in their early stages the epics must have involved a good deal of improvisation, supported by an extensive repertoire of ready-made formulas that helped ensure that the poem's metre and momentum were maintained while enabling the poet to focus his attention on advancing his story. No two performances would have been quite the same. An accomplished jazz pianist operates in much the same way.

Yet it would be wrong to regard constantly repeated formulaic phrases and passages as a shortcoming of early Greek narrative poetry. On the contrary, they are an important integral part of it, not merely accepted but indeed expected by those to whom Homer's poems were first recited. And of course this particular feature of the storyteller's technique is by no means confined to Homeric epic. One of my granddaughter's favourite stories consists almost entirely of a formula of words repeated over and over again, with the storyline progressing only a little at a time between repetitions. Yet if in telling the story I ever attempt to shortcut the process and leave out some of the repetitious bits, my granddaughter becomes extremely cross. The story is incomplete if not told in its entirety, all repetitions included.

There are also occasions when a formulaic phrase appears to have been used not merely as a standard element in the storyteller's stock-in-trade, or for metrical convenience, or to help fill a gap in the narrative. Rather, it has been deliberately chosen for its poetic effectiveness within a particular passage. So, too, there are a number of passages in which an epithet applied to a Greek hero is directly relevant to the context in which it is used, and has been selected primarily for this reason. The Homeric poems almost certainly reflect conscious creative activity by a single artist – or two such artists if we allow for the possibility that the *Iliad* and the *Odyssey* had different authors. To be sure, we can point to inconsistencies in detail in each poem. Thus iron is sometimes treated as a rare and precious metal, as it was in the Bronze Age, sometimes as a commodity in regular use, as it was in the eighth century. There are also a number of linguistic and syntactic anomalies. Most notably, while the Greek dialect of the poems is predominantly Ionic, other dialect forms also appear, sometimes in the same line!

At the very least, some scholars have argued, large sections of the poems should be regarded as interpolations by later writers. Undoubtedly there *are* interpolated passages in the *Iliad*, including, very likely, the whole of Book 10, the so-called *Doloneia*, and possibly also the so-called Catalogue of Ships in Book 2 (discussed on pp. 25–6). But by and large interpolationism is not much in fashion these days. And the *Iliad*'s and *Odyssey*'s numerous inconsistencies in matters of detail can most readily be explained as a reflection of the centuries of dynamic oral tradition that preceded and underpinned the composition of the poems. They are also an indication of the poems' original status as oral compositions, which might well account for the persistence of a number of minor anomalies likely to have been identified and smoothed out if the poems had begun life in written form.

Let us concede that the *Iliad* is not without its rough edges. But in so doing, we must stress that its unity of theme, its structural integrity, the high degree of consistency in the portrayal of its characters and the seamlessness of its narrative (with a few exceptions) point clearly and unequivocally to a single creative genius, albeit one who derived much of his content and inspiration from the many generations of his bardic predecessors.

We still cannot be sure when Homer's poems were first committed to writing. It may well have been in Homer's lifetime, or not long before, that the alphabet was introduced from Phoenicia into the Greek world. There is, however, only one apparent reference to writing in the Homeric poems. It is a letter containing the death warrant of the Greek hero Bellerophon, which Bellerophon himself conveyed, unaware of its contents, to the king of Lycia in south-western Anatolia.[9] One has the impression from the way Homer refers to it in this episode that writing is still a new and strange phenomenon in the Greek world,[10] unless he is intentionally putting it in the context of an earlier age, an heroic age of illiterate warlords. In any case, it is open to question whether within the space of Homer's own lifetime literacy could have developed to the point where either the poet himself was able to put his compositions into writing, or at least dictate them to someone who could. We shall consider this further below.

The earliest clear evidence we have of the poems actually being written down does not occur until the mid-sixth century BC, when the Athenian tyrant Pisistratus commissioned a version of them for recitation at Athens' annual Panathenaic festival.[11] But was this the first time that the poems were committed to writing?

Some scholars have suggested that the new technology of literacy was actually introduced into Greece so that the Homeric epics could be preserved in written form. Even if we dismiss this suggestion, as many have done, is it still possible that writing had reached a stage already in Homer's lifetime where it could have been used to record his poems? The letters making up the first Greek alphabet were crudely and laboriously formed, and initially quite unsuited, it would appear, to the task of writing down, whether from one's own head

14

or from dictation almost 28,000 lines of verse, the combined total of the *Iliad* and the *Odyssey*. Even if this were feasible, it would have taken almost a lifetime to accomplish it. And perhaps it did! We cannot completely discount the possibility that while Homer himself may have remained illiterate to the day of his death, there were those amongst his contemporaries who managed to compile over many years a written record of the entire body of Homeric epic, if not from the bard's own lips then from those who heard and memorized the performances he gave.

That is one possible scenario: 28,000 lines of epic verse recorded in crudely shaped letters. But what were they inscribed on? Did the Greek world already, at this time, have access to supplies of papyrus from Egypt, perhaps via Byblos in the Levant?[12] That is possible. But we need to remember that the Egyptians generally took great care to preserve their control of the papyrus market. They may well have prohibited their overseas customers from selling on the product, threatening to cut off supplies to them if they attempted to do so. In that case, the Greek world may not have had access to papyrus until around the middle of the seventh century, when regular direct trade with Egypt began, via the Greek trading settlement established at Naucratis on the Nile Delta. Prior to that, the only other feasible writing material for the Homeric epics was animal hide, which would have made each copy extremely bulky and exorbitantly expensive. In our attempts to determine when the poems were first committed to writing, the availability of writing materials is clearly a factor of major importance.

In any case, we know that the tradition of oral poetry continued well after the introduction of writing into Greece and that there were professional reciters whose repertoire included, primarily, the epics associated with the name Homer. Notable amongst these was a group of rhapsodes called the Homeridae ('sons of Homer'), who claimed descent from the great bard himself, declaring that he, like them, originated from the island of Chios, and who specialized in performances of his poetry. (They believed that their alleged links with Homer gave them a special insight into his poems and therefore priority over others in performing them on public occasions.) Given the existence of such persons who kept alive the process of oral transmission for many decades after Homer's own lifetime, it is quite possible that this process accounted largely if not entirely for the preservation of the epics until the first clearly attested written record of them in the mid-sixth century.[13] Of course, no matter how faithfully the tellers of the tales tried to adhere to the original compositions, variations were bound to creep in with each retelling. And, as we have remarked, Homer himself probably never told the same tale in exactly the same way twice. None the less, all indications from the poems themselves point to their being substantially the creation of one artist, and were, with only minor variations, faithfully preserved by a number of generations of professional reciters until achieving what we call fixity of text in the sixth century.

By this time the epics were widely known throughout the Greek world. But who were the poet's audiences when the epics were first composed?

HOMER'S AUDIENCES[14]

In attempting to answer this question, we begin with the assumption that the *Iliad* and the *Odyssey* were compositions by an Ionian Greek poet who lived on or near the western coast of Asia Minor during the eighth or early seventh century. It is within this setting that the poet's first audiences heard his tale of Troy. Homer himself speaks of the bards and minstrels who entertained the courts of Mycenaean kings and noblemen.[15] Almost certainly, his own audiences represented similarly elite elements of the society of his own day and his own world, half a millennium after the Mycenaean kingdoms had come to an end.

There is no doubt that Homer was himself a Greek, very likely a descendant of one of the families who migrated eastwards from the Greek mainland during the last two centuries of the second millennium, and resettled on the Asia Minor coastlands and offshore islands.[16] Their migrations occurred in the wake of the upheavals which accompanied the collapse of the Bronze Age civilizations throughout the Greek and Near Eastern worlds in the late second millennium. But we should not overestimate the extent of cultural discontinuity caused by these upheavals. The so-called 'Dark Age' that spans the period between the end of the Bronze Age and the emergence of the Iron Age civilizations in the early first millennium is taking on an increasingly lighter hue. Evidence continues to emerge of cultural survival and continuity across the chronological divide between the Bronze and early Iron Ages, as illustrated by the persistence of many Late Bronze Age elements in the early first millennium civilizations of southern Anatolia and northern Syria.

Almost certainly too there was marked continuity between the Bronze Age cultures and ethnic groups of western Anatolia and the emerging cultures and population groups of the region in the early first millennium. Anatolia's Aegean coastal fringe had provided an important interface between the Near Eastern and Greek worlds for much of the Late Bronze Age and, to a lesser extent in earlier periods as well. In addition to the evidence for numerous Mycenaean commercial contacts along this fringe, we know that Miletus, near the mouth of the Maeander River, became an important centre of Mycenaean influence and culture within the Anatolian region, par- ticularly in the thirteenth century, the period in which the Trojan War is most commonly set. A Mycenaean presence is also indicated at several other western Anatolian sites in this period, notably at Iasus and Müskebi (the latter's ancient name is unknown) to the south of Miletus.

Our evidence indicates close political and commercial interaction between western Anatolian and Greek elements in the Late Bronze Age that can hardly have failed to produce some degree of cultural interaction as well. And although Mycenaean political influence in western Anatolia seems to have been abruptly terminated towards the end of the thirteenth century, it is most unlikely that all effects of the Mycenaean presence in the region disappeared along with it. When Ionian Greeks settled in western Anatolia in the decades before the turn of the millennium, they were entering a region that already had a tradition of interaction between eastern and western cultures, and was still occupied, even if now in relatively small num- bers, by descendants of the Bronze Age inhabitants of the region, of both Greek and native Anatolian origin. Homer's immediate contemporary world was neither exclusively Greek nor exclusively Anatolian. It was a mixture of the two. And, as such, its polit- ical and cultural orientation was neither exclusively Greek nor exclusively Anatolian. It was a mixture of the two.

Like the bards who performed for Mycenaean kings and noblemen, Homer too probably enjoyed the patronage of a number of great families – families who constituted the local aristocracies of western

Anatolia in the early centuries of the first millennium. Many were undoubtedly of Greek origin. In some cases their Anatolian connections may have extended back to the period of Mycenaean settlement in the region. But in the majority of cases, the families were probably part of the new wave of Greek settlers who arrived in Anatolia in the post-Bronze Age era. Though by Homer's time two or more centuries had passed since they had departed their ancestral homelands, their descendants still retained a strong sense of their Greek identity, as reflected in their religious practices, social systems, folk traditions and domestic architecture. But many generations of living in an Anatolian environment, in close contact with local Anatolian peoples and cultures, cannot have failed to make a significant impact on their character, outlook and cultural orientation.

In addition to families of Greek origin, the elite elements of western Anatolian society in Homer's day may also have included indigenous families, whose entrée into the world of the local aristocracy probably carried with it the necessity of adopting Greek as a lingua franca. Perhaps too, Homer's patrons included persons of mixed origin, the product of Greek–Anatolian marriage alliances. Greek tradition supports this. Herodotus talks of the marriages of aristocratic Ionian migrants on their arrival in Miletus with Carian women, allegedly after murdering their prospective wives' fathers, husbands and children. He also tells us that some of the Ionians were subject to the authority of indigenous Anatolian rulers – descendants of Glaucus, the Second-in-Command of the Lycian contingent at Troy.[17]

It was before the members of such families, whether of Greek or Anatolian or mixed origin, that Homer's poems were almost certainly first recited. Within the western Anatolian world, these were the persons who would most readily have identified with the elite class from which the warriors came who confronted each other upon the plains of Troy; it was they who would most readily have understood the code of honour which Homer's warrior heroes embodied and shared.[18]

An honour code shared. We should not miss the significance of this. Though the Trojan War is of international dimensions, bringing as it does coalitions of Greek and non-Greek forces into armed conflict, in no sense does Homer present it as a contest between conflicting cultures or ideologies or belief systems. The whole thing turns upon a single point of honour. A Spartan princess has been abducted – whether willingly or unwillingly is in itself of no great moment. Honour requires that those from whom she has been taken should retrieve her, and that those who have taken her in should defend her, no matter what the cost. It is this which has led to a conflict to the death between the two opposing forces, a conflict that has arisen out of each side's faithful adherence to the same ideological concepts, the same code of honour.

Homer shows no bias towards or against either of them. His heroes on both sides display a mixture of strengths and weaknesses, from the Lord of Mycenae downwards. In the second book of the *Iliad*, Agamemnon cuts an impressive and authoritative figure, well deserving of his role as Greek Commander-in-Chief, a supreme, towering presence at the mustering of the combined Greek forces for the expedition to Troy. But elsewhere he appears pompous and arrogant, intransigent and indecisive by turns, and it is his petulant, selfish behaviour at the beginning of the *Iliad* which provokes Achilles' wrath and sets in motion all its disastrous consequences. Achilles himself is no model of integrity. Justly infuriated by Agamemnon's insult to his honour, he carries his fury to unreasonable lengths, not merely withdrawing his services from his comrades-in-arms but also requesting that Zeus inflict heavy casualties upon them so that they will have all the more cause to regret his absence from the field. When finally he takes up arms again and rounds off his orgy of destruction with the slaughter of Hector, his brutal desecration of Hector's body shocks even the gods. Yet elsewhere he displays a compassionate nature and a nobility of spirit, qualities which are particularly on show in the last book of the *Iliad* when he is filled with pity for Priam and returns to him his son's body for burial.

On the Trojan side, even Alexander Paris, with whom the blame for the war principally lies, is not without redeeming heroic qualities. His indolence and self-indulgence invite the scorn of Trojan and Greek alike. Even his brother Hector addresses him with contempt. Paris himself admits that he far prefers taking his pleasures in the embrace of the beautiful Helen, the gift to him from golden Aphrodite, than joining his comrades on the field of battle. Yet when he does rally to the call to arms, his courage and military prowess are beyond question. He even volunteers to meet Menelaus, his paramour's cuckolded husband, in single combat, putting his own life directly on the line in order to resolve the entire conflict and restore peace between Greeks and Trojans without further bloodshed.

Above all others who fought on the plains of Troy, the Trojan Hector, eldest of Priam's sons, might be regarded as the archetypal Homeric hero. Devoted to his family, unswervingly loyal to his comrades, he is the bravest and the most brutally effective of all the warriors of Troy, repeatedly wreaking havoc amongst the Greek forces and well deserving of his oft-quoted epithet 'killer of men'. Achilles alone of all the Greeks can match him. And once the Greek hero returns to the field, a showdown between the pair becomes inevitable. But then there is a major surprise. When Achilles does finally confront Hector, the bravest, the noblest of all the warriors of Troy suddenly loses his nerve. In sheer panic, he takes to his heels in a most undignified way – completing three circuits of the walls of Troy with Achilles in hot pursuit, like a farmyard rooster in terror-stricken flight from its axe-wielding executioner. But a Homeric hero cannot be allowed to die in such a way, with his back to the enemy. In the final moments of his life, Hector's true nature reasserts itself. He turns to face his pursuer and arch-enemy, in time to make one last stand against him, and die a heroic death upon his spear.

As Homer makes clear through his characterization of the combatants, neither side outdoes the other in terms of the moral and physical attributes that its heroes display or the weaknesses to which they succumb. And neither side consistently has the upper hand in the conflict. The Greeks' final victory is assured, but this is really quite incidental to the *Iliad*'s tale. Indeed in the tale itself it is the Trojan warriors who take the initiative more often than not, repeatedly driving the Greek forces in disarray from the field of battle, forcing them back to their last line of defence before their ships. When Hector is killed, the greatest obstacle to the Greeks' ultimate victory is removed. Troy's fall is imminent. But the Trojan's death provides no occasion for rejoicing. The opportunity for a panhellenic celebration is set aside as Achilles attends to the funeral rites of his beloved Patroclus. The mood of the last two books of the *Iliad* is a sombre one, lightened, for a time, by the vigour and excitement of the games held in Patroclus' honour. Then in the epic's closing stages we return to King Priam and his family. Dismissing all thoughts of his own safety, ignoring the appeals of his wife Hecuba, the aged king goes to the Greek camp to meet with Achilles in person, fully aware of the great dangers to which he is exposing himself. His courage is rewarded when Achilles relents and surrenders to the old man his son's body. Then, for the poem's last scene, we are back in Troy. For a Greek audience, this is enemy territory. But we have reached a point in the story where the setting is really quite incidental. The poem is no longer about a conflict between Greeks and Trojans. Our concern is purely with a grief-stricken family mourning the loss of a beloved son and husband whose body they prepare for burial. In the *Iliad*'s last lines, the distinction between Greeks and Trojans ceases to be significant. This is where Homer leaves it.

That he should end his epic in this way probably says a great deal about the audiences before whom the tale was first recited – audiences whose sympathies were, in the case of the Greeks, as much with the legendary heroes of their adoptive homeland as with those of their ancestral homeland. The actual outcome of the story of Troy was already well known by Homer's audiences. It was one which they might well have viewed in a detached, disinterested way. It provided an explanation for the derelict ruins that were all that remained of the once mighty citadel on the site they believed was Priam's Troy. But the real interest in Homer's epic lay in the poet's telling of the final events which preceded Troy's destruction, in the treatment that the poet gives without favour or bias to both parties to the conflict, in the portrayal of the chief heroes on each side, with all their strengths and weaknesses on display, in the heroic code of conduct that underpinned the conflict. Homer was no doubt well attuned to what pleased his audiences and what their expectations were – as indeed he needed to be if they were made up of persons or families whose patronage he enjoyed. All this must have had an important bearing on the shaping of the *Iliad*.

The social and cultural environment in which Homer lived was strongly Greek in character. But long-standing Anatolian beliefs and traditions, preserved in one form or another to Homer's own day, also contributed to the poet's cultural background. Reflections of this can be seen in both the *Odyssey* and the *Iliad*. The procedures Odysseus must follow in summoning up the spirits of the dead in

Book 11 of the *Odyssey* echo those of the chthonic rituals preserved in Late Bronze Age Hittite texts.[19] In the *Iliad*, inhumation and cremation are both used as a means of disposing of the dead, as in many parts of Bronze Age Anatolia, including Troy itself. Homer's dead heroes, Greek as well as Trojan, are generally consigned to the pyre. This practice appears to have had no precedent in the kingdoms of Mycenaean Greece, but is well attested in the Anatolian world that was contemporary with it.[20] Most striking is the similarity between Patroclus' burial rites[21] and those prescribed in the funerary texts of Hittite kings. In both cases, the deceased's body is consumed upon a pyre; the pyre's smouldering embers are quenched with wine before they are sifted for the bones of the deceased; the bones are immersed in a vessel of oil and then wrapped in fine linen. Though the procedure outlined in the Hittite tablets was specifically prescribed for deceased kings and queens, there is nothing to indicate that it was confined exclusively to them or to the immediate members of their family, or indeed to the Hittite aristocracy in general. The parallels with Patroclus' burial suggest that it may have had a wider currency, quite possibly amongst the elite elements of various local Anatolian kingdoms, and perhaps survived even down to Homer's own time. It could be that in his account of Patroclus' funeral Homer was describing funerary rites of a kind practised by the aristocratic families whose patronage he enjoyed. This would at least be consistent with the many clear instances we have of social customs and cultural traditions that originated in a Bronze Age context and then persisted well down into the early centuries of the first millennium.

In the same period, a number of cultural links spanned the geographical divide between the Near Eastern and Greek worlds. Close connections have long been recognized between the Kumarbi poems, a song cycle of Bronze Age Hurrian origin, and passages in the poem called the *Theogony* ('Birth of the Gods') by the late eighth-century Greek poet Hesiod. Scholars have also pointed to a number of parallels between specific episodes in Homer's poems and the Mesopotamian epic of Gilgamesh, composed in Babylon in the early second millennium.[22] These are sufficiently close to suggest that Homer either knew the epic itself or at least had heard tales from it. We may recall here the words of the second-century AD satirist Lucian who informs us that Homer was not in fact a Greek, but a

Babylonian. His name was originally Tigranes, but he changed it to Homer when he became a captive, or hostage (*homēros*), of the Greeks. This, he claims, he heard from the poet's own lips.[23] Of course Lucian is writing with his tongue planted very firmly in his cheek. Even so, Homer lived at the interface of the Greek and Near Eastern worlds during the so-called orientalizing period of Greek civilization, and westward-moving Near Eastern literary and folk traditions such as those associated with the Mesopotamian hero Gilgamesh may well have formed part of his own cultural heritage. He in turn became one of the agents in the process of east–west cultural transmission. The process, which may already have begun many centuries before in the Late Bronze Age, led eventually to the incorporation into Greek literature of a number of traditions whose origins lay in Mesopotamia, Syria and Anatolia.

I very much doubt that Homer actually saw himself as an agent in this process, nor do I believe that a grand panhellenic vision underlay his poems. He composed with one main purpose in mind – to please, entertain and enlighten his audiences. That is to say, he composed to satisfy the expectations of a socially elite class of mixed but predominantly Greek origins who lived in the Ionian region of western Asia Minor. The cities of this region provided one of the earliest and most important breeding grounds for Greek philosophy and science as well as a range of other Greek arts. Already in the eighth century Homer's prime audience was almost certainly a relatively sophisticated one. The markedly contemplative character of the final book of the *Iliad*, with its reflections on human destiny and human mortality, was judged to be a fitting end to the epic by a poet well attuned to the intellect, tastes and expectations of his audiences.

THE PANHELLENIC DIMENSION

How then did the Homeric epics, particularly the *Iliad*, come to acquire their panhellenic status? Certainly they were widely revered throughout the Greek world (Socrates referred to Homer as 'best and most divine of poets'[24]), even if one stops short of crediting them with an impact on this world similar to that of the Bible on the Judaeo-Christian world. And certainly they vastly overshadowed all other early Greek compositions, such as the poems of the so-called epic cycle which, by the end of the fourth century BC, were beginning to fade into obscurity. The same fate had been suffered much earlier by the two epics based on the Theban cycle of legends.

Artistic merit may well go some way towards explaining the reputation that the poems enjoyed, along with the sheer monumentality of the compositions. They began as, and were to remain, the most ambitious compositions in verse in the entire corpus of Greek literature, more than twice the length of the lost Theban epics. They also allegedly provided a repository of moral precepts – perhaps the reason why schoolboys, so it seems, were obliged to learn at least parts of them by heart.[25] Of course there is almost as much to be condemned in the conduct of the heroes as there is to be admired and emulated – just as there is much to be condemned in the behaviour of the gods. None the less, the heroic ideals as articulated in the *Iliad* undoubtedly served as a major source of inspiration for Greek and later Roman artists, poets and philosophers throughout the history of the Graeco-Roman world.[26]

Artists, in particular, found many of their themes in the epic's subject matter and treatment of its main characters. The wrath of Achilles, the battle at the Greek ships, the deaths of Sarpedon and Patroclus, Achilles' slaughter of Hector and the mutilation of his body, Priam's ransoming of Hector's body, were popular subjects on Greek painted pottery. The participation in the Trojan War of warriors from the island of Aegina is depicted in a relief scene in Aegina's temple of Aphaea-Artemis. Yet artistic inspiration came from other sources as well. The marriage of Peleus and Thetis, the judgement of Paris and the abduction of Helen are all alluded to in passing in the *Iliad*, but depictions of these episodes in Greek art were almost certainly based on other literary works to which they were more central. So, too, the traditions on which Aeschylus' *Oresteia* was based and several of the plays of Sophocles and Euripides that deal with themes related to the Trojan War were derived from non-Homeric sources. The *Iliad* and the *Odyssey* had no monopoly on the inspiration they provided to later artists and writers. (In fact in the fifth century, Athenian playwrights, painters and sculptors may have deliberately bypassed Homer as a source of inspiration; see p. 157.)

Perhaps the main key to the *Iliad*'s success lay in its panhellenic inclusiveness. Though the epic is not a celebration of an all-Greek triumph, none the less its panhellenic compass makes it virtually unique in ancient Greek literature. This undoubtedly contributed to its popularity in the Greek world. But in no sense does it reflect a spirit of panhellenic nationalism. City-state parochialism was far too strong for any such spirit to be widely or enthusiastically embraced, as fifth-century Athens and fourth-century Macedon became all too aware. Sanctuaries such as Delphi and festivals such as the Olympic Games helped remind the Greeks of their fundamental kinship across city-state boundaries. But it was a matter of individual city-state pride to be seen to be contributing to the maintenance of the Delphic sanctuary and to be providing athletes, preferably successful ones, for competition in the panhellenic games. So, too, participation in the expedition against Troy was a matter of city-state pride. To receive a mention in the *Iliad* was to acquire a sense of identification with it, and every state so mentioned, every state that could claim it had ancestors who fought in the war, helped contribute to the poem's popularity.

Everyone wanted a piece of the action, even if only in retrospect, and no doubt a poet dependent on the patronage of his audiences was only too willing to oblige. The well-known Catalogue of Ships in Book 2 of the *Iliad* provided just such an opportunity.[27] The Catalogue lists a total of 164 places that sent troops and ships to join Agamemnon's expedition against Troy. As we have noted, a combined Greek fleet of 1,186 ships was assembled at Aulis for this purpose, with an estimated fighting force of 100,000 men.

The Catalogue itself has provoked much scholarly debate. There are, however, a number of points on which most scholars agree. First, if a combined Greek armada did in fact set out for Troy with hostile intent, the size attributed to it in the *Iliad* is a gross exaggeration.[28] We shall have more to say about this in Chapter 8. Second, the very earliest songs of the Trojan War almost certainly did contain a list of the peoples and places who allegedly joined the Greek alliance. Third, many, if not all, of the places listed in the Catalogue may well have had an authentic Bronze Age origin. Some of these places were apparently abandoned at the end of the Bronze Age and not resettled again, or were only resettled after the lapse of some centuries.[29] Further, there is no proof that *any* of the places named in the Catalogue were not inhabited until *after* the Bronze Age. Fourth, the Catalogue was almost certainly created independently of the *Iliad* and was at some point rather carelessly inserted into it. Nor was it compiled out of pieces of information obtained from other parts of the *Iliad*. In fact, some of the information it contains is inconsistent with information elsewhere in the poem.

What, then, was the scenario for its creation? The following is one of a number of proposals which various scholars have made: the Catalogue was the work of a Boeotian poet who lived in the late eighth century. With the express purpose of compiling such a list, the poet undertook a series of pilgrimages through the homelands of the Greek heroes who allegedly fought at Troy. Though politically divided, the peoples of these homelands, including all the small districts and backwaters, were none the less very conscious of their common ethnicity and cultural heritage. And everyone visited by the poet wanted their ancestors to be included in the war, if Homer had not already put them in, or to be given a more prominent part if they felt that Homer had given them less than their due. In either case, the poet, singing for his supper, was happy to oblige, though he gave pride of place to his own Boeotian countrymen who headed the list of allies and from whose harbour at Aulis the Greek fleet set forth. Hence the Catalogue came about, in the process taking on a life of its own and swelling out of all proportion to any conceivable historical reality.[30]

Yet the *illusion* of historical reality is one of the *Iliad*'s strongest points. We shall discuss later the question of whether or not the story has any historical basis. But there is no doubt that Homer told this story so powerfully and presented the participants in it so graphically that he convinced many succeeding generations of his fellow Greeks and their Roman successors, and indeed some of the most astute scholars of recent times, that there really was a Trojan War pretty much as he has described it. This too helps explain the poem's revered status. Homer was not merely the Greek world's first great poet. He was also its first great recorder of history. So many believe!

He did, however, have his critics. Amongst the earliest of these was the fifth-century historian Herodotus. Herodotus had no doubt that a Trojan War did in fact take place, some 800 years before his own time. But he claimed that Homer misled his audiences on a matter of fundamental importance to the story. Following a version of it told to him by Egyptian priests, Herodotus declared that the ship in which Paris and Helen had fled from Greece was blown by violent winds onto the coast of Egypt. Here the Egyptian king Proteus detained Helen until such time as her husband Menelaus could fetch her home.[31] So the Trojan War was really based on a misunderstanding. Far from heroically defending the woman who had fled with their prince, the Trojans assured the Greeks that they could not hand Helen back to them because she was not nor ever had been in Troy! This, Herodotus believed, was the true version of the tale, as Homer himself well knew. But it lacked dramatic potential. By using it, Homer would have deprived his story of its grand underlying romantic motive. And so he rejected it. Even Thucydides, a younger contemporary of Herodotus and a rather more astute and much more sceptical historian, had no doubts about the basic historicity of the Greek–Trojan conflict and cited Homer as the main source for it. He believed, however, that Homer, being a poet, exaggerated the size of the expedition. Elsewhere he included Homer amongst those 'whose words may delight us for the moment, but whose estimation of facts will fall short of what is really true'.[32]

Throughout the Greek world, the Homeric poems were sung by successive generations of rhapsodes (amongst whom the self-styled 'sons of Homer' – the Homeridae – claimed pride of place), and their appearance in written form, *perhaps* no earlier than the sixth century, assured them of wider circulation still. Even if originally intended for the banqueting halls of the aristocracy (and of that we cannot be entirely sure), their performances must now have ranged from public orations at state festivals to recitations by tellers of tales in market squares and harbour-side taverns.

High-born families from every part of Greece could claim ancestors in the *Iliad*'s lists of all those who fought and died at Troy. But the poems must have had great appeal for the common man as well. They transported him into a world totally removed from his own, one peopled by gods and godlike beings of beautiful appearance and prodigious powers. These beings even spoke as gods might speak, using an elevated diction and a mix of strange dialect forms almost unintelligible to him. But that simply increased the mystique, the aura of wonder that surrounded them. Like untutored peasants who suddenly find themselves in the presence of great art or great architecture, many of those who gathered to listen must have experienced an overwhelming sense of awe as the teller recited his tale. They became totally absorbed and fascinated by the words he sang, without fully comprehending all that they were about.

After several centuries of written transmission, many versions of the epics must have been in circulation, and no doubt discrepancies were developing between them. It was this that prompted scholars at Alexandria in Egypt, most notably Aristarchus, who became head of the library of Alexandria in the second century BC, to produce standard and definitive texts of the poems. These were to become the ancestors of the ones we have today. During this century too, and perhaps even earlier, the influence of the poems was extending further afield. Westwards across the Adriatic, a civilization had arisen that was taking an increasing interest in the Greek world and becoming ever more receptive to Greek cultural influence. The focal point of this civilization was a city that was born about the same time as Homer himself – the city of Rome.

2

THE EARLY CITIES OF
TROY (LEVELS I TO V)

THE REDISCOVERY OF TROY

In the last decades of the eighth century BC, Aeolian Greeks from
the island of Lesbos set out in their boats for the short crossing to
the Anatolian mainland. Here they made their way to the ruined
site occupying a mound which the Turks now call Hisarlık, meaning
'fortress'. Close by, to the north, lay the narrow corridor of water
known in Classical times as the Hellespont, today's Dardanelles. The
remains of stone fortifications, now thickly overgrown, gave evidence
of a once great fortress on the mound. It was derelict, except for a
scattering of inhabitants whose forebears had occupied it in the years
following its destruction. Campfires among the ruins betrayed their
presence and primitive lifestyle.

The Greeks had come here not merely as visitors but as new
settlers. This place had special associations for them. They were well
acquainted with stories of a great war fought by their prehistoric
ancestors against a people called the Trojans, a war that ended with
the destruction of the Trojans' mighty citadel. The most famous
of all the accounts of this war had but recently been composed by
a poet called Homer, who had lived, and was perhaps still living, a
little further down the coast. He himself may well have visited the
site. Whether he did so or not – and he appears to have had detailed
knowledge of the region's topography[1] – the new settlers had no
doubt that the place they were now preparing to occupy was the
fabled setting of the Trojan War. In Greek bardic tradition, the city
of the Trojans was called both Troy and Ilios. The Classical name
for the site, Ilion, was almost certainly first used by the Aeolian
settlers there, though attestations of the name, in inscriptions and
on coins, belong to a later period.

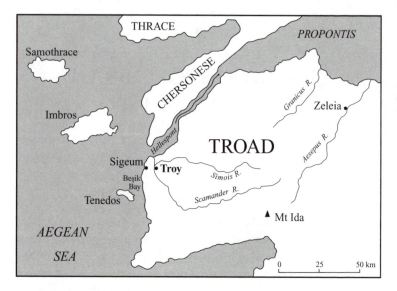

Map 2.1 The Troad.

Three thousand years later, in 1868, another visitor came to Hisarlık. He too became convinced that this was the site of Troy. And he had the determination, and the resources, to prove it. He was a wealthy German merchant called Heinrich Schliemann.

Schliemann's story is a highly romantic one – at least as he tells it. Already in his very early years, he claims, his father had fired his imagination with stories of Troy. He recalls with particular fondness an engraving in a book that his father gave him before he was eight years old. It depicted the Trojan prince Aeneas fleeing the burning city of Troy, with his father Anchises on his back and his son Ascanius by his side. This image profoundly affected the young Schliemann. It was one of the things that inspired his dream of seeking out and digging up the city of Troy. Many years and several personal fortunes later, he was in a position to realize that dream. Secure in his conviction that Hisarlık was Troy, he obtained permission to excavate the site, using his personal fortune to do so. He began work in 1871. By the end of May 1873, he found what he believed was dramatic confirmation that here indeed was Troy. With the help of his beautiful Greek wife Sophia, he discovered a large cache of treasure in the city wall. This he believed was the treasure of the ill-fated Trojan king Priam, whose kingdom had fallen to the Greek forces under the command of Agamemnon, Lord of Mycenae.

How much truth is there in all this? Schliemann's credibility, both as an archaeologist and more generally, has been closely scrutinized in the past few decades. His supporters and his detractors have crossed swords (or rather pens) on numerous occasions. Already a

Figure 2.1 Heinrich Schliemann, from the BBC Hulton Picture Library.

Figure 2.2 Aeneas fleeing Troy, engraving by Georg Ludwig Jerrer from his *Die Weltgeschichte*, 1819.

great deal has been spoken and written on this topic,[2] and we shall confine ourselves here to some general comments. To begin with, there is no doubt that Schliemann did have a considerable predilection for romanticizing, exaggerating and even falsifying aspects of his life and archaeological work. There are a number of occasions in his diaries, letters, books and reports where fiction and reality have become hopelessly entangled. Even the story of his childhood dream of finding Troy appears to be an invention of his later years. Of course, to be caught out playing fast and loose with the truth even on relatively trivial matters inevitably raises doubts about one's overall credibility. In the case of someone like Schliemann, who was to claim spectacular results from his excavations, this becomes a major issue.

But if we are to assess fairly Schliemann's claims, achievements and shortcomings, we need first to see them from the perspective of the period to which their author belonged. The nineteenth century was an age of great outreach and enterprise, of exciting advances in the field of human knowledge, due as much to intrepid adventurers and explorers as to men of science and learning. It was an age when a succession of new discoveries captured the popular imagination and were widely acclaimed, an age when intellectual curiosity and challenges to existing orthodoxies came into head-on conflict with entrenched cultural, intellectual and religious conservatism. Darwin's radical new theories of evolution, the voyages of exploration and discovery that inspired much of his thinking and the storm of debate and controversy that his theories provoked encapsulate much of the spirit and temper of this new age. So too do the great expeditions undertaken by Sir Richard Burton and John Hanning Speke in their search for the source of the Nile, and their subsequent public and highly acrimonious dispute that ended so abruptly and tragically with Speke's mysterious death.

It was an age when the exploration of the ancient world was still largely the preserve of amateurs: wealthy dilettantes fired with the ambition of digging up an ancient city, adventurers lured by the fascination of exotic lands and the lost civilizations that they contained, treasure-hunters intent, above all else, on plunder. Flamboyant, larger-than-life characters appeared amongst this crop of looters and would-be archaeologists – such as the gigantic Italian Giovanni Battista Belzoni of Padua, who was employed as a barber, trained as a hydraulics engineer and performed as a theatre strongman (dubbed 'the Patagonian Samson') before setting out upon his first expedition to the Land of the Nile. Though little better than many of the site-robbers who infested Egypt in the first half of the nineteenth century, Belzoni has, at least, left us with a useful written record of the discoveries he made in the pyramids, tombs and temples of Egypt and Nubia. No less colourful a figure was the Englishman Austen Henry Layard, who swashbuckled his way across Europe and the Near East, leaving a trail of broken heads, broken hearts and empty wine flagons in his wake, coming within an inch of his life on more than one occasion and finally establishing himself as one of the great pioneers of Assyrian archaeology.

In 1835, several years before Layard made his first expedition to the east, a British soldier called Henry Creswicke Rawlinson embarked on an enterprise that led to one of the greatest break-throughs in nineteenth-century scholarship. In the course of his military duties in Persia, Rawlinson visited the small Persian village of Bisitun (historical Behistun), was fascinated by the enormous 1,200-line trilingual cuneiform inscription carved on a cliff face near the village and undertook the task of copying and deciphering it. The inscription in Old Persian, Babylonian and Elamite belonged to the reign of the Achaemenid king Darius I (522–486 BC). Rawlinson's success in deciphering the Old Persian text led to the translation of the other two versions, thus opening up to scholarship the vast surviving storehouse of cuneiform literature.

A close scrutiny of the Bible as history was an important consequence of this, for scholars could now directly compare biblical tradition with actual historical texts. The outcome was mixed. Some claimed that the cuneiform texts provided striking confirmation of the biblical narratives. Others found worrying inconsistencies. There was a further concern. A number of cuneiform texts seemed to indicate that the Bible had taken over, and claimed as its own, traditions that initially belonged to quite different cultures and religious systems and had originated in much earlier periods. The episode of the Great Flood was one case in point; the story of Moses another.

Those whose faith in the literal truth of the Bible remained strong were confronted with what appeared to be threats to the very foundations of this faith, such as Darwinism and the newly emerging world of cuneiform literature. In an age that saw the development of rational, scientific enquiry as a basis for many fields of endeavour, faith needed to be reinforced by tangible, compelling evidence. For the champions of biblical tradition, archaeology could serve as a means of providing this evidence. Thus a principal aim of the Egypt Exploration Fund (which was joined on its 1890 campaign by a teenager called Howard Carter) was to examine the monuments and civilization of ancient Egypt with a view to demonstrating archaeological support for the stories of the Bible. This, too, was an important motive, up until quite recent times, of many archaeological campaigns in the 'Holy Land'. The Bible was used as a kind of archaeological manual or tourist guidebook to the ancient sites of Israel and Palestine, which were in turn seen as confirming the truth of biblical tradition.

It was with a similar sense of mission that Heinrich Schliemann embarked in 1871 on the first of his seven excavation campaigns at Hisarlık. His Bible was Homer's *Iliad*, his mission to prove beyond doubt that the ruins on the Hisarlık mound were the remains of the mighty citadel of Priam's Troy.

Of course such single-minded conviction, whether in biblical or Homeric archaeology, or any other field of archaeology for that matter, often runs counter to the spirit of objective scientific enquiry – and can seriously affect the outcome of such enquiry. The archaeologist who looks only for evidence that will support a conclusion he or she has already reached risks overlooking or destroying much valuable material likely to provide more comprehensive information about a site and the civilization to which it belongs. In this respect Schliemann was certainly not without fault. Yet he was no worse than many other nineteenth-century venturers into the fledgling field of archaeology – and he was a good deal better than most of them.

Swashbuckle and flamboyance are not qualities that immediately leap to mind when one sees photographs of this diminutive, dour-looking German businessman. Schliemann lacked the style and dash of a Belzoni or a Burton or a Layard. But he was undoubtedly a romantic with a flair for the dramatic. Indeed, this was almost a requirement of any archaeologist seeking to capture public attention in an age that had grown accustomed to spectacular discoveries in the fields of science, geography and the ancient civilizations. It was in such a context that Schliemann, upon unearthing the shaft graves at Mycenae, grandly announced in a telegram dated 28 November 1876, to King George of Greece:

> With great joy I announce to Your Majesty that I have discovered the tombs which the tradition proclaimed by Pausanias[3] indicates as the graves of Agamemnon, Cassandra, Eurymedon and their companions, all slain at a banquet by Clytemnestra (Agamemnon's wife) and her lover Aegisthus.

(Schliemann never spoke or wrote the words famously attributed to him: 'Today I have gazed upon the face of Agamemnon.') In fact, the shaft graves were several centuries too early for any conceivable date for a historical Agamemnon, Clytemnestra et al. But through his imagination-capturing reports, Schliemann succeeded in bringing to public notice the splendid civilization of Late Bronze Age Greece – during a period when he was in bad odour with the Turkish authorities for smuggling out of their country the finds he had made at Troy.

To prove the historical reality of Homeric Troy remained the overriding ambition of Schliemann's archaeological career. This was no easy task, particularly since archaeology had yet to be fully accepted as a serious professional discipline. Many still looked upon it as an activity engaged in primarily by amateurs. And in the world of Classical scholarship there were plenty of sceptics who regarded the Trojan War and the place where it was allegedly fought as no more than poetic fantasy. It was the professional scholarly world first and foremost that Schliemann, the amateur archaeologist, had to convince.

He was of course far from being the first to identify the ruins at Hisarlık with Homer's Troy/Ilios. Almost certainly they were so identified from at least the time when Aeolian Greeks took up residence there in the late eighth century, calling the site Ilion. That could well have been a Hellenized form of a long-standing local name for the site, as we shall discuss in Chapter 5. In 1801, some sixty-seven years before Schliemann first visited Hisarlık, the British traveller Edward Daniel Clarke confirmed that it was the site of Classical Ilion, on the basis of coins and inscriptions found there. And twenty years later, in 1820, a publisher from Edinburgh called

Charles Maclaren declared it to be the site of Homeric Troy. Of course the fact that the Classical Greeks called it Ilion did not necessarily mean that it was the site of Homeric Troy. The Greek geographer Strabo, who lived during the early Roman empire, claimed that the Greeks had made a mistake, that Homeric Troy did *not* lie there.[4] Proof of the identification was needed. And the credit for embarking on the search for this proof must go unequivocally to Frank Calvert, a British citizen then residing in the area, who bought part of the site and carried out preliminary excavations upon it in 1863 and 1865.

A great deal has been written in recent years about the importance of Calvert's role in the identification of Hisarlık with Homeric Troy, the thoroughly ungracious way in which Schliemann treated Calvert and the bitter acrimony that developed in the relationship between the two.[5] We need not retrace here the ground already covered by the British expatriate's modern-day supporters,[6] beyond noting that Calvert had to talk an initially sceptical Schliemann into accepting the Hisarlık–Troy identification, that Schliemann took full credit for the identification himself, and that in many other respects he neglected or refused to give Calvert the recognition that was his due.

One of Calvert's chief concerns was the crudity of Schliemann's methods of excavation, which undoubtedly led to the destruction of much valuable material on the site. It had become clear from preliminary excavations that the mound contained a number of occupation levels, representing different periods in the settlement's development and extending over many centuries. By the end of Schliemann's final season in 1890, nine major levels had been identified, each of which were divided into a number of sub-levels (forty-one or more) with a total height of more than 20 metres. Apart from the fact that Schliemann lacked the skill, the techniques, the resources or the patience for a thorough systematic excavation of each layer in turn, his overriding concern was to lay bare the Troy of the *Iliad*. He sacrificed all else to this one goal. And to achieve it, he employed a large workforce to dig an enormous trench through the mound from top to base in his search for the Homeric level. Contrary to what was to become standard archaeological practice, he numbered the levels from the bottom-most upwards, that is, from the earliest (which he called Level I) to the latest (Level IX).

37

Mistakenly identifying the level for which he was searching as Troy II, the second-oldest level, he cleared all that lay on top of it – in order to find the proof of Homeric Troy. In fact Priam's Troy was of a much later period. There is some irony in this. In his seach for proof of the Trojan War, Schliemann destroyed much of the level that came closest to providing it.

A question raised from time to time is whether Schliemann eventually came to accept, very shortly before his death, that his Troy II was 1,000 years too early to be the city of Priam. Troy VI, as proposed by his assistant Wilhelm Dörpfeld, was a much more likely candidate, both in chronological as well as in archaeological terms. Some scholars believe that Schliemann finally realized the truth. Others maintain that he clung stubbornly to his original identification until his last days. The answer appears to lie in a recently published letter that he wrote not long before he died. While he was still loath to give up his Troy II identification, a post-script to the letter indicates that he had now become resigned to accepting Troy VI as the city contemporaneous with the kingdom of Agamemnon, and thus the city of the Trojan War.[7]

Dörpfeld continued his work at Hisarlık for another two seasons, in 1893 and 1894, with the support of funds provided by Schliemann's widow, Sophia. Work resumed on the site in 1932 and continued until 1938, under the direction of Professor Carl Blegen, who headed a team from the University of Cincinnati. Though Blegen was a much better archaeologist than Schliemann, he still shared with his predecessor an implicit belief in the historical truth of a Trojan War:

> It can no longer be doubted, when one surveys the state of our knowledge today, that there really was an actual historical Trojan War, in which a coalition of Achaeans, or Mycenaeans, under a king whose overlordship was recognized, fought against the people of Troy and their allies.[8]

The most recent excavations on the site are those that have been carried out by an international team, from 1988 onwards, under the direction of Professor Manfred Korfmann from the University of Tübingen. Korfmann reports that more than 350 scholars, scientists and technicians from almost twenty countries have collaborated on the project. In spite of all this expertise, the Korfmann-led excavations have generated considerable controversy and criticism. We shall return to this later. In the context of the current excavations, the question of whether or not there was a Trojan War continues to surface. Korfmann frequently alludes to it, particularly in his more general publications; despite his cautious statements, one cannot help feeling that he, like Schliemann and Blegen before him, believes implicitly that Homeric tradition reflects a specific historical event. It is very easy to fall under the spell that Hisarlık casts upon those who have immersed themselves in Homer and the place where his story is allegedly set. Is the magic of Troy entirely illusion without substance?

Let us now take a closer look at this place and its history – to begin with, through the eyes of the archaeologist.

TROY'S FIRST TWO LEVELS

As we have noted, Troy is not one city but nine, each superimposed upon its predecessor. The time span it covers is vast – more than 4,000 years, from the beginning of the Early Bronze Age, around 3000 BC, down to at least the first millennium AD.[9] Indeed, Troy has the distinction of being one of the longest continuously inhabited settlements in the whole of human history. We become particularly conscious of this as we note what else was happening in the world of Troy's neighbours, near and far, as the city passed through its various phases.

Troy I contained ten sub-levels that extended over a period of some five centuries, from c.3000 to 2500 BC. It thus occupied the first half of the Early Bronze Age. The small settlement, less than 100 metres in diameter, was fortified by a wall approximately 2.5 metres thick and was entered through a gate flanked by square towers. The settlement had very much the character of a village community. Residential architecture included rows of long houses made of mudbrick on stone foundations. The earth floors of the houses were probably covered with woven mats and animal skins to provide seating for the occupants. Infant burials were found beneath house floors as well as in other areas of the citadel. Adult burials were apparently restricted to areas outside the walls. Artefacts included tools of copper and stone and handmade pottery.

Spinning and weaving figured amongst the crafts practised in this as in the later levels of the site. The inhabitants of Troy I, like their successors in later levels, enjoyed a varied diet of meat, fish and grain products. Artefacts identical in type to those of Troy I, especially handmade pottery, have been found at various other sites, including Poliochni and Thermi (on the islands of Lemnos and Lesbos respectively). These indicate that Troy in this period was part of a wider culture that extended from the north-western region of the Anatolian mainland to the islands that lay off Anatolia's northern Aegean coast.

The settlement was destroyed by fire and replaced almost immediately by its successor, Troy II (some 125 metres in diameter), which extended over a period of approximately 200 years, from c.2500 to 2300 BC. The second city of Troy began its existence about the same time as a little village appeared on the east bank of the Euphrates in southern Mesopotamia. It was called Bab-ilim, 'Gate of the Gods'. We know it better as Babylon. Troy II was the most distinguished of the Early Bronze Age settlements on the site. It was home to a highly prosperous community with an advanced metal technology. Access to the citadel was via two main gates, one lying to its southeast, the other to its south-west. The latter is the better known and better preserved of the two. It was approached by a steeply rising monumental ramp paved with limestone slabs and flanked by stone walls. The citadel's impressive fortifications of stone surmounted with mudbrick superstructure were flanked by towers and gate rooms. They had a distinctive slope to their outer surface, a feature we will have cause to comment on in our discussion of Troy VI (Chapter 3).

Inside the enclosure was a complex of courtyards and large buildings, dominated by the so-called 'Great Megaron'. This was a hall of substantial proportions, some 400 square metres in area. 'Megaron' is an ancient Greek term used for an architectural form that originated in the Near East. It eventually found its way into the Greek world where it became the central feature of Mycenaean palace architecture. The Great Megaron at Troy was a large columned rectangular building with a central hearth and was entered via an open portico. Very likely it served as a public reception hall where the citadel's ruler held council and gave audience to important visitors. Possibly it was used for important religious

Figure 2.3 Paved ramp of Troy II.

ceremonies. A nearby structure may have been the residence of the ruler of Troy and his family. Other spacious buildings of megaron type reinforce the impression that the citadel was now the preserve of a powerful and wealthy elite class.[10] During the Troy II period, a large megaron was the dominant feature of Poliochni on the island of Lemnos. It, too, was presumably a public building, perhaps a ruler's residence. Poliochni in this period was an impressive well-planned settlement, with a long main street flanked by blocks of houses. It was twice the size of the known area of Troy II, though the latter's actual boundaries may well have extended a considerable distance beyond its citadel's walls.

One of the hallmark technological innovations of Troy II was the potter's wheel, which led to the manufacture of wheelmade pottery alongside the traditional handmade ware. Amongst the wheelmade vessels of this period were a number that depicted human faces. The grimness of the facial expressions led Blegen to believe that the occupants of this level were a dour, austere people, with little fondness for gaiety, geniality or good humour. That may be a quite unwarranted assumption. On the same basis, one wonders what conclusions might be drawn about the people who produced the contemporary

Cycladic figurines with their bland, expressionless faces. In any case a more common type of pottery associated with Troy in this period was the so-called *depas amphikypellon*, a slender, two-handled goblet so named after Nestor's cup in the *Iliad*. This type of ware is found distributed throughout central and southern Anatolia, Syria, the Cyclades, the Greek mainland, Thrace and Bulgaria, an indication of Troy's widespread trading contacts in this period. We cannot of course be sure that all such vessels came from Troy itself, but the type may well have originated there, and subsequently provided a model for production in local centres.

An even more significant development in this period was the introduction of the metal alloy bronze, consisting of copper mixed with a small percentage of tin. Throughout the Near Eastern world this development was to have a profound impact on many aspects of life – social, cultural, commercial and political – and was to play a major role in shaping the course of the civilizations that made up this world until the Bronze Age had run its course.

It is appropriate at this point to step back from the settlement on the mound at Hisarlık and take a look at what was happening in the wider world as Troy approached the climax of its development in the Early Bronze Age.

TROY'S EARLY BRONZE AGE CONTEMPORARIES

The little fortified village of Troy had come into existence at the very dawn of what we call the historical era of human society – the era of the written record. Writing made its appearance at roughly the same time, though probably independently, in Egypt and southern Mesopotamia. The earliest evidence of written records in Egypt was found in a tomb in Abydos dating to the end of the predynastic period – i.e. the late fourth millennium. In Mesopotamia the first known examples of writing appeared on tablets found in the temple district of Uruk (biblical Erech). These tablets can be assigned to the end of the so-called Uruk period and thus also belong to the late fourth millennium. In both Egypt and Mesopotamia writing was one of the most important innovations associated with the growth of cities and the development of political and administrative structures that enabled authority to be exercised over them. It was

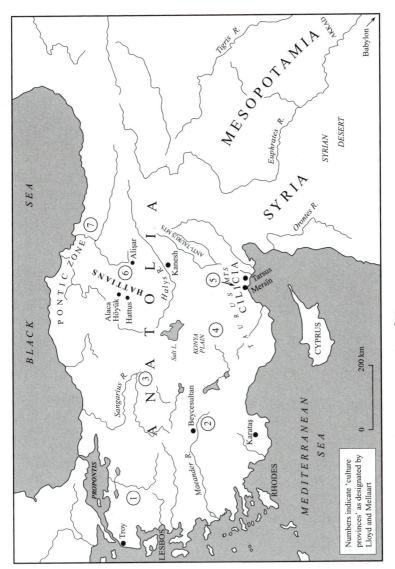

Numbers indicate 'culture
provinces' as designated by
Lloyd and Mellaart

Map 2.2 Early Bronze Age contemporaries of Troy.

closely linked with the beginning of Egypt's Early Dynastic Period, which saw the union of Upper and Lower Egypt around 3000. It was also one of the defining features of the Sumerian civilization of southern Mesopotamia, whose origins around 2900 marked the beginning of the Early Dynastic Period in Mesopotamian history.

Troy was thus born about the time Egypt was first united under a single ruler. It was probably at least one hundred years old before the Sumerian city-states began to emerge, the states that provided (so we are told) the cradle of Western civilization. And by the time the first foundation stone of the first of the pyramids – those archetypal symbols of remote antiquity – had been laid, Troy had passed its 300th birthday. It was already of venerable age. But what did it have to show for its years? The small settlement lay at the opposite end of the Near Eastern world to both Egypt and Mesopotamia, far removed from contact with the advances in human society and civilization that were taking place there, including the art of writing. It was to be more than 1,000 years – not until the early second millennium – before this new communications technology penetrated *anywhere* into the Anatolian region. How long, then, did it take to reach a small community perched on its furthermost edge? Indeed, how sure can we be that writing was introduced into Troy at *any* time during the Bronze Age? These are questions to which we shall return.

Throughout the Bronze Age, much of the stimulus for the social, cultural and political development of the Near Eastern world came from Egypt and the civilizations of Mesopotamia. The latter, in particular, passed on to the lands lying to their west many of their social and cultural traditions, along with the art of writing that enabled these traditions to be recorded and, in some cases, transmitted further westwards. But local developments complemented this process. Undoubtedly the second millennium civilizations of Anatolia, particularly of eastern Anatolia, were much influenced by the contemporary and earlier civilizations lying to their south-east. But we should not underestimate the important contributions which their own predecessors made to them, specifically the civilizations of the Early Bronze Age.

On the basis of similarities and differences between various groups of sites, we can think of Early Bronze Age Anatolia as consisting of a number of 'culture provinces' lying within broadly definable geographical regions. Each was dominated by one or two major settlements.[11] Troy was clearly the most important site of the north-west province, in the region later called the Troad. Beycesultan, near the source of the Maeander River, was the most prominent settlement in the province lying to its south. The north-central region of Anatolia, within the bend of the Classical Halys River, contained the Early Bronze Age sites of Alaca Höyük and the settlement called Hattus in Middle Bronze Age records. Tarsus and Mersin were major settlements within a south-east culture province, located in the region of Classical Cilicia. Other culture provinces were located in the Konya Plain and the Pontic zone.

By the middle of the third millennium, in the Early Bronze II phase, the sites to which we have referred had become major centres of civilization in their regions and, very likely the seats of wealthy ruling houses. Throughout the entire Bronze Age, Beycesultan, whose origins date back to the Late Chalcolithic period, seems to have been one of the most flourishing of all western Anatolian communities. Of the forty main levels on the site, as identified by its excavators Seton Lloyd and James Mellaart, fourteen (XIX–VI) have been assigned to the Early Bronze Age. At the height of its development in this period, Beycesultan was a prosperous fortified settlement which shared a number of features, such as its megaron-type architecture, with Troy. Its prosperity was probably due in no small measure to its strategically advantageous position at the headwaters of the Maeander River. Very likely it lay on major routes of communication that linked it with the Troad as well as with the central Aegean coast and perhaps also with places lying to its east. Such a favourable location would have contributed much to Beycesultan's commercial development and general prosperity.

Location must also account for the high level of prosperity of Early Bronze Age Tarsus, whose origins extended back to the Neolithic period. Situated as it was on Anatolia's south-eastern periphery, Tarsus provided a link between the Anatolian region and the countries lying further to the east. The *depas amphikypellon* type of pottery found at Tarsus indicates trading contacts with Troy II, and there was also an abundance of pottery on the site originating from Cyprus, Syria and Mesopotamia. Impressive private dwellings in the city at the height of its Early Bronze Age development reflect the existence of an elite class that had almost certainly built its wealth on commerce.

North-central Anatolia was the homeland of the Hattians, an indigenous people with their own distinctive language, culture, folklore and religious rites. The most impressive Hattian settlement, at least from an archaeological viewpoint, occupied the site now known as Alaca Höyük, located some 200 kilometres north-east of the modern Turkish capital Ankara. It began its life in the Late Chalcolithic Period, reached its peak in the Early Bronze II period and continued as a flourishing city down to the end of the Late Bronze Age. It is perhaps to be identified with the city called Arinna in Late Bronze Age Hittite texts, the city of the great Sun Goddess. The most significant remains of the Early Bronze Age settlement are thirteen 'royal' shaft graves which contained spectacular grave goods.[12] They are generally dated to c.2300–2100,[13] and are thus roughly contemporary with the 'treasure' discovered by Schliemann at Troy, which we shall refer to on pp. 49–52. Other important settlements in the region were Hattus, on the site of the later Hittite capital Hattusa, Alişar lying 80 kilometres to the south-east of Hattus (it was probably the ancient Ankuwa) and Kanesh (modern Kültepe) just below the southern bend of the Halys River, where the Assyrian merchants established the headquarters of their Anatolian trading operations early in the second millennium.

Thus the overall picture of Anatolia around the middle of the third millennium is one of prosperous regional centres, linked often by trading enterprises. The development of regular commercial interchange between and within the various regions of Anatolia no doubt contributed much to these regions' material prosperity, or at least to that of their major centres. Trading enterprises must also have extended considerably further afield, particularly given the increasing importance of bronze technology in the third millennium. Much, if not all, of the tin required for bronze manufacture in Anatolia may have had to be imported from distant sources in the east and brought along routes linking the Anatolian communities with Mesopotamia and the lands beyond it. A growing demand for raw materials from far-off lands must have led to increasingly complex trading networks, creating the need for an increasingly high level of coordination and cooperation in trading enterprises. No doubt this helped stimulate the development of administrative hierarchies responsible for the overall management of a centre's trading operations, especially when these involved negotiations and agreements with distant trading partners or with authorities in the towns or regions through which goods had to pass, en route from place of origin to final destination. Such factors may well have provided the context for the emergence of ruling houses in centres like Troy, Beycesultan, Tarsus and Alaca Höyük.

Regular inter-regional trading activity presupposes a politically stable and relatively peaceful environment. Around the middle of the third millennium, conditions obviously favoured fairly extensive commercial operations through the various regions of Anatolia to which we have referred. But we should remember that many of the settlements in these regions were heavily fortified at this time. We have noted the impressive fortifications of Troy II. Beycesultan was also a fortified settlement, as was Hattus in central Anatolia. And the inhabitants of Tarsus built two successive walls around their city as a defence against enemy attack. Commercial prosperity had its downside. The wealthier a city became, the greater its attraction as a military target.

Across the Aegean, the third millennium witnessed comparable developments in parts of mainland Greece, where the term 'Early Helladic' has been adopted to designate the Early Bronze Age civilizations of the region. Here too the Early Bronze II, or Early Helladic II (EH II) phase, was characterized by a number of major advances, including the emergence of fortified urban centres with monumental buildings, the development of metal technology and the production of distinctive new pottery types (though not as yet wheelmade), such as the hard, thin-walled Urfinis ware with glazed surface. Typical pottery shapes of the period include the 'sauceboat' and the long- and thin-necked jug. Though the economy of the Early Helladic world remained essentially an agricultural one, commercial enterprises also contributed much to its prosperity. The trading links of the Early Helladic II communities extended to Crete and Anatolia as well as to the islands of the Cyclades, thus bringing these communities into contact with other civilizations that were themselves in the process of major change.

Lerna in the Argolid region was probably the most important and the wealthiest of all Early Helladic II sites. Founded originally in the Neolithic period (represented by Levels I and II on the site), it was abandoned at the end of this period and was subsequently reoccupied at the beginning of Early Helladic II (Level III).

47

Excavations conducted by Professor John Caskey between 1952 and 1958 brought to light a settlement with planned layout and large, robustly constructed buildings surrounded by a double ring of walls punctuated by gates and towers. The site was dominated, successively, by two monumental building complexes. The second, built over the first, is the well-known 'House of the Tiles' (so-called because of the schist and terracotta tiles used in the construction of its gabled roof). It was a two-storeyed structure, 28 by 14 metres in area, and on its ground floor were two large rooms flanked by corridors and a series of smaller rooms. Whether these buildings are to be identified as palaces or community assembly halls, they clearly reflect a prosperous and well-organized society, perhaps under the control of a single ruler whose authority extended over the surrounding district and its commercial, industrial and agricultural activities.

Lerna is clearly comparable to Troy (with which it almost certainly had commercial contacts), to other major urban centres of Anatolia and to centres like Poliochni and Thermi on the islands of the eastern Aegean – when all were at the peak of their Early Bronze Age development. Other principal centres of Early Helladic II Greece include Eutresis and Orchomenos in central Greece, in the region later called Boeotia. At Tiryns, located a few kilometres to the north-east of Lerna, an enormous circular building, almost 28 metres in diameter, was discovered beneath the later Mycenaean palace. Whether it too was a palace or a community meeting place, or a religious and ceremonial centre, or even a granary remains unknown. All have been suggested.

Troy had significantly changed its character from the original village community it had been in the first phase of its existence. The spacious buildings now occupying its acropolis left no room for residences of a common sort. Here dwelt the elite of Troy. The territory outside the walls was very likely occupied by beings of a lower order who made up the bulk of Troy's community, subjects of the ruler whose residence lay within the citadel. Perhaps in time of enemy threat at least some of the peripheral population was brought within the walls. In any case, the citadel was almost certainly the administrative centre of a region over which Troy exercised control, one which probably extended some kilometres from the citadel and consisted of a spread of farmlets and small villages whose produce contributed to the sustenance of the entire kingdom.

This was probably typical of settlement patterns and administrative structures elsewhere in the Near Eastern world during the third millennium, as illustrated by the Sumerian city-state complex of southern Mesopotamia. The complex was characterized by a network of urban centres, each of which exercised authority over the districts, farmsteads and villages lying within a 10 to 15 kilometre radius from it. In eastern Anatolia, the kingdoms referred to in Assyrian merchant texts of the early second millennium had almost certainly originated in the Early Bronze Age. To judge from the Assyrian records, each of these kingdoms had as its focal point a chief city whose ruler exercised authority over the districts and communities lying within the territory that surrounded it.[14] Further evidence of Early Bronze Age kingdoms in this region *may* be provided by a text which records a rebellion of seventeen rulers, including the kings of Hatti and Kanesh, against Naram-Sin, an Akkadian king who in the twenty-third century ruled an empire that extended from the Persian Gulf to central Anatolia.[15] Though the text is a late one, *c.*1400 BC, and its historical reliability is questionable, none the less the notion that already in the Early Bronze Age kings ruled over various parts of Anatolia is quite consistent with the archaeological evidence, which indicates the growth of prosperous and relatively large urban centres, particularly from the middle of the third millennium. As we have suggested, these may well have been the seats of wealthy ruling dynasties.

THE TREASURES OF TROY

Evidence of Troy II's wealth was provided by the treasure trove that Schliemann claimed to have unearthed, in Level IIg, on 31 May 1873, during his third excavation season at Hisarlık.[16] The collection of weapons, gold, silver, electrum, copper and bronze vessels, gold jewellery, including thousands of gold rings, and a range of other objects made of precious materials apparently came to light close to the outer side of the city wall near the building which Schliemann designated as the royal palace.[17] He had no hesitation in labelling the hoard as 'Priam's Treasure'. It provided dramatic confirmation, so he believed, that Troy II was indeed the city of

Priam, the city of the Trojan War. A famous photograph depicts Schliemann's wife Sophia wearing earrings, a golden diadem and other jewels from the hoard – the so-called 'jewels of Helen'. Schliemann smuggled the entire hoard out of Turkey and then debated what he should do with it. Greece, England, the USA and Russia were all considered possible destinations before Schliemann finally settled on his native Germany. Here the treasures were housed in the Berlin Museum for Prehistory and Early History until May 1945, when the Red Army took possession of them and spirited them away to Russia.

For almost fifty years nothing more was heard of them. Indeed there were grave fears that they had been lost forever, perhaps even destroyed in the bombing of Berlin. Finally, in 1993, the Russian Minister of Culture, Evgeny Sidorov, announced that they were safely stored in an underground chamber in Moscow's Pushkin Museum. Three years later, in April 1996, they were put on display at a special exhibition in the museum. Debate still continues over where their final resting place should be. One might well argue that they belong in Turkey, whence they were illegally removed in the first place. Certainly Turkey has as great a claim to them as Greece has to the Parthenon sculptures.

To add one further element to the controversies surrounding the treasure, doubts have been expressed as to whether it is in fact genuine. David Traill, one of the leading sceptics, believes that Schliemann actually salted the site with the hoard, after quietly collecting over a period of time the pieces of which it was composed so that he could claim a single spectacular discovery.[18] Schliemann's tendency to be loose with the truth may lend some support to this view. Certainly his claim that Sophia was at his side when he made the discovery was false. She had returned to Greece at the beginning of May because of the death of her father, as one of Schliemann's own letters (now in the British Museum) makes clear.[19] But few now doubt that the hoard itself is, by and large, genuine, though it perhaps included items gathered over several weeks.

What conclusions can we draw from it about the Troy to which it belonged? Clearly, it is far too early for Priam's Troy. Most scholars assign to it a date between 2400 and 2200 BC, though some would go 200 years earlier, others two or more centuries later. Much of its material may well have been of local manufacture, produced within Troy itself or its surrounding region. Very likely it reflects a tradition of jewellery-making within the context of a local metallurgical arts and crafts industry.[20] Yet for all the hoard's fame, and the admiration that it has attracted, the quality of workmanship is not so fine – some of it has in fact been described as 'somewhat pedestrian' – as that which we find further east, in the royal tombs of Alaca Höyük. The goods from those tombs – consisting of bronze and copper mirrors, silver combs, gold pins, necklaces, bracelets, ear pendants, diadems, beautiful long-stemmed gold cups, jugs and 'fruit-stands' and, most impressive of all, the disc or arc standards incorporating stylized bulls or stags inlaid with silver or gold – completely overshadow, in both variety and quality, the treasure of Troy. Does this indicate a degree of refinement and sophistication in the central Anatolian cultures superior to that of the cultures further to the west? This is a question to which we must return when we consider who the actual makers of these cultures were.

Troy II was destroyed by fire, which seems to have struck the citadel with lightning rapidity. The inhabitants apparently had to flee at a moment's notice, leaving their household possessions scattered about. At this time, very likely, the 'Treasure of Troy' was hastily and successfully hidden as the city was consumed by flames. We do not know what, or who, was responsible for the destruction. Around 2300, there are indications in various parts of western and southern Anatolia of violent change and major conflagration, and the disappearance of many of the Early Bronze Age II communities. Hostile invaders, sackers of cities, may have been the cause of these traumatic events. Was Troy II one of a number of communities that fell victim to enemy attack? That is quite possible. However, Troy III rose directly from the ashes of Troy II, and the new level showed virtually no cultural break with its predecessor. So if enemies had attacked and sacked the city, they had either simply moved on, allowing its original inhabitants to rebuild it, or else (and less likely) they now mingled with the original inhabitants and absorbed their culture.

There is a third possibility. The city was indeed destroyed by attack, but one carried out by attackers who belonged to the same region and culture. Perhaps the destruction occurred during a local uprising, leading to the overthrow of the current ruling dynasty and the installation of a new regime. The concealment of the treasure at the end of Troy II may have some bearing on this. If Troy's destruction was due to a natural disaster from which its population fled, later to return and rebuild the city, why was the treasure not retrieved? The fact that it was not suggests that the persons who had hidden it had not survived, taking with them to the grave the secret of where the treasure now lay. In this scenario, they could of course have been killed – or kidnapped – during an enemy sack of the city. But it is equally possible that they fell victim to an uprising against them by their own people.

THE SUCCESSORS OF TROY II

Though Troy III maintained continuity with its predecessor, its material civilization was markedly inferior, and markedly less prosperous. We do see a gradual improvement through the Troy IV and V levels, but none of the sub-levels of these phases reached the heights of Troy II. Living conditions were much more crowded in Troy III. Single free-standing houses were now largely replaced by blocks of housing units fronting on to narrow streets. The citadel was no longer the preserve of an elite ruling class, and the crowded conditions indicate that larger numbers of the local population now lived within the walls. Troy III apparently lasted about a century, from c.2300 to 2200. Its successor, Troy IV, though larger in size, again experienced fairly crowded living conditions, with irregularly built housing units separated by narrow winding streets. Troy V seems to have enjoyed a general improvement in living standards. Conditions were less crowded, and the houses were better constructed and more spacious – though they still showed the same basic features in their layout as their predecessors in Troy I.

The end of Troy V marked the end of the first major era in Troy's history, one which lasted some 1,300 years, spanning both the Early and Middle Bronze Ages, from the settlement's beginnings around 3000 until the conflagration to which the fifth city succumbed around 1700. As we have noted, Troy I and Troy II had also been destroyed by fire. In these cases, however, the city had been rebuilt with no perceptible break in its culture, an almost certain indication that the same population group continued to occupy it. We have suggested that, if the fires were not purely accidental, they were due to internal political upheavals rather than to an enemy who simply melted away after putting the city to the torch. But the latter possibility cannot be ruled out, and indeed the destruction of Troy II around 2300 would not be inconsistent with the pattern of destructions elsewhere in western and southern Anatolia in the same period.

The city reached the first peak in its development during its second phase, when it became the most important urban centre in north-west Anatolia, and perhaps in western Anatolia as a whole. Clearly its status declined after the destruction of Troy II, as reflected in the material deterioration evident in Troy III, and, though conditions improved and the city grew in size during the two successor levels, neither of these levels reached the impressive heights of the second city. Troy became something of a backwater in the last three centuries of the third millennium and the first three centuries of the second. This was a period that saw great changes and the emergence of new forces in many parts of the Near Eastern world. Troy had no role in these. Its remote geographical location helped ensure its isolation from, and its insignificance in, a world that was undergoing substantial transformation. It is to this wider world that we shall now return.

THE WIDER NEAR EASTERN SCENE

Around the time of the destruction of Troy II and the emergence of Troy III, a man called Sargon (2334–2279), ruler of the kingdom of Akkad in northern Mesopotamia, took a step unprecedented in world history. He built an empire. Earlier rulers of the Mesopotamian city-states may have exercised temporary hegemony from time to time over their immediate neighbours. But no one had succeeded in establishing, or even conceived the idea of establishing, permanent power over a region that incorporated lands lying far beyond the confines of the two rivers. At its greatest extent the empire founded by Sargon and expanded by his grandson Naram-Sin (2254–2218) stretched southwards through Mesopotamia to the Persian Gulf and westwards across northern Syria to the lands of eastern Anatolia. Yet in the reign of Naram-Sin's son Sharkalisharri (2217–2193), the Akkadian empire fell apart, after a lifespan of less than one and a half centuries. Eight decades later, there followed the equally illustrious and even shorter-lived empire of the Third Dynasty of Ur. Founded by Ur-Nammu (2112–2095), it lasted just over century before the sun set finally upon it in the reign of its fifth king, Ibbi-Sin (2028–2004).

These first experiments in empire-building were mounted on fragile foundations, for the authors of them, notwithstanding their prowess in the field of battle, lacked the experience, the administrative expertise and the resources necessary to maintain lasting control over the large expanses of territory that had fallen to them by the sword. But they were pioneers in the field of imperial enterprises. They had demonstrated to others the rewards of such enterprises. The days of the independent city-state and petty kingdom were now very largely at an end. Subordination to one or other of the major powers that arose and followed in the wake of the first empires was almost inevitable. The early second millennium saw the emergence of a number of rival kingdoms, such as those of Isin and Larsa, whose imperial aspirations led to fierce competition for political and military supremacy in northern Mesopotamia and Syria. Each flourished briefly, and then fell.[21]

The most distinguished among them was undoubtedly the kingdom of Assyria, whose international commercial operations were to have a profound impact on the lands lying to its west. For it was in this period, the so-called Middle Bronze Age, that a network of Assyrian merchant colonies was established, along the trade routes from the Assyrian capital Assur to the communities and kingdoms of eastern Anatolia. Trading fine woollen textiles and tin in exchange for Anatolian gold and silver, the Assyrian merchants indirectly helped shape the political development of the regions in which they operated. The kingdoms within these regions, called *mātu* in Assyrian texts, almost certainly originated in the Early Bronze Age, and probably coexisted on relatively peaceful terms for several centuries – up to the period of the Assyrian merchant colonies. Passage by the merchants from one local kingdom to another necessitated cooperation between the rulers of these kingdoms, and a greater consciousness of territorial boundaries. Given the heavy tolls and taxes that merchant caravans were subject to in each kingdom through which they passed, territorial demarcation between kingdoms acquired much significance. Boundary disputes arose, sometimes involving wayward subject communities in the border regions between the kingdoms. Tensions mounted, conflict became inevitable.

It was in this context that the first Anatolian empire arose. The empire was the creation of a local dynasty that established the seat of its power at Nesa/Kanesh, south of the Halys River, and from there imposed its control by military force over much of the eastern half of Anatolia, from the Pontic zone in the north to the region east of the Salt Lake in the south. Through their dealings with the Assyrian merchants, the local Anatolian rulers had become fully aware of the great empire which lay to their south-east, of the wealth and power of the Great King who controlled it. Assyria may well have inspired the first Anatolian essay in imperial enterprise. The founder of the dynasty that embarked on this enterprise was a man called Pithana. His son Anitta extended his conquests and, in so doing, became master of the first empire in Anatolia.[22]

Anitta's reign serves to highlight an even more momentous development in the history of the Anatolian region: the introduction of the written record. Writing had made its first appearance in Anatolia at the beginning of the Assyrian colony period, several generations before Anitta's reign. It has survived on many thousands of tablets (mainly unearthed at Kanesh) written by, for, or to Anatolia-based Assyrian merchants who kept copious records of their commercial transactions in their own language. They wrote in the cuneiform script, the script that had been developed in Mesopotamia more than 1,000 years earlier. Anitta also used this script for recording his and his father's achievements, which were originally carved on a stela set up in the gate of his capital Nesa. But although the script on the stela was adopted from the Assyrian merchants, the language Anitta used in his inscription was that of his own people. It was called 'Nesite'.

The first Anatolian experiment in empire-building was short-lived. Anitta's empire barely outlasted his death. With its disintegration, the Assyrian merchants, nervous at the best of times about trading in politically unstable areas, disbanded their colonies and went home. Literacy disappeared along with them. This happened around 1750 or a little later, about the time Troy V came to an end. Several decades were to pass before a major new development took place in the history of Anatolia: the rise of the kingdom of the Hittites in the early years of the period we call the Late Bronze Age.

The new age was characterized by great changes in Anatolia as well as elsewhere in the Near Eastern world. But there was also continuity with what had gone before. By no means was the break with the past a complete one. The Middle Bronze Age kingdoms and communities of eastern Anatolia had benefited enormously from their contacts with their more sophisticated neighbours in northern Syria and Mesopotamia, particularly the Assyrians. And while the cultural and political momentum generated by these contacts may have slowed, it never completely ceased. Henceforth, the eastern Anatolian regions would become ever more closely engaged, politically, commercially and culturally, with the countries and civilizations lying to their south-east. Other important legacies were passed on from Middle to Late Bronze Age. The first Anatolian empire had arisen in the Middle Bronze Age and had flourished briefly before sputtering out. But its creator, Anitta, was adopted into Hittite royal tradition and, under the early Hittite kings of the seventeenth century, the concept of empire was reborn. The language used by Anitta, Nesite, became the official language of the Hittite kingdom. Writing was reintroduced into Anatolia, the cuneiform script used by the Hittites being adopted from northern Syria, and became an essential element in the Hittites' administration of their expanding kingdom. In the Middle Bronze Age, north-central Anatolia had become the political centre of gravity of the entire Anatolian region. It was to remain so until the end of the Late Bronze Age.

In the early centuries of the second millennium, the lands of western Anatolia appear to have remained largely isolated from the political and commercial developments taking place amongst their eastern Anatolian neighbours. There was no Assyrian commercial penetration of the western Anatolian regions, nor did the Assyrian presence in the eastern kingdoms have, as far as we can determine, any beneficial flow-on effects for the west. There is no evidence of writing in the west in this period, nor indeed do we have any tangible evidence for it in this region at any time during the remaining centuries of the Bronze Age, except towards its end. But while the western lands had at best only marginal contact with the developments taking place in the east, they appear also to have remained free of the political and military upheavals that frequently accompanied these developments. Troy was a case in point. Its walled defences throughout the period of Levels III to V indicate that the city was never entirely secure from the threat of attack. But threat may never have become reality. The city's uninterrupted if unspectacular development through these levels, each occupying a more extensive area and accommodating a larger population than its predecessor, suggests that for some six centuries it enjoyed a relatively tranquil existence, along with a modest amount of progress.

Peace and stability provide conditions beneficial to a society's growth and development. Yet instability and violent disruption of the existing order of things often pave the way for much more substantial progress. By the end of the Middle Bronze Age, Troy had reached the end of one era and was about to enter upon another. Dramatic change was soon to usher in the most distinguished phase of its history.

3

THE KINGDOM OF PRIAM
(LEVELS VI TO VII)

WHAT THE NEW CITY LOOKED LIKE

From the ashes of Troy V a splendid new settlement emerged, which, at the height of its development, far overshadowed its predecessors in size and magnificence, and provided the setting for the most famous epic in Western literary tradition. For this was the place where Homer located the kingdom of Priam. Before its walls, Greek and Trojan forces repeatedly clashed, and Achilles and Hector fought to the death. At least that is what the tradition tells us.

Impressive new fortifications built of squared limestone blocks protected the citadel of Troy VI. The walls, surmounted by mudbrick breastwork, once reached a height of over 9 metres. Several watchtowers were built into these walls, the most imposing of which is the huge north-eastern bastion, which served to reinforce the citadel's defences as well as affording a commanding view over the Trojan plain. It calls to mind Homer's great watchtower in the *Iliad*. Five gateways provided access to the citadel, the most important of which was the southern gate, 3.3 metres wide, protected by a tower and giving access to a broad way ascending steeply into the citadel. Archaeologists have suggested that this was the famous Scaean Gate, where Hector bade his wife Andromache farewell and where Paris inflicted the fatal wound upon Achilles' heel.

The buildings within the citadel were constructed on a series of terraces rising up towards the centre of the site. Today there are remains only of the structures on the outer terrace, but these provide some indication of the overall character of the citadel in this phase of its existence. The huddled residences of the previous phase have given way to spacious, free-standing, two-storeyed houses, with solid stone walls. The pillared megaron was, once more, a feature of this level. Very likely the houses became ever more imposing as one approached the citadel's summit, where the citadel's crowning feature, the royal palace, was located.[1] Unfortunately, this and the buildings closest to it are now irretrievably lost to us. Schliemann is only partly to blame. Much of the citadel's surface had been cleared already in late Greek and in Roman times to make way for the construction of a new sanctuary in honour of the goddess Athena. Whether or not the survival of palace remains would have furnished further archaeological support for the historical reality of a King Priam and his family is something we shall never know.

In very broad terms, Homer's description of Troy is not inconsistent with what is left of Level VI and what can be deduced about the parts that have been destroyed. The citadel of the *Iliad* is steep and lofty, entered through monumental gateways with bolted doors of close-fitting timber planks. It has a great square tower to which Hector's wife Andromache goes, grief-stricken at the news of Trojan reverses, and from where Priam sees Achilles creating havoc amongst Troy's warriors. It is a city of well-laid streets through which Hector hastens, to find Andromache and bid her a final farewell. Husband and wife meet at the Scaean Gate before Hector goes forth into the enemy's midst. Priam's palace is a many-roomed mansion with polished stone colonnades and fifty sleeping apartments flanking an inner courtyard. Here resides the king's large family, including his sons and daughters and their spouses. Close by, his eldest sons Hector and Paris have beautiful palaces of their own. A dominant feature of the citadel is the temple of the goddess Athena. Homer's references to it inspired one of the site's most enduring traditions. Troy's early first-millennium inhabitants built a temple to the goddess, allegedly where an original temple to her stood. Together with the image that it housed, Athena's sanctuary was to become one of Troy's most revered institutions, honoured by a succession of pilgrims and distinguished visitors, for the remainder of the city's history.

The overall Homeric concept of Troy, allowing for some degree of poetic embellishment, certainly reflects some of the features of Troy VI, particularly its lofty fortifications and monumental gateways and square towers, and its spacious free-standing houses rising up towards a central palace. Yet these features are by no means exclusive to Troy. Other Bronze Age sites both in the Near East and in contemporary Mycenaean Greece – such as the acropolis of the Hittite capital Hattusa and the citadels of Mycenae and Tiryns – could also be thus described, to a greater or lesser extent. Nor of course are these architectural features confined to the Late Bronze Age. At best, Homer's portrayal of Priam's Troy is based on a poet's assumption of what such a city might have looked like at the height of its power. But his representation of the city is not, perhaps, entirely the product of a poetic imagination. What he tells us about Troy fits far better with the remains of the sixth settlement than with those of any earlier or later period in Troy's Bronze Age history. That may not be without significance.

One feature of Troy VI that has often attracted comment is its sloping walls. In the *Iliad*, the Greek warrior Patroclus makes four attempts to mount them. He fails each time, but not because of the walls themselves. It is because Apollo keeps dislodging him, before finally persuading him to give up the enterprise.[2] The slope in Troy's walls gives some credibility to Homer's account of Patroclus' efforts to scale them, a feat which would have been beyond even the most agile warrior, especially one bearing weapons, had the walls been

Figure 3.1 The sloping walls of Troy VI.

vertical. Of course Troy VI had no monopoly on sloping walls. We have already noted this feature in Troy II (it was also a feature of other early levels of the citadel), and we could compare the so-called Yerkapı rampart in the fortifications of the Hittite capital Hattusa. Dr Jürgen Seeher, current Director of Excavations at Hattusa, has commented that soldiers could easily have clambered up the slope of this structure at a run – though he believes that the rampart was erected primarily as an architectural monument rather than as an element in the city's defence system. In any case, Troy's walls were much steeper.

THE 'LOWER CITY'

One of the long-standing concerns about identifying the ruins at Hisarlık with Homer's Troy is that even at the height of its development the site was small, no more than 200 metres in diameter (c.20,000 square metres in area). How could such a tiny place have warranted a massive panhellenic invasion, let alone withstood for ten years a siege mounted by what Homer would have us believe were the greatest warriors of the age – even if we allow for much poetic exaggeration in the telling of the tale? More to the point, we have remarked that at the height of its development, the citadel of Troy VI probably housed a ruling class consisting of no more than a few hundred people. How could a small and evidently prosperous elite group have maintained itself without a support population large enough to generate its prosperity, through agricultural, mercantile and skilled handicraft activity? Moreover, the settlement at Hisarlık lay in a very fertile, arable region. Given both its natural wealth and its proximity to the sea, this region could have supported a much larger number of people than the citadel was able to accommodate at any stage of its existence.

It follows that Troy must have had a relatively large peripheral population, even if this proved difficult to substantiate on the basis of the surviving material remains. For that matter, the same could be said of many Bronze Age sites whose known material remains are confined very largely to the area occupied by their ruling elites. In the case of Hisarlık, Schliemann was convinced of the existence of a settlement outside the citadel and planned to search for it in 1891, but died before he had a chance to put his plans into effect. Dörpfeld subsequently took up the investigation, but without conclusive results. It is only in the most recent series of excavations that the matter has become a prime focus of attention.

One of the most important results claimed by Professor Korfmann from his excavations at Troy since 1988 is the identification of a lower city of Late Bronze Age date. It spans the entire period of Levels VI and VIIa, from the seventeenth to the twelfth century. Extending to the south and east of the citadel, the lower settlement was discovered, and its layout revealed, by magnetometer surveys. Thus Korfmann reports.[3] He has concluded that this lower city was protected, at least in the thirteenth century, by a fortification system consisting of a mudbrick wall marking the city's perimeter and, beyond it, by two ditches, the first located *c*.400 metres to the south of the citadel, the second 100–150 metres further south again.[4] The ditches, he suggests, served as initial lines of defence which an attacking enemy had to negotiate before reaching the wall itself. But the purpose of the ditches remains unclear. We cannot be certain that they were in fact defence works. Critics of Korfmann's proposals have argued that they had nothing to do with defence, but functioned as a water drainage and reservoir system.[5]

In the course of Korfmann's investigations south of the citadel, remains of stone or wooden houses belonging to Levels VI and VII have been identified, some with very large dimensions, below strata belonging to the Hellenistic and Roman levels (Levels VIII and IX), and on a quite different alignment to them. The finds of lower-city habitation are understandably meagre, given their predominantly mudbrick and timber construction and the fact that in Graeco-Roman times any stone materials belonging to earlier levels would simply have been quarried for reuse.

If Korfmann's overall findings and conclusions are accepted, then his excavations appear to have dramatically increased the size of the known area occupied by Troy, from some 20,000 square metres (the citadel on its own) to approximately 200,000 square metres. Korfmann claims that the layout of the lower settlement has been confirmed by an intensive and systematic pottery survey conducted in 2003.[6] He estimates that Troy's entire population, enclosed within his proposed city wall and including the residents of the citadel, was somewhere between 4,000 and 10,000 inhabitants at the height of Level VI's development. But the number of persons belonging to the kingdom of Troy may well have been significantly larger, allowing for an extra-mural population who lived and worked in outlying rural areas that perhaps formed part of the kingdom's territory.[7]

It must be said that Korfmann's work and the claims he has made have become the subject of considerable heated criticism. The controversy received wide publicity in 2001. It was triggered largely by an exhibition that had recently been staged in Germany called *Troia, Traum und Wirklichkeit* (*Troy, Dream and Reality*). One of the chief features of the exhibition was a large model depicting a complete reconstruction of the citadel and 'lower city'. Critics of Korfmann's reconstructions, and his findings in general, have been led by Professor Frank Kolb, one of Korfmann's colleagues in the University of Tübingen. The main thrust of the criticism is that Korfmann has greatly overestimated the importance of the site and the significance and extent of his discoveries outside the citadel, that he has misinterpreted the evidence and that his reconstructions are largely products of his imagination. He has allegedly exaggerated his results in order to build up media and public interest and to produce outcomes satisfactory to the financial sponsors of what is a very expensive project.

After the debate had already generated much heat and (some would say) little light, the University of Tübingen organized an academic symposium with the disarmingly neutral title 'The Meaning of Troy in the Late Bronze Age'. It was held on 15–16 February 2002. The symposium focused on the Korfmann controversy, with invited speakers, thirteen in all, taking one side or the other. As might be expected, little was achieved by way of consensus on the main issues of the controversy, and the opinions already held by the scholars who participated remained as firmly entrenched as ever. Later in 2002, a group of British scholars who attended the conference, D. F. Easton, J. D. Hawkins, A. G. Sherratt and E. S. Sherratt, wrote a detailed review of Korfmann's findings and the case made by his critics.[8] In this review, published in the journal *Anatolian Studies*, they expressed a number of reservations about Korfmann's conclusions and reconstructions and, on certain matters of detail, saw some justification in the case made by his critics. But overall they judged that his findings were largely valid and the criticisms against him largely unfounded.

In 2004, two of Korfmann's critics, Professors Hertel and Kolb, published a response in *Anatolian Studies*, reasserting their arguments and disputing many aspects of the British scholars' generally positive assessment of Korfmann's work.[9] Once more, they strongly criticized Korfmann's representation of a densely built-up 'lower city', pointing out the sparseness of the actual remains of Late Bronze Age residences and emphasizing that 95 per cent of Korfmann's reconstruction is pure conjecture. While acknowledging the existence of small habitation areas outside the citadel, they denied that this was evidence for the existence of a coherent lower city. They dismissed as mere fiction the proposed fortification system that, Korfmann believes, defined the limits of such a city.

As in many debates where opinions become strongly polarized, the truth probably lies somewhere between the two extremes. Korfmann's detailed reconstructions and conclusions appear to require substantial modification and a much clearer distinction between fact and supposition. But the overall concept of a royal citadel to which was attached a lower settlement of significant proportions may well be valid. It is difficult to believe that the impressive Late Bronze Age level on the mound at Hisarlık was no more than an aristocratic residence, as Hertel and Kolb suggest, rather than the centre of a kingdom whose status was similar to that of the major kingdoms of the Mycenaean world and a number of regional kingdoms of the Near Eastern world. Of course, without unequivocal archaeological evidence, this remains largely a matter of faith. It will be the task of a later generation of excavators at Troy, working in a more dispassionate environment, to determine whether such faith reflects reality.

THE FATE OF LATE BRONZE AGE TROY

Troy VI came to a violent end when it was in its eighth sub-level, Level VIh. The large amounts of Late Helladic IIIA pottery found in the destruction deposits, together with a small quantity of Late Helladid IIIB1 pottery, suggest that VIh fell some time after 1300, probably in the early decades of the thirteenth century.[10] This would accord quite well with the dates assigned by various ancient sources to the Trojan War.[11] Already in the nineteenth century, Schliemann's assistant and successor, Wilhelm Dörpfeld, firmly believed that Level VI represented the city of Priam. But subsequently Carl Blegen concluded from his own excavations in the 1930s that Homer's Troy was in fact the first phase of the seventh major level – Troy VIIa.[12] He did so primarily on the assumption that Troy VIh had been destroyed by earthquake, not by human agency as required by Greek tradition. Cracks in the citadel's fortifications and subsidence in surface levels *may* provide evidence of earthquake activity at the end of Troy VIh.[13] But even if we could prove that an earthquake did occur at this time, we would still be unable to tell whether it was on a scale large enough to cause the destruction of the entire citadel. A compromise has been proposed. If we cannot choose between two alternatives, why not combine them? The proposal is that Troy's fortifications were seriously weakened by earthquake, to the point where the citadel became vulnerable to enemy conquest; it was a combination of both factors that brought about Troy's destruction. Like many compromises, this is unlikely to satisfy the supporters of either of the alternatives it seeks to combine.

What *is* certain is that Troy VI was brought to an end by a major traumatic event. If this was not due to the forces of nature, then enemy attack is the most obvious alternative – and a rather more appealing alternative, since it would clearly fit better with the tradition of a Trojan War. Some evidence for hostile action against the city has been found in the form of arrowheads and spearheads embedded in the walls and a few human skeletons whose mutilated condition makes it likely that they were victims of human violence. But the quantity of such finds is very small, understandably so on a site that continued to be occupied for another two and a half millennia.

There is, however, another possible explanation for the destruction. Though covering a larger area than any of its predecessors, the citadel of Troy VI, with its spacious layout and large free-standing buildings, could have been occupied by no more than a few hundred people. It was clearly the preserve of a small, elite class – as Troy II had apparently been. Whoever the builders of Troy VI were, the nature of the citadel in this period suggests a much sharper division in society than had been the case in Troys III to V. The citadel once more became the exclusive preserve of a privileged minority. All other persons considered residents of Troy and, probably, subjects of its ruling elite, must have lived outside the citadel walls. Was the destruction of the citadel of Troy VI caused by an uprising of the local population? We have suggested the possibility of a similar end for Troy II.

Let us consider the aftermath of the destruction. Troy VIIa quickly rose from the ruins of its predecessor, with no perceptible break in the population or the basic culture. The fortification walls were repaired, old houses were rebuilt and new ones were added. But there was a marked change in the character of the citadel. The fine, spacious houses of Troy VI disappeared. Smaller, meaner structures were now crowded within the citadel's walls. Inside a number of them, large vessels for storing food and drink were sunk into the ground, presumably in anticipation of siege or famine. Trading activity, particularly with the Mycenaean world (see Chapter 4), went into decline. All this is suggestive of a city which, though still occupied by its previous inhabitants, had suffered a severe setback of one kind or another from which it never fully recovered. The area outside the citadel continued to be occupied, but the encroachment of common dwellings within the citadel walls indicates either that the ruler of Troy could no longer guarantee the local population's safety beyond the citadel – or, just possibly, that a new, more broadly based regime had taken control and swept away the remnants of the previous elite ruling class.

So, was the end of Troy VI due to a popular uprising – one which led to the storming of the citadel and the destruction of the buildings within it? Could the people of Troy have turned against their own rulers (which has in fact been suggested as the principal reason for the destruction of the Mycenaean palaces)? This scenario could well explain the material conditions of Troy VIIa. Indeed, contemporary written records may provide more specific indications of local uprisings in the kingdom during the thirteenth century (see Chapter 8). In any case, the crowding within the citadel, the sunken food storage containers within the houses and the decline in overseas trade contacts suggest that the period of VIIa was one of growing insecurity and instability in the Troad, as in many other parts of the Near Eastern world.

VIIa also suffered destruction by fire, around 1180, this time almost certainly the result of enemy attack, though too late to be linked with a concerted Mycenaean invasion from the Greek mainland.[14] We are now in the Bronze Age's declining years, the period when many centres of civilization in the Greek and Near Eastern worlds collapsed and disappeared. Yet, though it was undoubtedly affected by the upheavals of the age, Troy survived them for a time. The same population continued to inhabit the site, found some protection behind its still impressive walls, continued to make substantial quantities of pottery of local type, once called Grey Minyan ware and now known as Trojan or Anatolian Grey Ware,[15] and even carried on some residual trade with Mycenaean merchants.[16] This last phase of Troy VII is divided into two sub-phases: Level VIIb1 and Level VIIb2. The distinction between them is marked by the appearance in the latter of a coarse ceramic knobbed ware referred to as *Buckelkeramik*, perhaps reflecting the arrival of an immigrant population group from south-eastern Europe.

But, even after their arrival, elements of the Level VIIb1 culture persisted alongside that of the newcomers. Troy VIIb2 also ended in destruction by fire, some time between 1050 and 1000, in the so-called Protogeometric period.

Excavations in Level VIIb1 have recently brought to light, in one of the buildings on the citadel, a find which *may* be of great significance. It is a biconvex bronze seal, inscribed on both sides in the Luwian hieroglyphic script. So far, this is the only piece of hard evidence we have for writing at Troy in the first 2,000 years of its existence.[17] The inscriptions upon the seal are among the very last of the Anatolian Bronze Age, post-dating the last known Hittite inscription by several decades. One side of the seal gives the name of a man and his profession as scribe, the other side the name of a woman. Both names are incomplete. The likelihood is that the pair are husband and wife.

Seals were regularly used as a form of personal signature in Late Bronze Age Anatolia by Hittite kings and other members of their families, by bureaucrats in the royal administration and by local rulers and officials in various vassal states. Often circular in shape, they were stamped on clay *bullae* as well as on a range of formal documents, including land-grants, records of goods purchased and treaties. The very late date of the context in which this particular seal occurs is in itself a matter of great surprise. But there is no indication that the context has been contaminated, no suggestion that the seal does not genuinely belong to this level. It may of course have been made a number of years before the period of its findspot, and we cannot be sure that it actually originated in Troy, given that such items are easily portable. The fact that we have the seal itself and not just an impression of it might strengthen the supposition of a Trojan origin. But this falls a long way short of proof.

We shall have more to say about the seal and its significance when we consider the question of the Trojans' language and ethnicity in Chapter 5.

Figure 3.2 Seal found at Troy (by permission of the Troia Projekt, Universität Tübingen). Reproduction by J. D. Hawkins.

TROY'S NEAR EASTERN
CONTEMPORARIES

Troy reached the peak of its development in the Late Bronze Age. But even in this, the most flourishing period of its entire history, it played no more than a tiny role in the Near Eastern world to which it belonged. Let us now turn our attention to what else was happening in this world as Late Bronze Age Troy rose, prospered and fell.

In Mesopotamia, half a century or so before the emergence of Troy VI, the final remnants of the first great Assyrian empire, well known for its extensive merchant operations in eastern Anatolia, were absorbed by Assyria's southern neighbour Babylonia. Under its most famous king Hammurabi (c.1792–1750), Babylonia became Mesopotamia's new superpower. Yet as Troy VI began its life, the empire which Hammurabi built was already beginning to contract, though it would remain for some time the supreme power east

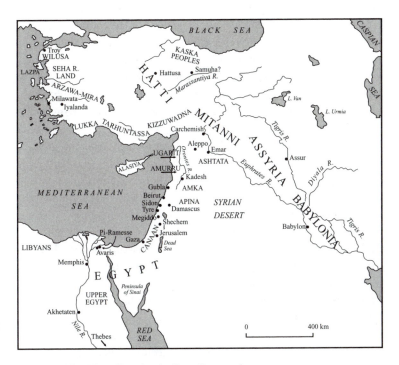

Map 3.1 The Near East in the Late Bronze Age.

of the Euphrates. In northern Syria the kingdom of Yamhad, administered from its royal seat at Aleppo, dominated much of the region lying west of the Euphrates, through a network of vassal states and appanage kingdoms which stretched from the Euphrates to the Mediterranean coast. In this period too a group of peoples called the Hurrians were making their presence increasingly felt in northern Mesopotamia and Syria. From them was to emerge, by the end of the sixteenth century, one of the major powers of the Late Bronze Age: the kingdom of Mitanni.

South of the Mediterranean, important changes had been taking place in the land of the Nile. As Troy VI rose, Egypt was passing through the last decades of four centuries of peace, unity and prosperity – the period of the so-called Middle Kingdom (c.2055–1650). A century of political fragmentation followed, the so-called Second Intermediate Period, probably brought about by a line of foreign kings known as the Hyksos, whose ancestral homelands lay in western Asia. Setting up their base at Avaris in the eastern delta, the Hyksos established Egypt's fifteenth dynasty. But they never succeeded in imposing their rule over the whole of the country and were finally overthrown and driven back to the lands whence their ancestors had come. Their conqueror, Ahmose, was the founder of a new era in Egyptian history. Spanning a period of almost half a millennium (c.1550–1069), it extended through Egypt's eighteenth, nineteenth and twentieth dynasties. We call it the New Kingdom.

Though its fortunes fluctuated, the New Kingdom was, at its height, the greatest phase in Egypt's long history. And the greatest of its rulers was, arguably, the pharaoh Ramesses II, who held sway over Egypt for much of the thirteenth century. The Trojan War – if there was such a war – would thus have been fought, far to the north, during the period Ramesses occupied his country's throne. Ramesses is also the pharaoh most commonly associated with the biblical Exodus story, which tells of the departure of the Hebrews from Egypt. If we accept this story as historically authentic, then Moses was a contemporary of King Priam (or Priam's historical prototype), and led his people from the land of the Nile about the time Troy fell to the Greeks. In any case, New Kingdom Egypt began as Troy was moving towards the peak of its development. It came to an end, after a long period of decline, when Troy VII was in its dying stages.

Figure 3.3 Ramesses II, Abu Simbel.

Across the Mediterranean from Egypt, another great power appeared on the horizon as Troy VI was being built. It reached its peak in the second half of the fourteenth century, by which time it had established supremacy over much of Anatolia and northern Syria. Based in central Anatolia, with an empire stretching from the Aegean to the Euphrates, it was called the kingdom of Hatti, better known to us as the kingdom of the Hittites. Already in the reigns of the earliest Hittite kings, the foundations of the Hittite empire were being laid. Hattusili I, who came to the throne in the second half of the seventeenth century, imposed his authority by military force over many parts of eastern Anatolia, conducted military expeditions into northern Syria, where he clashed with the kingdom of Yamhad, and carried his battle standards across the Euphrates through northern Mesopotamia almost to the banks of the Tigris River. His grandson and successor, Mursili I, completed the conquest of the kingdom of Yamhad and destroyed its capital Aleppo, before marching his troops east to the Euphrates and south to Babylon. Mursili's sack of this royal city brought to an abrupt and violent end the dynasty of King Hammurabi (c.1595) and paved the way for the emergence of a new line of rulers in Babylonia, the Kassites. Hatti further consolidated its Great Kingdom status in the Near East when its warrior king Suppiluliuma (c.1350–1321) destroyed the Hittites' greatest rival for supremacy in northern Syria and eastern Anatolia, the Hurrian kingdom of Mitanni.[18]

In the late fourteenth century, when Troy VI had entered upon the last century of its lifespan, authority over much of the Near Eastern world was exercised by four kingdoms: Egypt, Babylonia, Hatti and Assyria, the last of these rising to fill the power vacuum east of the Euphrates caused by the destruction of the Mitannian empire. The rulers of these lands styled themselves 'Great Kings', and addressed each other as 'My Brother'. They communicated regularly through correspondence and diplomatic missions, their bonds of 'brotherhood' reinforced by marriage alliances and regular exchanges of gifts between their royal houses. But relations between them were not always amicable. In the final years of Troy VI, Egyptian and Hittite forces fought a famous battle at Kadesh on the Orontes River in Syria (1274), under the respective commands of Ramesses II and his Hittite counterpart Muwattalli II. There were heavy casualties on both sides and, though the Hittites emerged as the long-term victors, the battle itself ended in a stalemate.

Fifteen years later, hostilities between the two powers were formally ended by a peace treaty, consolidated by a marriage alliance between Ramesses and the daughter of the current Hittite king, Hattusili III. The boundary between their respective subject territories in Syria lay in the region of Damascus. The territory including Damascus and the area lying to its south belonged to Egypt, the territory to its north to Hatti. Across the Euphrates Assyria was taking on an increasingly threatening aspect as it absorbed within its expanding empire the remnants of the Mitannian kingdom, clashed on more than one occasion with its southern neighbour Babylonia and menaced Hittite subject territory west of the Euphrates.

The kingdoms of Egypt and Hatti were indisputably the greatest military powers of the age, rulers of a substantial network of vassal states. Egyptian territory extended northwards from Ramesses' new capital at Pi-Ramesse in the Egyptian Delta as far as Damascus and southwards through the lands of the Nile to the southern limits of Nubia. Hittite territory stretched across the face of Anatolia through northern Syria to the western fringes of Mesopotamia. Each kingdom could muster a formidable array of troops from all parts of its empire to protect and control the vast regions that lay beneath its sway.

Politically, militarily, commercially and culturally, the Anatolia-based Hittite kingdom was firmly oriented towards the regions that lay to its south-east. Above all, a substantial presence in Syria-Palestine was essential to the maintenance of its Great Kingdom status.[19] Suppiluliuma devoted much of his career to replacing Hurrian with Hittite authority in the region and to imposing vassal status upon many of the local principalities. He also established viceregal seats at Carchemish and Aleppo. His grandson Muwattalli put forces of almost 50,000 into the field against Ramesses at Kadesh to protect and maintain the territories won by his predecessors and contested by Egypt. Muwattalli's brother and second successor, Hattusili, was ever prepared for a fresh outbreak of conflict with Egypt during the first part of his reign, up to the time of his treaty with Ramesses. He also faced the prospect of an Assyrian invasion of his territories from across the Euphrates. There was the further need for constant vigilance against the threat of uprisings in the local states upon which Hittite sovereignty had been imposed. The maintenance of the Great King's authority throughout the region meant a substantial ongoing commitment of resources for military operations, with the capacity for rapid deployment of troops likely to be called upon at any time to re-establish Hittite control over often highly volatile subject territories.

Yet in spite of their eastern focus, the Hittites sought also to establish and maintain a strong influence in the lands lying to their west. From c.1400 onwards, they conducted a series of military expeditions in these lands, often under their king's personal command, and eventually imposed vassal status upon a number of them. Almost inevitably, their western campaigns brought them into contact with Troy.

The contact was by no means insignificant. As we shall see, it was probably with a king of Troy that Muwattalli drew up one of his western treaties (the only western treaty to have survived from his reign) prior to his showdown with Ramesses at Kadesh. And it was probably because of a dispute over Troy that his brother Hattusili was willing to go to war in the west, while still keeping his troops in constant readiness for further major campaigns in Syria. Of what possible interest could Troy have been to the Hittites, especially when their commitments in other regions made such heavy demands on their far from inexhaustible resources? Let us remember that Troy was situated in the most remote part of the Near Eastern world, at the opposite end to where the Hittites' prime interests lay. Its population numbered a mere few thousand, not much more than the size of a modest Hittite expeditionary force. Why did the Hittites bother with it at all?

In order to answer this question, we must deal first with an important population group who spread widely through western and southern Anatolia from the third millennium onwards and who did much to shape the history of the regions where they settled.

THE LUWIANS[20]

During the Early Bronze Age, large numbers of newcomers arrived in Anatolia. One of the features they had in common was that they spoke a language, or languages, that belonged to the so-called Indo-European language family. Unfortunately, there is still no consensus among scholars as to their original homeland or as to the nature and date of their entry into Anatolia. Nor can we determine whether they arrived en masse over a relatively short period of time or came in a series of migrations spread throughout the third millennium. If they arrived in a single movement, they must have begun to disperse shortly afterwards into various parts of Anatolia. In either case, the languages they spoke, while retaining a number of common elements, became increasingly differentiated.

We can identify three main groups on the basis of these languages. One of the groups appears to have mixed with an indigenous population of central Anatolia called the Hattians. This group became part of the basic stock of the later Hittite kingdom, its language, called Nesite, acquiring the status of the kingdom's official chancellery language. We now call this language 'Hittite'. A second group, the Palaians, were located to the north-west of the land of Hatti, within the region later known as Paphlagonia. We call their language Palaic. The third group, speaking a form of Indo-European called Luwian, dispersed widely, over a period of many centuries. By the time of Troy VI's beginning, *c.*1700, they had occupied large areas of western and southern Anatolia.

We have noted that Troy II, along with the many other Early Bronze Age II sites, came to a violent end around 2300. Predatory newcomers to the region may have been at least partly responsible for their destruction. If so, Troy II perhaps fell victim to marauders from among the Luwian-speaking groups who were probably already occupying parts of western Anatolia before the end of the third millennium. But since there is no appreciable break in the material culture between Troy II and Troy III, we have suggested in Chapter 2 that, if Troy was attacked by outsiders, its attackers simply moved on after their sack of the city; or, if some of them did remain, they were absorbed into the local culture and became an indistinguishable part of the population of Troy III. This of course is all very speculative and, in suggesting a possible link between the destruction of Troy II and a hostile Luwian penetration of the region, we do need to stress that no one has yet been able to determine when or where Luwian-speakers first arrived in Anatolia. Indeed, they may already have entered the north-western part of it by the beginning of the third millennium. Right from its foundation, Troy could conceivably have had a Luwian population or, at least, a Luwian element within its population.

We can be sure, however, that by the early years of the Late Bronze Age extensive areas of Anatolia in the west and south were being settled by Luwian-speaking peoples. Indeed the earliest version of the Hittite Laws uses the term 'Luwiya' to designate a large part of western Anatolia.[21] Some of the major Late Bronze Age settlements in the west may well have been inhabited by Luwian settlers, such as Beycesultan II and, quite possibly, Troy VI. We have noted that the material culture of Troy VI indicates a major break with what had gone before. Perhaps it was only now that Luwian peoples in a world of expanding commercial opportunity saw the advantages in taking over a site like Troy for themselves. Can we conclude, then, that the Trojans, the inhabitants of Priam's kingdom, were one of the Luwian-speaking population groups of western Anatolia? If so, they would have been relatively close cousins of the Hittites, and much more distant cousins of the Mycenaean Greeks who also spoke an Indo-European language. We shall return to this question in Chapter 5.

Some time during the first century of the Late Bronze Age, the term 'Luwiya' appears to have dropped out of use, at least in Hittite texts, which replace it with the name 'Arzawa'. This new designation may reflect new political developments in the western Luwian-speaking areas, and the emergence of states or kingdoms there. Arzawa was the generic term for a complex of territories collectively known as the Arzawa lands, with a population that was probably largely, though by no means exclusively, made up of Luwian-speaking peoples. To judge from information provided by our Hittite texts, Arzawa, or the Arzawa Lands, incorporated up to five individual states or kingdoms: 'Arzawa Minor', Mira (with its later extension Kuwaliya, attached to it as frontier territory), the Seha River Land, Wilusa and Hapalla. These were apparently the main Luwian-speaking states in western Anatolia. They were ruled by kings, and they appear to have been independent of each other, though from time to time they may have formed confederacies for military and other purposes under the overall leadership of the kings of one of them. The ruler of what we have called Arzawa Minor (to distinguish it from the term Arzawa used in the broader sense) may have played such a role in the first half of the Late Bronze Age.

Each of the Arzawa Lands had a royal seat from which its king ruled. We know, for example, that the capital of Arzawa Minor was a city called Apasa, almost certainly the Bronze Age predecessor of Classical Ephesus. We have suggested, provisionally, that Troy VI was occupied by Luwians. It very likely ranked as one of the most important cities of western Anatolia in the Late Bronze Age and, given the prominence of Luwian-speaking population groups in this region at this time, we might reasonably suppose that Troy was the royal seat of another of the Arzawan kingdoms, even without further evidence to this effect. In fact, the majority of scholars now hold the view that Troy was the capital of the Arzawan kingdom called Wilusa. This possibility was first suggested in the 1920s by the Swiss scholar Emil Forrer who noted references to Wilusa (Wilusiya) in the Hittite texts. One reference in particular was juxtaposed with the name 'Taruisa'. Forrer believed that Wilus(iy)a was the Hittite way of writing the Greek name Wilios, an archaic form of Ilios before the dropping of the Greek letter digamma (commonly represented as 'w'),[22] and that Taruisa was the Hittite form of the Greek name Troia (Troy).

His identifications provoked much controversy and met with strong opposition, particularly from the German scholar Ferdinand Sommer, who refused to accept that the name similarities were any more than mere coincidence. The matter remained in dispute and the unfortunate Wilusa found itself shifted from one location to another on the map of western Anatolia according to scholarly whim. To be sure, the Troad remained the most strongly favoured candidate for its location, though purely as a matter of faith in the absence of any clear supporting evidence. Such evidence has gradually been coming to light over the past couple of decades. To demonstrate this, we need to look at the emerging picture, in its entirety, of the political configuration of Anatolia during the period of the Hittite kingdom.

THE GEOPOLITICAL LAYOUT OF LATE BRONZE AGE ANATOLIA

At the height of its power in the fourteenth and thirteenth centuries, the kingdom of Hatti incorporated large areas of Anatolia and northern Syria. The core territory of the kingdom, commonly referred to as the Hittite homeland, occupied the region in north-central Anatolia that lay within the confines of the Halys River.

The Hittites called this river the Marassantiya. Its modern Turkish name is the Kızıl Irmak. From their capital Hattusa, which lay 160 kilometres east of the modern Turkish capital Ankara, the Hittites exercised control over a large assortment of subject states ruled by local vassal rulers who owed their allegiance directly to the Great King himself. There were also substantial parts of Anatolia that were never subject to Hittite control. The mountainous region south of the Black Sea and north of the Hittite homeland, the Pontic zone, was inhabited by tribes called the Kaska peoples, who constantly menaced the Hittites' northern frontiers, often crossing these frontiers and, on more than one occasion, attacking and sacking the Hittite capital itself. Two regions, known as the Upper and Lower Lands, served as buffer zones for the Hittite homeland against enemy encroachment, but these proved to be of only limited effectiveness.

The Hittite kingdom waxed and waned dramatically through the 500 years of its existence. At its peak it claimed sovereignty over much of western, southern and eastern Anatolia and northern Syria. At its lowest point, it was reduced to little more than the area around Hattusa itself and, indeed, lost this to the enemy on at least two occasions before its final abandonment at the end of the Bronze Age. The political configuration of the Anatolian world was a very fluid one.

At a conference on Troy held in the University of Sheffield in 1977, James Mellaart spoke of 'the guessing game known as Hittite geography'. This has become a much quoted statement. It refers to scholars' numerous inconclusive and often conflicting attempts to work out the political geography of Anatolia in the Late Bronze Age. The basic problem can be quite simply stated. Hittite texts unearthed mainly from the archives of Hattusa provide us with hundreds of place names of the rivers, mountains, communities, cities and kingdoms of Anatolia in this period. However, relatively few of them can be anchored to precise or even approximate locations. Countries and cities have been shifted around in the scholarly literature, like pieces on a chessboard, with bewildering rapidity. Mellaart understandably called the process a game – though it was one in which he himself never hesitated to participate. Each scholar has his or her own views. Many have devised their own geopolitical schemes of things – and have often showed much ingenuity in manipulating the available information to fit their theories.

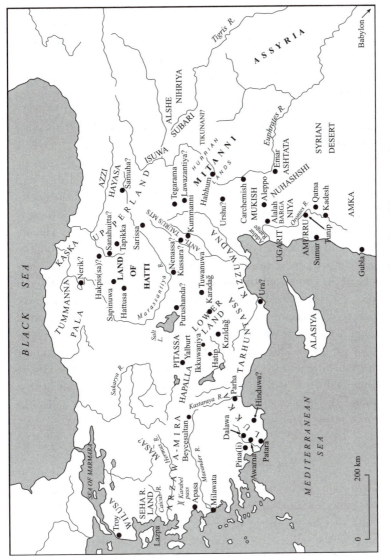

Map 3.2 Late Bronze Age Anatolia, northern Syria and northern Mesopotamia.

Yet recent developments in the field of Hittite scholarship, particularly in the past two decades, have substantially improved our knowledge of the layout of Late Bronze Age Anatolia. And, as we shall see, this has a major bearing on the identification of Troy in Hittite records. Increasingly, though still in small numbers, place names that occur in the texts are being linked with actual sites. Within the Hittite homeland itself, the archaeologist's spade has uncovered several regional administrative centres of the kingdom, each with tablet archives that enable the sites to be identified with names long known from Hittite texts – Sapinuwa (modern Ortaköy), Tapikka (modern Maşat) and Sarissa (modern Kuşaklı).[23] In other cases, accumulating textual information has provided a range of circumstantial evidence that points fairly unambiguously to particular locations. Some locations have long been established and accepted on this basis. We know that to the north-east of the homeland lay the country of Azzi-Hayasa and to the north-west the country of Pala-Tummanna in the region of the later Paphlagonia. Though as yet no specific material evidence of these countries has come to light in archaeological excavations, we can be confident of their general locations on the basis of information provided by our texts. So too, textual information makes clear the location of the country of Kizzuwadna in south-eastern Anatolia, in the region of Classical Cilicia. It was occupied by both Luwian and Hurrian population groups and fluctuated in its allegiance between Hatti and the Hurrian kingdom of Mitanni until its annexation by the Hittite king Tudhaliya early in the fourteenth century. Subsequently, around the middle of the century, Suppiluliuma put it under the direct authority of his son Telipinu.

The countries of southern Anatolia

Kizzuwadna's location, once thought to be in the north of Anatolia, was firmly established by Albrecht Goetze in an important monograph that he published in 1940.[24] But for many years after this, much of the political geography of southern and western Anatolia remained in doubt. There were almost as many opinions on the subject as there were scholars who wrote about it. Then came an important discovery in the Hittite capital. Underneath a pavement near Hattusa's southernmost entrance, the so-called 'Sphinx

Gate', a bronze tablet was unearthed in 1986, completely intact.[25] It was a treaty drawn up between the Hittite king Tudhaliya IV (c.1237–1209), son of Hattusili III, and his cousin Kurunta, whom Hattusili had appointed as ruler of the appanage kingdom of Tarhuntassa. This kingdom appears to have been created by Muwattalli when he relocated the Hittite capital there prior to his war with Ramesses.

Amongst other things, the tablet provides important information about Tarhuntassa's boundaries. We learn that the kingdom bordered Kizzuwadna in the east and, from there, extended westward along Anatolia's southern coast. Covering the region of Classical Cilicia Aspera and much of Classical Pamphylia, it terminated in the west with the Kastaraya River (Classical Cestrus) and the city of Parha (almost certainly Classical Perge). It may also have extended north to the Konya Plain. A group of hieroglyphic inscriptions has been discovered in this region, on a mountain-top sanctuary now called Karadağ and on a site called Kızıldağ where the remains of an ancient city are located.[26] More recently, a hieroglyphic inscription on a rock relief discovered at Hatip, 17 kilometres south-west of Konya, may define part of Tarhuntassa's northern boundary. The inscription features Kurunta, referred to above, who is called 'Great King' and may for a time have actually occupied the throne in Hattusa.[27] It is possible that Hittite Ikkuwaniya, which appears in the bronze tablet as a neighbour of Tarhuntassa, was located on the site of Konya (Classical Iconium).[28]

Parha and other names in the boundary description are juxtaposed in another text with a region called the Lukka Lands.[29] The Lukka people figure several times in the Hittite texts, and once also in an exchange of correspondence between the kings of Egypt and Alasiya (Cyprus). They were one of the Luwian population groups of western Anatolia and, as we shall see, they may well have contributed to the tradition of a Trojan War.[30] By a process of association, the bronze tablet helps us establish a location for Lukka: it extended from the western end of Pamphylia into the regions which the Greeks later called Pisidia and Lycia.

A number of cities in first-millennium Lycia clearly derive their names from Bronze Age settlements or districts that lay in or at least close to Lukka territory. Arñna (the Lycian name for Lycia's chief city, located on the Xanthus River and better known by its

Greek name Xanthus) is the Lycian derivative of Late Bronze Age Awarna. Pinara, which lies to the west of the Xanthus River, is the Lycian derivative of Pina(li). Awarna and the forerunner of Pinara appear together in the so-called Yalburt inscription. Unearthed in 1971 at Yalburt to the north-west of Konya, the inscription records Tudhaliya IV's conquests in the Lukka lands.[31] Tlawa (the Lycian name for Tlos) is derived from Bronze Age T/Dalawa, Kandyba (the Greek name for Lycian Khãkbi) perhaps from Bronze Age Hinduwa. Dalawa and Hinduwa were the names of cities probably belonging to the Lukka Lands that rebelled against Hittite rule early in the fourteenth century. Pttara (Greek Patara) is derived from Patar(a); a Mount Patara is referred to in the Yalburt inscription.

Of course, we cannot be altogether sure that places so called in the first millennium were in fact Bronze Age foundations of the same name, or indeed that they were built on sites with an earlier level of human habitation. In some instances, duplication of names may well have been due to population movements, groups of peoples shifting from one region to another and naming their new settlements after their old. And it has to be said that Bronze Age finds in Lycia have been meagre in the extreme. But the textual evidence is more promising, particularly when it is used in conjunction with the sites of first-millennium Lycia. We have in this case a cluster of first-millennium names of Bronze Age origin denoting Lycian cities that lay in close proximity to each other. This cluster can be paired with a similar cluster of names of Bronze Age settlements that we know lay in the same region. Groups of corresponding names are much more likely to indicate direct continuity between second- and first-millennium settlements than would be the case if we had only one or two name pairs. We can be reasonably confident that a region broadly definable as the Lukka Lands occupied the south-western corner of Anatolia in the Late Bronze Age, covering Lycia and the western end of Pamphylia and extending beyond that to parts of the later Pisidia, Isauria and perhaps even to Lycaonia. The inhabitants of this region were a Luwian-speaking people, and their link with the later inhabitants of Lycia is indicated by the fact that the latter's native language, attested in their inscriptions, was closely related to Bronze Age Luwian.[32]

We have now 'blocked out' the southern coastlands and their immediate hinterlands in our map of Late Bronze Age Anatolia and can proceed to the countries of western Anatolia. But before doing so, it is as well to remind ourselves of what precisely we are doing. In almost all the cases with which we are dealing, we are drawing conclusions based entirely or almost entirely on written information. In many cases this information is compelling. However, no proposed location for a country, no proposed identification of a particular site with a particular city known from our texts, can be regarded as absolutely certain until we have clear tangible proof, produced by the archaeologist's trowel or spade, from the location or the site itself. And even when we can with a high degree of confidence locate a country or a kingdom on our map, we can often only guess at where its actual boundaries lay – where it ended and its neighbour began. With these provisos in mind, let us move on to the west.

The countries of western Anatolia

To the north-west of Lukka, in the region of Classical Caria, lay the land of Milawata (otherwise called Millawanda). Its location has been confirmed by the now assured identification of the city of Milawata with the site of Classical Miletus at the mouth of the Maeander River. Excavations at Miletus have brought to light three main building phases in the site's Late Bronze Age history. The first of these reveals strong influence from Minoan Crete and, almost certainly, the settlement of Milawata by migrants from Crete in what archaeologists refer to as the Middle Minoan IIIb Period, c.1600. As we shall see, the Minoan presence at Miletus was replaced by a Mycenaean presence in the city's subsequent phases.

However, the main countries of western Anatolia were the Arazawa Lands, whose relationship with Hatti varied markedly from one period to another. At one time they were enemies of the Hittites and challenged their political and military supremacy in Anatolia. Later they became vassal states of Hatti – though some rebelled from time to time against Hittite overlordship and allied themselves with external enemies. The biggest thorn in the Hittite side during the first half of the Late Bronze Age was Arzawa Minor, a kingdom that clashed repeatedly with the Hittites until it was destroyed in the late fourteenth century by King Mursili II. In the aftermath of its destruction, tens of thousands of its population were transported back to the Hittite homeland. The royal seat of the kingdom was called Apasa, which we believe was located on or near the site of Classical Ephesus. Late Bronze Age pottery and parts of what is very likely a Late Bronze Age fortification wall have recently been discovered there, on the acropolis of Ayasuluk. This was probably the location of pre-first-millennium Ephesus.[33] After the dismemberment of Arzawa Minor, much, if not all, of its territory was almost certainly reassigned by its Hittite conqueror to the adjacent Arzawan land called Mira, whose ruler apparently supported the Hittites in their campaign against its troublesome neighbour. Mira's territory may thus have been greatly expanded, so that it now reached the coast, where it probably incorporated Apasa and, from there, extended a considerable distance inland, where it encompassed the land of Kuwaliya. Beycesultan, on a branch of the upper Maeander, may have been Kuwaliya's chief city.[34]

We can now very likely fix part of the northern boundary of Mira-Kuwaliya. The key to this location is an inscription carved on a rock-cut monument next to a relief of a human figure in a mountain pass called Karabel, some 28 kilometres east of Izmir (Classical Smyrna), which lies on Turkey's central Aegean coast. The relief, which overlooks the pass, depicts an adult male armed with a bow, spear and a sword with a crescent-shaped pommel. On his head is a tall peaked cap. The inscription has long been known. It was referred to by Herodotus in the fifth century BC, who identified the sculpture with an Egyptian prince called Sesostris and translated the inscription: 'With my own shoulders I won this land'.[35] Professor Hawkins has now provided an authentic translation of the inscription, which is written in the Luwian hieroglyphic script: 'Tarkasnawa, king of the land of Mira, son of (?) (reading uncertain), king of the land of Mira, grandson of [. . .], king of the land of Mira'.[36]

The monument may well be a frontier marker (though we cannot be certain of this), located on Mira's northern border. Rock-cut inscriptions found in the Latmus mountain region (at the mouth of the Maeander, north-east of Miletus) and containing the names of princes of Mira provide further tangible indications of the territory that Mira covered.[37]

One of the countries that almost certainly bordered upon Mira was the Arzawan country of Hapalla. It was located between Mira to its west and the Hittite buffer zone called the Lower Land to its east. It seems also to have lain close to the country of Pitassa, a land

Figure 3.4 The Karabel relief (photograph by J. D. Hawkins).

apparently independent of Hittite authority and probably lying just to the west of the Salt Lake in the region of Classical Pedasa. The bronze tablet refers to Pitassa in the border definition of the land of Tarhuntassa.

From another text we can deduce that Mira shared a border to its north with the Arzawan kingdom called the Seha River Land.[38] The latter lay beyond the Karabel Pass, if the monument found there marked Mira's northern boundary. Its name must have come from one of two main rivers in the region – either the Caicus (modern Bakir) or the Hermus (modern Gediz) as they were called in Classical times.[39] One of these was presumably the Seha River. From yet another text, we learn that a place called Lazpa was a dependency of the Seha River Land.[40] The identification of Lazpa with the island of Lesbos off Anatolia's north-west coast provides a further indication of the Seha River Land's location. (Lesbos was sacked by Achilles, according to Homer.)

Only one other country classified as an Arzawa Land remains to be located on our map. This is the country called Wilusa. We now have a clearer indication of Wilusa's location. A letter written to the Hittite king by his vassal Manapa-Tarhunda, ruler of the Seha River Land, indicates that trouble had broken out in Wilusa and that a Hittite expeditionary force had been sent to the region to deal with it.[41] The Hittites came first to the Seha River Land and, from there, proceeded directly into the land of Wilusa. It seems very likely that Wilusa and the Seha River Land were neighbouring kingdoms. And since the latter shared a border with Mira to its south, Wilusa can only have lain to its north. This would almost certainly place it in the region called the Troad in Classical times, where the kingdom of Priam has been located. We now have strong grounds for identifying this kingdom with the historically attested Wilusa, one of the Arzawan states of the Late Bronze Age. Troy VI would thus have been the royal seat of the kingdom of Wilusa.

This identification will provide the basis for a later stage in our investigation of the Trojans and their neighbours. But we should be quite clear about its status. Though the evidence in favour of it is strong, none the less it is circumstantial and will remain that way until such time as incontrovertible proof of it turns up. For the time being, the premise on which the identification is based is a matter of assumption rather than established fact.

4

THE AEGEAN
NEIGHBOURS

MINOAN CRETE

After twenty years of fighting and wandering, Odysseus has just
returned to his homeland, Ithaca. He is disguised as a beggar, his
true identity unknown even to his wife Penelope. She asks him who
he is and whence he has come. Pretending to be of Cretan origin, he
fondly describes to her the land of his alleged birth: 'Out in the
wine-dark sea there lies a land called Crete, a rich and lovely land,
sea-girt and densely peopled, with ninety cities.'[1]

This rich and lovely sea-girt land was the home of what we now
call the Minoan civilization, the civilization of Bronze Age Crete. It
reached its peak in the so-called Palace period, which spanned the
first six centuries of the second millennium – the Middle and part
of the Late Minoan periods in archaeological terms. The use of 'Palace'
as a chronological label comes from the monumental building
complexes that were constructed at Cnossus, Phaestus and the site
now called Mallia (ancient name unknown), originally around 2000.
These complexes apparently served as administrative and cultural
centres of the Minoan civilization during the Middle and Late Bronze
Ages. But their precise nature and functions have been a matter of
some debate. It has been suggested, for example, that they were
temple communities,[2] or even burial cities. Whatever the merits of
these and other suggestions, we should acknowledge that 'palace'
may not be an altogether appropriate term – though for want of
something better, we shall continue to use it as a matter of conven-
tion and convenience. There were two phases in the Palace period.
Phase I came to an end when the complexes were destroyed, probably

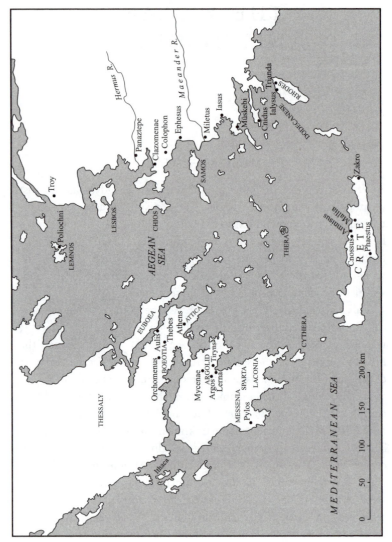

Map 4.1 The Aegean neighbours

due to natural causes, around 1700. Their prompt rebuilding ushered in Phase II of the Palace period, about the same time as the emergence of Troy VI.

Crete's palace-centred civilization flourished during the most prosperous period of the island's history. Its prosperity was due to several interrelated factors – thriving agricultural and craft industries, a long period of peace and stability and, most importantly, a vigorous international trade network. The term 'thalassocracy' commonly used in reference to Minoan Crete reflects a widely held assumption that the Minoans enjoyed commercial and perhaps also some degree of political dominance in the Aegean and eastern Mediterranean regions through much of the first half of the second millennium.[3] In exchange for imported raw materials, including copper, gold, silver and tin, the Minoans exported a range of finished products that were highly prized on overseas markets: textiles, ceramic ware, wine, oil, spices, perfumes and jewellery. Via Near Eastern emporia like Ugarit on the Levantine coast, many of these products found their way into the homes of wealthy families in mainland and island Greece, Mesopotamia, Syria, Anatolia and Egypt.

Contacts between Egypt and Minoan Crete in the Second Palace Period are indicated by fragments of Minoan-style wall paintings found on the site of Tell el-Dab'a (ancient Avaris) in Egypt's eastern delta. They date to the reign of the pharaoh Ahmose (c.1550–1520), founder of the eighteenth dynasty. The paintings were executed either by Minoan artists living in or visiting Egypt, or by Egyptian artists imitating Minoan artistic techniques and themes.[4] In the following century, not long before the end of Crete's Second Palace Period, paintings in the tombs of nobles in western Thebes depict the presence in Egypt of representatives from the Minoan world.[5] They are almost certainly members of trade missions, though Egyptian propaganda represents them as 'bringers of tribute'.

Many scholars believe that the name 'Keftiu' or 'Kaptaru' which appears in a number of texts from Bronze Age through to Greek and Roman times refers to Crete, though identifications with other parts of the eastern Mediterranean world have also been proposed.[6] The name appears, for example, amongst a list of Aegean places on a statue base in the temple of the pharaoh Amenhotep III at Kom el-Hetan. The list is in two parts. On the left-hand side are names of mainland Greek sites, including Mycenae, Nauplion, Messenia, Elis and Cythera, and Minoan sites, including the palace centres Cnossus (together with its port Amnisus) and Phaestus, and also the town called Cydonia (modern Khania). On the right-hand side, the names Dnj and Kftw (Keftiu) are inscribed. It is possible that these names designate the lands where the places in the left-hand list were located. Dnj has been equated with a hypothetical 'Danaya', perhaps the name, or one of the names, used of mainland Greece in the Bronze Age.[7] (We recall that Homer sometimes referred to the Greeks as 'Danaoi'.) Other Egyptian texts refer to ships of Keftiu in the context of Late Bronze Age international trade. Clearly Keftiu/Kaptaru played an important role in the world of international sea commerce, which would of course be fully consistent with its identification with the homeland of the Minoan civilization.

The Minoans were active in the eastern Aegean already in the First Palace Period, as indicated by the finds of Middle Minoan I–II pottery on the islands of Rhodes and Samos, as well as on the Anatolian mainland at Miletus, Iasus, and possibly Cnidus. At Iasus, finds of the beautiful Kamares pottery date to this period. Subsequently, in the Middle Minoan IIIB period, around 1600, the Minoan presence in the region becomes increasingly marked, particularly at Miletus, the land called Milawata or Millawanda in Hittite texts. Excavations here have revealed three main building phases in the Late Bronze Age history of the site. The first of these indicates strong influence from Crete, as illustrated by Minoan stone vessels, pottery of Minoan type, Minoan wall frescos and Minoan masonry techniques and architecture. Of particular interest is the appearance of three signs from the Minoan Linear A script on the fragments of a clay vessel – the earliest evidence we have for writing in western Anatolia. The presence of all these features indicates, almost certainly, the settlement of Milawata by migrants from Crete in the Middle Minoan III period. In the same period, there is evidence of Minoan connections with other sites in the region, such as Iasus on the Anatolian coast to the south of Miletus, and with the islands of the south-east Aegean, such as Rhodes.[8] In these cases, however, it is uncertain whether the Minoan connections reflect actual Minoan settlement.

THE ANCESTORS OF THE GREEKS

Through its network of trading contacts, Troy was almost certainly in contact either directly or indirectly with the Minoans as well as with other Aegean peoples, though material evidence for such contact is at present very meagre. That situation changes dramatically when, in the late fifteenth century, the Aegean world takes on a very different character. For reasons that still mystify scholars, the Second Palace period of the Minoan civilization came to an abrupt end at the close of what archaeologists call the Late Minoan IB period. Around 1450,[9] the major palace centres on the island, Phaestus and Mallia, and perhaps also Cnossus, suffered violent destruction.[10] Scholars cannot yet agree on the cause or causes of this destruction – whether it was due to natural forces or human agency or a combination of the two. But it clearly had a devastating effect on the island's population, economy and way of life. Phaestus and Mallia were abandoned for all time. But Cnossus was to receive a new lease of life. Some years after the catastrophe, in the so-called Late Minoan II period, it was occupied by peoples from the Greek mainland. The new occupants rebuilt and remodelled the palace centre, retaining many elements of its earlier existence, but imposing upon it their own distinctive character.

Who were these mainlanders? This question brings us into the world of a people who had a great deal more to do with Troy than their Minoan predecessors: the Greeks of the 'heroic age'. Most scholars now believe that the ancestors of these Greeks first arrived in mainland Greece around 2100. We have seen that the Early Bronze Age civilization here reached its peak during the so-called Early Helladic II phase, whose most prominent site was Lerna (Level III) in the Argolid. The sudden end of this phase was marked by the violent destruction of Lerna, reflecting a pattern of destruction that spread to and overwhelmed many other sites on the Greek mainland at this time. We have noted a similar pattern of destruction in western and southern Anatolia at the end of the Early Bronze II period. The period that followed in the wake of these traumatic events was characterized by smaller and poorer settlements, reduced trading contacts and a reversion to a more rudimentary, subsistence-type lifestyle. Two new pottery types now make their appearance, a matt-painted ware, and the so-called Minyan ware; the latter, so named by Schliemann and once wrongly believed to be of western Anatolian origin, is a very distinctive type of grey, wheelmade pottery, with a metal-like sheen and a soapy feel.

What can we conclude from the destructions and their aftermath? Widespread devastation in a region followed by a distinct break in its culture often heralds the arrival of a new population group. That provides us with a possible context for 'the coming of the Greeks'. But there are many uncertainties about the date and manner of their coming, about who they were to begin with, and where they came from. Let us remember that we are dealing with a period before we have the benefit of written records, that mute artefacts on their own can give rise to a wide range of interpretations and conclusions. Carl Blegen claimed that the Greeks did not enter Greece until the beginning of what he called the Middle Helladic period, around 1900; John Caskey, the excavator of Lerna, believed that there were two waves of immigrants: one at the end of Early Helladic II, the other at the end of Early Helladic III. More recently, Robert Drews has argued that the first Greeks did not appear until around 1600, at the beginning of the Late Helladic period. Differences of opinion are bound to persist – and scholars would not want it otherwise! None the less, there is a broad scholarly consensus that the break between Early Helladic II and III, around 2100, marks the arrival of the 'first Greeks' in their new homeland: mainland Greece.

If that conclusion is correct, can we in any way tie their arrival to events in western Anatolia around the same period? Attempts to establish direct links between the immigrants into Greece and the peoples of western Anatolia through ceramic and linguistic evidence (the latter primarily on the basis of place names in both regions with -*nth*- and -*ss*- infixes) have proved either unsustainable or at best inconclusive. Of course, the idea of some kind of connection between violent upheavals in Anatolia at the end of the Early Bronze Age II period and similar upheavals in mainland Greece at the end of the Early Helladic II period is an attractive one, with plenty of dramatic potential. It is tempting to conjure up an image of marauding hordes sweeping southwards and westwards across Early Bronze Age Anatolia, with one of the northernmost groups pausing only long enough to destroy and pillage Troy II before continuing upon its path of destruction into the Greek mainland where it wreaks havoc amongst the settled communities there.

But we should not too readily assume that the end of the Early Bronze II period in Anatolia correlates closely with the end of the Early Helladic II period in Greece. There may have been a time gap of some decades, or even a century or two, between them. It is impossible to assign anything like precise dates. Quite apart from this, invasion theories are not much in fashion these days. Scholars now prefer to think in terms of more gradual processes, of newcomers entering and settling in a region over a period of years, decades or even centuries, gradually amalgamating with the already established peoples in the region. Undoubtedly disputes broke out between original inhabitants and newcomers, and perhaps sometimes escalated into major conflicts. But any notions of massive invasions by marauding barbarians, such as those that brought the Roman empire to an end many centuries later, must be firmly discarded.

The early Greeks were probably spreading through mainland Greece around much the same time as Luwians were occupying various parts of western Anatolia. One thing the groups had in common was that both were of Indo-European stock. So if the Late Bronze Age Trojans were predominantly of Luwian origin, many of the inhabitants of Troy VI would have belonged to the same language-speaking family as their neighbours across the Aegean. But that is a far cry from claiming that they were closely related. Let us not be misled by the virtually identical customs and beliefs of Greeks and Trojans in the *Iliad*, or by the ability of Agamemnon's and Priam's warriors to converse directly with each other without the aid of interpreters. These are purely conventions, and Homer's audiences would have had no trouble in accepting them as such, just as today no one would expect a movie audience at a biblical epic to believe that God's first language was English, spoken with an American accent. Greeks and Trojans were no more than very distant cousins, speaking languages quite unintelligible to each other.

Present indications are that the Middle Helladic period in Greece (*c.*1900–1600) was one of relative cultural stagnation and reduced outside contacts, perhaps due to the disappearance of the major centres of civilization in the last century of the Early Helladic period and the intrusion of new population groups, 'proto-Greeks', around the same time. But we cannot be sure whether these new groups were responsible for the disappearance of these centres, or merely occupied the vacuum that their disappearance had created. Moreover, it is hard to believe that all communications with the world beyond the mainland were lost in this period. Very likely, trade of some kind continued with the islands of the Cyclades and probably also some sporadic contact was maintained with western Anatolia, including Troy. However, we have yet to find evidence of Middle Helladic peoples engaged in maritime trading ventures.

THE MYCENAEANS

Around 1600, a century or so after the emergence of Troy VI, new developments in mainland Greece marked the beginning of what is now called the Late Helladic period. The stimulus for this, the most illustrious period in the history of the Greek Bronze Age, is – once more – a matter of debate. According to Drews, *this* was the time of entry of foreign intruders into Greece who were to transform the civilization of their new homeland; Greece was now taken over by a charioteering people who came from the lands south of the Caucasus and launched a seaborne invasion of the Greek world; it is to them that the sudden surge in the material civilization of the Greek world was due, to them the establishment of widespread trading contacts between the Greek world, the lands of the eastern Mediterranean and the lands beyond it.[11] However, most scholars take the line that the evolution from Middle to Late Helladic, substantial though it was, should be attributed to the already existing inhabitants of mainland Greece. Certainly, Drews has a point when he claims that evidence for a peaceful internal evolution from Middle to Late Helladic is very slight and questionable. But we could also say the same about his own theory of a sudden and dramatic overthrow of the existing order in Greece by external invaders. We have yet to find a convincing explanation for the sudden florescence in the material civilization of mainland Greece around 1600.

The most prominent of the Late Helladic sites is Mycenae in the Argolid Plain. Mycenae was the first such site to be excavated, by Heinrich Schliemann in 1876. It was apparently the richest and most powerful settlement in Late Helladic Greece, and in legendary tradition it was the home of Agamemnon, leader of the combined Achaean forces against Troy. For all these reasons, its name is commonly used as a convenient label for the Late Helladic civilization as a whole. The first phase of this civilization is represented by six shaft

Figure 4.1 The Lion Gate, Mycenae.

graves, dating to the sixteenth century, which were unearthed on the citadel of Mycenae. All but one were excavated by Schliemann. Their undisturbed contents contained the remains of nineteen persons of both sexes, adult and child, clothed in magnificent funeral garb and richly bedecked with jewellery, much of it of pure gold. Also included amongst the grave goods was a large array of weapons (some with exquisite inlays), armour, tools and beautifully wrought domestic vessels of precious metals – leaving us in no doubt that already in this first phase of its Late Helladic existence, Mycenae was a place of great wealth. From the shaft graves alone, it is clear that Homer's description of it as *polychrysos*, 'rich in gold', is well justified.

That raises a question. How do we account for Mycenae's wealth, given that the region in which it lay was poor in natural resources, particularly mineral and agricultural resources? If, as generally supposed, it lay at the hub of a major communications network, strategic location probably had much to do with its apparent affluence. It may have played a leading role in the distribution of the raw materials – commodities such as copper and tin, precious metals such as silver and gold – that were much in demand in the Aegean world and that had to be obtained primarily or exclusively from outside sources.[12] Fine textiles and spices (such as cumin and sesame), ivory from Syria, along with a range of exotic luxury items – ostrich eggs from Nubia, lapis lazuli from Mesopotamia, alabaster and faience from Crete, amber from the Baltic region[13] – were also amongst the goods regularly imported into the Mycenaean kingdoms.

Certainly Mycenae itself must have been actively involved from very early in the Late Helladic period in wealth-producing activities far beyond the limits of its own territorial confines, activities both of a peaceful commercial nature as well as of a warlike and piratical nature. But would not its inland location have been a distinct disadvantage for such enterprises? The question of why Mycenae became so prominent and how it achieved its wealth is not one we can readily answer.

Apart from Mycenae, there was a burgeoning of many centres of Mycenaean civilization throughout Greece, such as Argos and Tiryns in the Argolid region, Pylos (discovered by Carl Blegen in 1939) in Messenia, and Athens, Thebes and Orchomenus in the regions later called Attica and Boeotia. Their roughly parallel development suggests a degree of interconnectedness between them. It is quite possible that on occasions some of them engaged in joint overseas enterprises, whether for trade or for war. A network of roads may have facilitated communication between them. Perhaps too there were groups of itinerant architects, artisans and artists who carried their skills and services from one region to another. This may partly account for the strong homogeneity of Mycenaean civilization, as reflected, for example, in the similar layouts of the palaces and in the close resemblances observable from one centre to another in Mycenaean paintings and in pottery styles and techniques. These, together with a marked uniformity in burial practices throughout the Mycenaean world and the widespread adoption of the so-called Linear B script for written records, depicting very similar bureaucratic practices in the different centres, indicate a pervasive cultural unity in the Late Helladic world, and indeed throughout Late Bronze Age Greece in general.

On the other hand, there is no evidence for anything approaching what we might call a Mycenaean empire, made up of peoples and states bound together under a single overlord. Rather, the political configuration of Mycenaean Greece was probably very much as Homer depicts it – small independent kingdoms, one of whose rulers might have acted from time to time as a kind of *primus inter pares* (first amongst equals) for collaborative enterprises. It may well be that confederations were formed between various kingdoms for particular purposes, much as the *Iliad* represents the combined Greek operations against Troy. The core of each kingdom was a palace centre. This was generally accommodated in a fortified citadel, which contained the residence and reception halls of the king who exercised authority over a region that included a number of villages and farmlands lying within a radius of a few kilometres of the centre.[14]

Each kingdom may not have been markedly different in size to the individual city-states of the Sumerians or the Early Bronze Age kingdoms of Anatolia or, indeed, the kingdom of Late Bronze Age Troy. None of these city-states or kingdoms were remotely comparable with the empires that had emerged in the Near East during the course of the third and second millennia: the Akkadian, neo-Sumerian, Assyrian, Babylonian, Mitannian, Hittite and Egyptian empires. The kingdoms of the Mycenaean world were small by comparison. In terms of their size and resources, they might more aptly be compared with some of the more prominent local kingdoms and principalities of the Near Eastern world.

In the Late Helladic III period, roughly 1400 to 1100, the Mycenaean civilization enjoyed its most extensive contacts with the outside world. Mycenaean products were widely distributed through-out this world, and Mycenaean settlements were established in a number of locations beyond the Greek mainland, including Crete, Rhodes, the islands of the eastern Aegean and the western coast of Anatolia. This period also witnessed the most impressive build-ing achievements of the Mycenaean civilization, as reflected in the monumental fortifications of the citadels in the Argolid plain, the palace architecture, and the widespread distribution of *tholos* tombs, the most spectacular of which were those of Mycenae itself. These were the material trappings of what may seem to have been great and powerful kingdoms whose activities and influence extended well beyond their own immediate territories.

The collapse of the Minoan 'palace' administrations may have helped pave the way for a major expansion of Mycenaean overseas enterprises at this time.[15] But in recent years there has been a tendency to scale down assumptions about the role played by the Mycenaeans themselves in international commercial operations. Their products were certainly widely available in Aegean and Near Eastern markets, but the evidence that they themselves were active agents in their distribution is surprisingly slight. For example, though trade items were exchanged between Egypt and the Mycenaean world throughout the Late Helladic period (Mycenaean items have been discovered at some twenty Egyptian sites), there is no evidence that Mycenaean traders themselves ever visited Egypt. By contrast, Minoans appear in Egyptian tomb paintings of the eighteenth dynasty, as we have noted, and other tombs of this period depict merchant vessels from Syria.[16] Mycenaeans or Mycenaean vessels are conspicuous by their absence in Egyptian paintings. Nor is there any evidence that Mycenaeans were ever present in the trading emporia of the Syro-Palestinian region, even though more than sixty sites in this region have produced Mycenaean pottery. Export and import traffic between the Mycenaean kingdoms and other parts of the Late Bronze Age world was very largely in the hands of others, such as Syrian merchants, acting as the agents for the distribution of Mycenaean products as well as for imports into the Mycenaean world.

Yet Mycenaeans were clearly active in a number of overseas enterprises throughout the Late Helladic period, with a marked increase in this level of activity in the period's third and final phase.[17] We have referred to the arrival of Mycenaean settlers in Crete, particularly at Cnossus, some time after the collapse of the Minoan palace centres. There were also Mycenaean settlements on the island of Rhodes and other islands of the Dodecanese, though these may have been no more than enclaves of merchants within a native population, at places like Trianda and Ialysus on Rhodes, who were perhaps quartered there to arrange the trans-shipment of goods to Cyprus and the Levant.[18] There is no evidence that Mycenaeans themselves were present in the Levantine region. Nor is there evidence that Mycenaean immigrants established settlements on Cyprus, called Alasiya in Late Bronze Age texts. References to the island in these texts indicate that it was much more closely linked, politically and culturally, to the Near Eastern world than it was to the lands of the Aegean.[19]

Anatolia's Aegean coast, on the other hand, provides substantial evidence of contact with the Mycenaean world. Mycenaean pottery is found at a number of sites along this coast, including (from north to south) Troy, Clazomenae, Panaztepe, Colophon and Ephesus. To be sure, at these and other sites north of the Maeander River, the finds indicate trading contacts rather than actual settlement. However at Miletus and Müskebi (south of the Maeander), Mycenaean architecture and Mycenaean tombs leave no doubt that these sites were inhabited by Mycenaean settlers. At Miletus, the Minoan elements of the city's first building phase were replaced by Mycenaean in its second phase, as illustrated by Mycenaean figurines and domestic pottery. Already in this second phase, which came to an end with destruction by fire (late Late Minoan I period), there may have been Mycenaeans among the city's inhabitants. But the evidence for Mycenaean settlement is much stronger in the city's third phase. In addition to the abundant quantities of Mycenaean pottery belonging to it (much produced from local clay), we now find chamber tombs of Mycenaean type containing Mycenaean grave goods. Iasus, which lay on the coast south of Miletus, may have been another site where elements of Minoan culture gave way to Mycenaean. But the evidence that Iasus actually became a Mycenaean settlement remains inconclusive.[20] Much more certain is the evidence for Mycenaean settlers in the Halicarnassus Peninsula, at the site of Müskebi, where forty-eight Mycenaean chamber tombs have been discovered.[21]

From the material evidence it is clear that Anatolia's western coast held much interest for Mycenaean Greeks. Which raises questions that archaeological remains on their own cannot answer. What attracted the Mycenaeans to this region, apart from the fact that it was for them the most accessible large overseas landmass? Who in the Mycenaean world initiated contacts with the region? Who established the settlements there? Kings? Trading consortia? Political refugees? Private adventurers? What impact did their presence have on the local populations? How did the kingdom of Hatti, which claimed sovereignty over many of these populations, react to their presence?

THE AHHIYAWA CONTROVERSY

Our search for answers to these questions brings us to one of the longest standing and most hotly debated issues of Hittite scholarship. Mycenaean activities in western Anatolia, even only on its fringes, could not have failed to bring those who conducted them into contact with territories subject to the kingdom of Hatti. Surely the Hittite texts, which deal extensively with western Anatolian affairs, have something to say about these intruders who were muscling in on, or at the very least threatening, their Great King's western states. If so, what do the texts call the intruders?

Again the name of the Swiss philologist Emil Forrer surfaces. In the 1920s, a few years after the decipherment of the Hittite language, Forrer claimed to have found Mycenaeans in a number of Hittite texts. Observing that Homer frequently uses the term 'Achaean' to refer to the Bronze Age Greeks,[22] he also noted that the Hittite texts contain references to a place called Ahhiyawa (earlier form Ahhiya). This, he concluded, was the Hittite way of designating the land of the Achaeans.[23] His claim sparked off a long and sometimes acrimonious debate, but it is now accepted by the great majority of scholars. Indeed the circumstantial evidence in favour of it seems overwhelming. As I have commented elsewhere, if the equation between Ahhiyawa and the Mycenaean world is not valid, then we have to accept that there were two quite separate Late Bronze Age civilizations with very similar names, in the same region and in the same period. One of them, Ahhiyawa, is attested by documentary evidence but has left no identifiable trace in the archaeological record; the other, the Mycenaean/Achaean civilization, has left abundant archaeological evidence but no identifiable trace in the documentary record. This goes beyond mere coincidence.

We can with some confidence proceed on the assumption that Forrer's identification is a valid one, while acknowledging that we still lack hard proof of it – and may never find such proof unless something like a cache of letters addressed to a king of Ahhiyawa turns up in the remains of one of the Mycenaean palaces.[24] Stranger things have happened in the world of archaeology!

If accepted, the identification has substantial historical implications. For the Hittite tablets that refer to Ahhiyawa provide our only significant source of contemporary written information about the history of the Ahhiyawan-Mycenaean world. To be sure, writing was known in the Mycenaean world, as illustrated by the thousands of Linear B tablets whose inscriptions are written in an early form of the Greek language. These tablets have come to light at a number of Mycenaean sites, most notably Cnossus after the Mycenaean occupation, and Pylos in the western Peloponnese. But valuable as these documents are for the information they provide about Mycenaean society, their contents are confined almost entirely to the affairs of the local palace bureaucracies: inventories of goods, muster rolls, land produce, items dedicated to the gods and so forth. Only very occasionally, and very indirectly, can we glean from them anything of broader historical value.

On the other hand, the Hittite tablets that refer to Ahhiyawa add a significant historical dimension to the field of Mycenaean studies. Archaeology indicates Mycenaean trading interests in western Anatolia, but little more. The tablets, ranging in date from the early fourteenth to the late thirteenth century, make clear that Mycenaean Greeks were also politically and militarily involved in western Anatolian affairs during the last two centuries of the Bronze Age. Inevitably they came into contact, and sometimes conflict, with the kingdoms and cities of the region.

Which leads to the question that scholars, archaeologists and film-makers have been repeatedly asking and attempting to answer: Do the texts that refer to the Land of Ahhiyawa indicate conflict between this land and Troy?

Before addressing this question, and by way of background to it, we will find it useful to review the range of information that our written records provide about Ahhiyawa – that is to say, about the world of the Mycenaean Greeks. The term is sometimes used in a very broad sense, perhaps in reference to the Mycenaean world in general. But in a number of texts, it is more specific – referring to an actual kingdom of Ahhiyawa which, for a period of time, exercised sovereignty over part of the western Anatolian coast. The ruler of this kingdom was the recipient of letters from the Hittite royal court.

The first written evidence for Ahhiyawan-Mycenaean involvement in western Anatolia introduces us to a 'Man of Ahhiya' called Attarssiya (or Attarissiya), one of only two Ahhiyawan persons who are actually mentioned by name in our surviving texts. Attarssiya was present on the Anatolian mainland around 1400 with a small army of infantry and 100 chariots. What was he doing there? Professor Niemeier has suggested that political pressures in the Mycenaean mainland connected with the rise of the centralized palace system may have been an inducement for displaced Mycenaean nobles to try their fortunes across the Aegean; Attarssiya, with his own private militia, was perhaps one of these displaced aristocrats, seeking to carve out a new homeland for himself and his followers in western Anatolia.[25] According to the Hittite text that records his aggressive activities in the region,[26] he later set his sights on Cyprus/Alasiya. Another suggestion is that men like Attarssiya (who is never accorded the title 'King') may have been agents of the new expanding Mycenaean palace centres whose rulers sought to extend their control to the Aegean islands and the south-west coast of Asia Minor; their prime purpose in doing so was to gain access to valuable resources in short supply or unobtainable in their homelands.

Such resources almost certainly included human labour. The large workforces required for the construction of the fortified citadels and palaces no doubt placed a considerable strain on local sources of supply. Much of the labour may therefore have come from external sources. Kidnapping and raiding were major facts of life in the society depicted by Homer, and in this respect at least Homeric tradition may well reflect common Mycenaean practice. We know from the so-called Tawagalawa letter, a well-known letter written by the Hittite king Hattusili III to his Ahhiyawan counterpart in the thirteenth century (to be discussed in more detail in Chapters 5 and 8), that some thousands of western Anatolians were taken from their homelands by agents of the Ahhiyawan king – willingly in some cases, forcibly in others – and resettled in territory ruled by their abductor. Very likely many of the males thus 'recruited' were used in citadel-construction labour gangs. Indeed, in an admittedly late tradition, we hear of 'giants' from western Anatolia being employed to build the great walls of Tiryns.[27] Further, we learn from the Linear B tablets of Pylos that women employed in textile manufacture in the palace workforces were obtained from a number of places in the eastern Aegean, including the island of Lemnos, and from Cnidus, Miletus and the cities of the Troad, including Troy, on Anatolia's Aegean coastal fringe.[28] All these references are compatible with the notion of Mycenaeans using western Anatolia as a recruiting ground for human labour, both male and female.

Apart from labour recruitment, access to mineral resources (gold above all), for which there was a high demand in the resource-poor Mycenaean homelands, may well have provided a major incentive for establishing contacts with, and in some cases control over, parts of the western Anatolian coast. To begin with, the Mycenaean enterprises in this region may have been largely private ventures carried out by traders and slavers acting on their own initiative. But the rewards that such enterprises offered no doubt paved the way for subsequent ventures conducted under the auspices of one or more rulers of the Mycenaean kingdoms. These ventures were certainly more than purely peaceful commercial operations.

The Mycenaeans were undoubtedly a warlike, aggressive people. This first becomes evident in the fierce aspect of Mycenae's shaft-grave warlords with their array of weapons about them and, subsequently, in scenes of warriors departing for battle and Mycenaean warships engaged in conflict, in the depiction of weaponry in Mycenaean frescoes, and in the massively fortified citadels of the Argolid plain. This militaristic image accords well with the ethos and character of the 'heroic' society depicted by Homer. It also provides a perspective of Mycenaean society that differs markedly from that of the intensely bureaucratic society represented in the Linear B tablets.

The elaborate defensive architecture of the Argolid citadels suggests growing tensions and rivalry during the Late Helladic III period between various palace centres, especially those located close to each other. As in other parts of the Late Bronze Age world, a kingdom that sought constantly to build both its material wealth and its military power no doubt found territorial expansion essential to the realization of its ambitions. Within the Argolid itself, attempts to acquire new lands meant competing with one's neighbours in a resource-poor region of limited extent.[29] No doubt conflicts over territory did occur in the region from time to time, and the massive fortifications of the citadels may well indicate the need to provide adequate defence against neighbouring kingdoms. But an ambitious Mycenaean king bent on increasing his wealth and power would have found far greater opportunities for achieving his ambitions by acquiring overseas territories, particularly ones that gave him access to resources highly sought after in the Mycenaean world. There is little doubt that at least one of the mainland Mycenaean kingdoms had its sights set firmly on expanding its power by taking possession of a number of eastern Aegean islands, as a step towards establishing its authority over territories on the Anatolian mainland.

This might be achieved by forming alliances with local states and kingdoms – in the case of states subject to Hatti, winning them away from their allegiance to the Hittite Great King. Prompt retaliation could be expected. Thus we learn of a Hittite expedition sent against Milawata in the third year of King Mursili II's reign, because it had tried to join forces with the king of Ahhiyawa. Milawata was sacked by the Hittites, according to Mursili's own record of the campaign. The devastation it suffered may be reflected in the archaeological record, which indicates the destruction of the city by fire at the end of its second building phase in the Late Helladic IIIA2 period,[30] around 1320 to judge from the historical record. In the same year, there was a further rebellion against Mursili, this time by Uhhaziti, the king of Arzawa Minor. The uprising, which very likely had Ahhiyawan backing, was crushed by Mursili, who led his troops into Uhhaziti's capital Apasa in pursuit of the rebel king. But his quarry escaped him. The islands to which, according to Mursili's own account, Uhhaziti now took flight presumably lay off the Anatolian coast and were under the control of the Ahhiyawan king, who gave asylum to the fugitive.

In the reign of Mursili's son Hattusili III, a renegade Hittite subject called Piyamaradu conducted insurrectionist activities in the west, aided and abetted by the king of Ahhiyawa. Piyamaradu may well have been acting as one of the king's chief agents for the expansion of Ahhiyawan influence and perhaps actual territorial control in western Anatolia. This was the subject of the letter we referred to above, the Tawagalawa letter, written by Hattusili to the king of Ahhiyawa, complaining about the latter's support for Piyamaradu, and demanding that he take all possible action to stop him harassing Hittite territory in the future. In the reign of Hattusili's son Tudhaliya IV, we hear of an uprising in the Seha River Land, another of the Arzawan states in the west, again with the support and perhaps direct assistance of the king of Ahhiyawa. Once more the Hittites crushed the uprising, its ringleader, the upstart Tarhunaradu who had seized power in the kingdom, very likely coming to a sticky end. The royal family whom he had displaced was restored to power.

A consistent pattern seems to emerge from all this. Kings of the land called Ahhiyawa constantly sought to roll back Hittite authority in western Anatolia by supporting local anti-Hittite insurgents and uprisings in preparation for the expansion of their own authority in the region. They met with some success. Some time after the Hittite sack of Milawata early in Mursili's reign, the city was rebuilt and became subject territory of the Ahhiyawan king. This happened either later in Mursili's reign or in the reign of his son and successor Muwattalli. The transfer of sovereignty is almost certainly reflected in the archaeological record. In this, its third building phase, Milawata/Miletus takes on the character of a Mycenaean settlement.

Given the growing menace the Hittites faced at the other end of their empire, with the rise of the aggressive Egyptian nineteenth dynasty, the Great King of Hatti may have decided to cede Milawata to his Ahhiyawan counterpart, in the hope that this would satisfy his territorial ambitions in Anatolia. There may even have been a treaty drawn up between Milawata's new overlord and the Hittite king, defining Ahhiyawa's territorial limits in the region. But as far as the Ahhiyawan king was concerned, the base he had now established on the Anatolian mainland was probably no more than a starting point in his development of an overseas empire in western Anatolia – whatever formal agreement he may have made with Hatti. The status he had already achieved was acknowledged by Hattusili III, who addressed him as 'Great King' and 'My Brother'. Both titles were forms of address accorded only to the most powerful rulers of the Late Bronze Age. Presumably for reasons of diplomatic expediency, there is no doubt that Hattusili overstated his royal brother's importance in addressing him in this way. No Mycenaean king possessed anything like the power or the resources of the mighty Near Eastern kingdoms of the age. But, as far as the Hittites were concerned, the kingdom of Ahhiyawa had the potential for becoming a very significant force and a very serious threat to Hittite interests in the west. It was as well to try to come to terms with it. But tensions between the two kingdoms, Mycenaean and Hittite, continued to smoulder, fanned from time to time by local dissidents against Hittite authority. The Hittites were acutely sensitive to any attempts to interfere in their subject territories, and the Ahhiyawan king showed little reluctance in supporting anti-Hittite activity in the region whenever he saw it was to his advantage to do so.

If we rule out any notion that the Mycenaean world at this time was under the control of a single ruler, then which of the Mycenaean palace centres was the actual kingdom of Ahhiyawa? The most likely candidate is Mycenae itself.[31] Quite possibly, at this time it did exercise some form of *primus inter pares* role in the Mycenaean world, and perhaps even some form of sovereignty over the kingdoms closest to it. In any case, references to Ahhiyawa in the Hittite texts almost certainly indicate the aggressive activities of a Mycenaean kingdom bent on establishing and expanding its authority over parts of the western Anatolian coastlands, and either supporting or leading a number of collaborative military enterprises against several of the western Anatolian kingdoms. Was Troy one of these kingdoms? Do we have in Ahhiyawa's activities in western Anatolia the basis of a Trojan War tradition? We must wait until the final chapter to address that question. In the meantime, let us look more closely at the question of how important Troy was, and what role it played, in the Near Eastern world of the Late Bronze Age.

5

TROY'S ROLE AND STATUS IN THE NEAR EASTERN WORLD

RELATIONS WITH THE NEIGHBOURS

This tablet which I have made for you, Alaksandu, must be read out to you three times every year, and you, Alaksandu, must know it (thoroughly).

Early in the thirteenth century, the Hittite Great King Muwattalli drew up a treaty with a man called Alaksandu, ruler of the kingdom of Wilusa. We have identified Wilusa with Ilios/Troy. On the understanding that this identification still lacks firm proof, we will use it as our starting point for investigating Troy's role in the history of the Late Bronze Age Near East and its relations with its Near Eastern contemporaries.[1] The treaty makes clear that Wilusa was a vassal state of the Hittite empire, and one of four western Anatolian kingdoms called the Arzawa Lands.[2] The other three were Mira-Kuwaliya, the Seha River Land and, further to the east, the kingdom of Hapalla. A fifth Arzawan state, Arzawa 'Minor', had probably been eliminated some three decades earlier by Muwattalli's father Mursili.[3]

As was the case with its fellow Arzawan states, Wilusa's relations with Hatti fluctuated markedly throughout the Late Bronze Age. Unfortunately, its fragmentary history is known to us only from information contained in Hittite texts. Wilusa itself has left no written records, at least none that have so far come to light. What we know about it is presented to us almost entirely from a Hittite perspective. It first appears, in the form Wilusiya, as the penultimate member in a list of twenty-two countries that had formed an anti-Hittite alliance in the reign of the Hittite king Tudhaliya I/II[4] early in the fourteenth century. From the name Assuwa, apparently a collective term embracing all these countries, the alliance is often referred to as the Assuwan Confederacy. Tudhaliya had earlier conducted a campaign to the west against a coalition of hostile states, which included several of the Arzawa Lands – Arzawa Minor, the Seha River Land and Hapalla – and was now obliged for a second time to deal with a coalition of anti-Hittite forces. On both occasions he was victorious, though the western states continued to threaten the security of the Hittite world.

Already in the reign of the first Hittite king for whom we have written records, Hattusili I (c.1650–1620), we hear of a Hittite campaign against Arzawan territory. Left unchecked, the military alliances which the western states were prone to form could eventually pose a serious threat to the security of the Hittite homeland itself, as was dramatically demonstrated in the dark days of Tudhaliya III's reign in the first half of the fourteenth century, when enemy forces from Arzawa invaded and occupied large portions of Hittite territory up to the boundaries of the Halys (Hittite Marassantiya) River.[5] What made the danger all the greater was the intrusion of a Mycenaean kingdom into western Anatolia and its readiness to support anti-Hittite insurrectionist activity there. Like it or not, the Hittites had to establish some form of permanent authority in the west, primarily for reasons of their own security. It was in this context that the Arzawan kingdoms, including Wilusa, had Hittite vassal status imposed upon them. Each was under the control of a local ruler who was bound by treaty to the Hittite king and swore to fulfil the obligations that the treaty assigned to him. In return, the Hittite king guaranteed to protect his vassal and his legitimate successors against both external enemies and dissidents within his own kingdom.

The last name after Wilusiya in the Assuwan Confederacy is Taruisa. As we have noted, Forrer attached much significance to the juxtaposition of these names, given their close resemblance to (W)ilios and Troia, which Homer uses as alternative names for Priam's city in the *Iliad*. Originally, Wilusiya and Taruisa were perhaps the names of adjoining but separate countries rather than alternative names for the one country. Wilusiya may subsequently have absorbed its neighbour, though local tradition (we may surmise) preserved the latter's name through the following centuries until it re-emerged as an alternative to Ilios in Homeric tradition.[6]

Taruisa crops up only once more in our sources – in an inscription of Late Bronze Age date carved upon a silver bowl, unfortunately of unknown provenance, now in the Museum of Anatolian Civilizations in Ankara. The inscription, in Luwian hieroglyphics, records the conquest of a place called Tarwiza (presumably the hieroglyphic form of Taruisa) by a king called Tudhaliya.[7] It is tempting to assign this conquest to Tudhaliya I/II's campaign against the countries of the Assuwan Confederacy, of which Taruisa was a member. Admittedly, the inscription would then be by far the earliest known example of a Luwian hieroglyphic text, apart from inscriptions on seals. But that in itself does not rule out the possibility that the silver bowl provides evidence for a Hittite conquest of Troy early in the fourteenth century.

In any case, it is clear that Wilusa was amongst the Hittites' enemies the first time it appears in written records, and its hostility towards Hatti is again indicated in the historical preamble to the Alaksandu Treaty, in the context of Hatti's war with the Arzawa Lands. It was some time after this – precisely when, we do not know – that it became a Hittite ally. From then on, to judge from the Alaksandu Treaty, Wilusa under pro-Hittite rulers remained loyal to Hatti – conspicuously so, for other Arzawan states continued to prove troublesome. Muwattalli states in the treaty that his grandfather Suppiluliuma launched an attack on Arzawa but remained at peace with Wilusa, whose king Kukkunni had maintained regular communication with him. At this time he may have done so as a

*This bowl Samaya, the man of the land of Hatti, **dedicated**(?) for himself before King Maza-Karhuha, when Tudhaliya Labarna **smote** the land of Tarwiza – it in that year he made.*

Figure 5.1 Hieroglyphic inscription on silver bowl (reproduced and translated by J. D. Hawkins).

Hittite ally rather than as a subject, for we have no clear indication that vassal status was imposed upon any of the Arzawan kingdoms until the reign of Muwattalli's father, Mursili II.

When dealing with the obligations which he expected Alaksandu to fulfil, Muwattalli made clear to his vassal that he could be called upon to provide troops for campaigns far away in the east, against Egypt or Babylonia or Assyria. Indeed Wilusans-Trojans may have taken part in the battle of Kadesh, along with other western Anatolian peoples, in the vast army of almost 50,000 infantry and chariotry which Muwattalli put into the field against Ramesses.[8] But Wilusa's king had an immediate role to fulfil as part of his treaty obligations. He was obliged to exercise constant vigilance in his region, reporting without delay any intelligence he received about anti-Hittite plots in nearby Hittite vassal states. He had also to be ready, when called upon, to provide troops and chariots to reinforce Hittite military expeditions sent to the west to put down uprisings there. Such obligations as these were standard features of the treaties that Hittite kings drew up with their vassal rulers. But in this case they took on an added urgency, because of the volatility of the western Anatolian region and the critical importance of keeping it peaceful and stable as the Hittites became ever more focused upon their confrontation with Egypt.

Wilusa makes another appearance in the reign of Muwattalli, in the letter which Manapa-Tarhunda, vassal ruler of the Seha River Land, wrote to his Hittite overlord. We have already used this letter as part of the evidence for locating Wilusa in the Troad. Unfortunately, the passage in which Wilusa appears is fragmentary and open to different interpretations. One possibility is that Wilusa had been occupied by the rebel Piyamaradu, another that it had staged an anti-Hittite uprising with or without Piyamaradu's involvement. All we know for certain is that Muwattalli had sent an expeditionary force to the kingdom to restore Hittite control over it. We shall have more to say about the passage and its interpretation in Chapter 8.

That Piyamaradu acted as an important agent for the extension of Mycenaean influence and perhaps ultimately territorial expansion in western Anatolia, and that the Mycenaeans had more than merely a commercial interest in Wilusa-Troy both become evident from one of the best-known Hittite documents. This is the so-called

Tawagalawa letter that we referred to briefly in Chapter 4.[9] Its author, Hattusili III, complains to the king of Ahhiyawa, the letter's addressee, about Piyamaradu's insurrectionist activities in Hittite subject territory and accuses him of supporting the insurgent. He makes what appears to be a significant statement about Wilusa in his letter: 'Now as we have reached agreement on the matter of Wilusa over which we fought'. The conflict between them, he says, is now well in the past, and he is anxious that Piyamaradu's activities should not lead to a renewal of it. He seeks to prevent this by urging the Ahhiyawan king to say to Piyamaradu: 'The King of Hatti and I – in that matter of Wilusa over which we were at enmity, he has converted me and we have made friends; [. . .] a war would not be right for us.'[10] Here, then, we seem to have clear evidence that an Ahhiyawan-Mycenaean king fought a war over Wilusa-Troy. But how much bearing does this actually have on the Homeric tradition of a Trojan War? This is a further question to which we shall return in Chapter 8.

The final reference we have to Wilusa in Hittite texts occurs in a letter that most scholars attribute to Hattusili's son and successor, Tudhaliya IV. Commonly known as the Milawata letter, its broken text has been augmented by an additional fragment discovered in 1981 by Professor Hoffner.[11] From the joined fragments, it seems that the addressee of the letter, probably the king of Mira, had collaborated with Tudhaliya in a successful attack on the land of Milawata (Bronze Age Miletus), and had now been established as the land's immediate overlord following a redefinition of its boundaries.[12] A most significant event, if we have correctly interpreted the letter. Up until the late fourteenth century, Milawata had been subject territory of the Hittites. But, probably by the time of the Alaksandu Treaty, it had come under Ahhiyawan-Mycenaean control. Though relations between Ahhiyawa and Hatti may then have been peaceful, there is little doubt that Milawata's overlord constantly sought to expand his influence in western Anatolia from his base in Milawata. That becomes even more evident from the Tawagalawa letter. But, subsequently, to judge from the Milawata letter, the Hittites had regained their sovereignty over Milawata, an achievement that very likely marked the end of any significant influence exercised by Ahhiyawa in western Anatolia.[13]

The text-join to the Milawata letter also provides one small item of information about Wilusa: we learn from it that the current king of Wilusa, a man called Walmu, had been deposed from his throne (by persons unknown), but was now about to be restored to it. He was at the time apparently in the custody of the letter's addressee. Tudhaliya had written asking that he be handed over to the Hittites, as a first step towards putting him back on his throne and had sent documents confirming the legitimacy of his claim to occupy it; the addressee was, however, to have continuing authority over Wilusa, as a kind of regional overlord acting in the interests of the Great King of Hatti.

TROY'S STATUS AND SIGNIFICANCE

In answer to the question of what we learn about Wilusa-Troy from contemporary historical records, the answer has to be not very much at all. There is certainly nothing to indicate that it stood out in any significant way from its western Anatolian neighbours. On the contrary, the few facts we have about it suggest that its history followed a very similar path to that of its neighbours. In its first appearance it was involved in action against Hittite armies, along with other Arzawa Lands and a number of other western states and communities. At a later date, it became a vassal state of the Hittite empire, along with the other Arzawa Lands. Its loyalty to its Hittite allegiance may well have fluctuated from one period to another, as was the case with other Arzawa Lands, and with the help of outsiders it may have occasionally overthrown its pro-Hittite rulers who were subsequently restored by Hittite force of arms. As a Hittite vassal state, its treaty obligations were much the same as those imposed upon other vassal states.

But let us not be unduly negative about the role Wilusa-Troy played in the Near Eastern world. The handful of scattered and mostly fragmentary pieces of information we have about it may do scant justice to its actual status and significance in its contemporary context. There may well have been much more to justify its enduring reputation in the traditions of a later age than mere serendipitous selection by Mycenaean Greek bards. A single new discovery could alter substantially our perceptions of this Late Bronze Age kingdom of the Troad. There are plenty of precedents for this in Near Eastern archaeology.

Even in terms of our present knowledge, Wilusa-Troy was by no means an insignificant place. In the thirteenth century, it was one of the three major kingdoms of western Anatolia whose lands extended to and along the Aegean coast. In political and military terms, Mira was the most important of these kingdoms. Its territory was probably much expanded by Mursili II after his destruction of the kingdom of Arzawa Minor around 1320. And as we have just observed, its king's status and power were further enhanced by the Hittite king Tudhaliya IV. Second in importance was the Seha River Land, which lay immediately to the north of Mira. It played a role of major strategic significance in the region, and Hittite kings set considerable store by ensuring that its throne was occupied by a local ruler on whose loyalty, ability and effectiveness they could count. Muwattalli paid its ruler Masturi the signal honour of giving him his sister's hand in marriage. To be wed to a Hittite princess was a privilege reserved exclusively for foreign Great Kings and the most highly valued vassals, such as the ruler of the Syrian kingdom of Amurru in the border region between Hittite and Egyptian territory.

Wilusa-Troy ranked third amongst the western kingdoms. Though it was smaller and more peripheral to the Hittite world than its two southern neighbours, the kings of Hatti did not hesitate to commit their military resources to maintaining their authority over it when the need arose. Why was it important to them? In spite of its remoteness, they considered it an integral part of the security network that they had built up in western Anatolia. Experience had shown that the most effective means of preventing the resurgence of anti-Hittite coalitions amongst the western kingdoms was to impose Hittite sovereignty over each of them. As vassal subjects of the Great King, each was obliged to report to their overlord news or even rumours of rebellions in neighbouring states and communities, to give support to neighbouring vassal rulers in the event of uprisings against them, to reinforce their overlord's expeditionary forces during Hittite campaigns in their region, and to ensure that their territory did not become a haven for dissidents against Hittite authority or a base for rebel attacks upon Hittite territory. This last may have been a particularly important consideration in the thirteenth century, given the activities of renegades like Piyamaradu. The events outlined in the Hittite documents we have referred to above make clear the potential such renegades had for destabilizing the entire network of Hittite subject-states in the west. Control of Wilusa helped to ensure the security of this network at its northern-most end. Without this control, Wilusa could have provided an ideal base for launching attacks on Hittite territories further to the south, either by land or by sea.

Further, the Ahhiyawan king was almost certainly looking for further opportunities to extend his territorial holdings in the western Anatolian coastlands, partly by forming strategic alliances. It is likely that he attempted to establish influence in or over the Seha River Land in this way, by supporting the ultimately unsuccessful coup staged in the kingdom by a rebel, Tarhunaradu, during the reign of the Hittite king Tudhaliya IV.[14] And Piyamaradu may well have paved the way for an attempted Mycenaean takeover of Wilusa to the north of the Seha River Land, a prospect that could have led to conflict between Hatti and Ahhiyawa.

Yet Wilusa was a prize worth taking for its own sake. Its capital, on the basis of its identification with Troy VI, was very likely one of the most impressive cities in western Anatolia. Where precisely it ranked in the hierarchy of western Anatolian urban centres is something we could assess more accurately had we a better idea of the size and nature of other major western cities of the period, such as Apasa and Milawata.[15] Of course, Troy was not in the same class as the great royal capitals of the Near Eastern world such as Babylon, Egyptian Thebes and Hattusa. Indeed, it has been commented that to anyone coming from the east, Troy would have seemed a somewhat ordinary town, medium to small by Hittite or Near Eastern standards.

But this assessment is too negative. Troy may well have ranked among the more significant regional centres of the Near Eastern world, such as the new city of Emar on the Euphrates and the capitals of some of the more important vassal kingdoms. It has, for example, been compared in area and population size with the city of Ugarit on the Levantine coast, one of the great international trading emporia of the Late Bronze Age. The comparison needs some quali-fication. To begin with, it raises once more the question of whether there was a lower city at Troy, at least on the scale proposed by Korfmann.[16] But that aside, Ugarit, in terms of both its material wealth and strategic location, was undoubtedly a jewel in the Hittite crown, with far more influence upon, and involvement in, the polit-ical and commercial affairs of the Near Eastern world than Troy could ever have hoped for. Nevertheless, in a purely material sense, Troy may well have been comparable with Near Eastern cities such as Ugarit, as well as with the largest of the Mycenaean palace centres.

WAS TROJAN SOCIETY LITERATE?

In one respect in particular, Troy contrasts strikingly with Ugarit. From the Levantine city, archaeologists have unearthed one of the most valuable repositories of written records of the entire Late Bronze Age. The archives of Ugarit have provided us with an extremely rich source of written information on the history and international relationships of the period, particularly within the Syro-Palestinian region. Excavations at Troy, on the other hand, have so far failed to produce one single tablet, or even a fragment of one, for any period in the city's Bronze Age history. It is far from unique in this respect. The same, unfortunately, has to be said of all the known Bronze Age sites of western Anatolia. Yet there can be no doubt that the Arzawan kingdoms of the region, including Wilusa, had chancelleries and scribal staffs. Hittite texts provide ample evidence of written communications, in the form of both treaties and letters, exchanged between the Hittite court and the king's western vassals. Such communications went both ways. As we have already seen, a number of letters written by the vassal rulers to their Hittite overlords were preserved in and have been unearthed from the archives of the Hittite capital.

We might explain the absence of evidence for literacy at Troy and other western sites by observing that writing materials are amongst the most perishable of all ancient artefacts. When records on clay tablets, which form the vast bulk of written material from the Bronze Age, are preserved, this is very largely a matter of chance. They have survived only because the originally unbaked tablets were accidentally fired in the great conflagrations that destroyed the buildings housing them. Even so, chance survival is by no means a rare phenomenon. Excavations of a number of Late Bronze Age sites have produced, almost from the beginning, caches of clay tablets – for example in the Hittite homeland region itself, the sites of (modern) Maşat, Kuşaklı and Ortaköy; from the last of these, a Hittite provincial administrative centre called Sapinuwa, more than 3,000 tablets have recently been unearthed. Bearing this in mind, we may quite reasonably be surprised that not one single scrap of an inscribed tablet has turned up in Bronze Age Troy, even allowing for a further 2,000 years of almost continuous occupation after the end of the Bronze Age and the crudity of the methods of excavation when the site was first comprehensively dug by Schliemann.

Failure to find tablets on the site has meant that we have no tangible evidence of what language was spoken by its Bronze Age inhabitants. By contrast, the Linear B tablets of the Mycenaean world, in spite of the extremely limited information that they supply about Mycenaean history, at least demonstrate that the Mycenaean people spoke a recognizable form of Greek. But before bemoaning too much the lack of similar evidence for identifying the language of the Trojans, we should sound a warning – in case Bronze Age texts do suddenly turn up at Troy. The likelihood is that these texts will be written in Hittite! This was in fact the language used in all communications with western Anatolia that have come to light in the Hittite archives, communications dispatched to the western states (of which copies were kept in Hattusa) and those received from these states. In a letter written on behalf of an Arzawan king to the Egyptian pharaoh Amenhotep III, the scribe who wrote the letter asked his Egyptian counterpart to put his responses henceforth into Hittite, presumably instead of Akkadian which was the international language of diplomacy in the Near Eastern world at the time.[17] The request is a significant one, particularly as it was made in the period when the Arzawan Lands were independent of Hittite authority.

The likelihood is that Hittite was the diplomatic lingua franca of western Anatolia thoughout the Late Bronze Age. It was used regularly in official communications between the countries of the region and the Hittite court and, perhaps, also in communications between these countries and other lands, to judge from the exchange of correspondence between Arzawa and Egypt. This does not, of course, mean that the Trojans themselves or the inhabitants of the other western Anatolian kingdoms spoke Hittite. Either it became the standard chancellery language that western scribes were expected to master, or else Hittite scribes were installed in the western kingdoms, or hired themselves out to these kingdoms, for the purpose of putting into writing communications between the Arzawan rulers and their correspondents in Hattusa. The use of Hittite in correspondence between Arzawa and Egypt, as well as between Hatti and

Ahhiyawa, indicates further extensions of the use of the language for diplomatic purposes, though still on a very much more limited scale than Akkadian.

THE LANGUAGE AND ETHNICITY OF THE TROJANS

What language or languages did the inhabitants of Troy speak? If we could answer this question, we might have a clearer indication of the Trojans' ethnic origins.

We have referred to the widespread distribution of Luwian-speaking population groups through western and southern Anatolia from the third millennium onwards. The Hittites, in the early versions of their Laws, used the term Luwiya as a broad ethno-geographical designation for the western Anatolian regions occupied by these groups. In later versions of the Laws, the term Luwiya was replaced by Arzawa. As we have seen, Arzawa came to be used as a generic name for five western Anatolian kingdoms, including Wilusa. Given the likelihood that the names Luwiya and Arzawa covered, very broadly, the same regions of western Anatolia, we might reasonably assume that the Arzawan kingdoms had Luwian-speaking populations. It would follow from this that the inhabitants of Wilusa, which in the Alaksandu Treaty was designated as one of these kingdoms, were of Luwian origin.

Linguistic support for identifying Wilusa as a Luwian kingdom may be provided by the fact that the oldest known form of its name, Wilusiya, is a Luwian formation, and the names of at least the first two of the three known kings of Wilusa – Kukkunni, Alaksandu and Walmu – could also be of Luwian origin. Moreover, the earliest piece of writing to be discovered at Troy, the inscription on the recently discovered seal dating to the second half of the twelfth century, is written in the Luwian hieroglyphic script.

All this appears to provide fairly strong evidence that the Trojans of Troy VI and VIIa were of Luwian origin (on the assumption, of course, that the Wilusa-Troy equation is valid), and thus part of the widespread Luwian ethno-cultural complex of western and southern Anatolia. But a number of scholars are sceptical. To begin with, Wilusa's connection with the Arzawa Lands has been described as tenuous.[18] The Alaksandu Treaty is the only text to categorize it as an Arzawa Land. In fact, the first time the name appears, in the text where it is listed as a member of the Assuwan Confederacy, it is quite separate from references to Arzawa. Second, the Luwian formation Wilusiya need not necessarily mean that the inhabitants of the region to which the name applied were themselves Luwian-speakers. Nor can we be sure that the personal names Kukkunni and Alaksandu were in fact of Luwian origin. Professor Güterbock remarks that there is no recognizable meaning for these words in Luwian, and that they could just as well be Greek.[19] Professor Melchert states that the name Alaksandu is at least as compatible with Lydian as it is with Luwian.[20] Similarly doubtful is the attempt to assign a Luwian origin to the name Priam.[21] More generally, Professor Neumann has expressed doubts about the assumption that the language of Wilusa-Troy was Luwian rather than another language belonging to the northern Anatolian language group, which included Hittite and Palaic and first-millennium Lydian.[22]

There has also been much debate about the significance of the Luwian seal found at Troy. The fact that its owner was a scribe might give us our first tangible proof of a chancellery in the Late Bronze Age city. But this is a very big assumption to base on a very small piece of evidence. In any case, the seal can hardly be used as evidence that the population of Troy spoke Luwian. Luwian was the language regularly used on seal inscriptions throughout the world ruled by the Hittites, irrespective of the language or languages spoken in the regions where the seals have turned up. Moreover, the fact that this particular seal was found at Troy need not indicate that Troy was its place of origin. Seals were portable objects that travelled with their owners. Given the period to which the seal belongs, in the last years of the Bronze Age, it is very likely that by this time palace bureaucracies had largely disappeared, and persons who still did possess scribal skills sold their services wherever and whenever there was a need for such services.

All this leaves us in much uncertainty about what the language and ethnic composition and culture of Wilusa-Troy really were in the Late Bronze Age. Are there other indications? What of the architecture and layout of Troy VI? Does it have any distinguishing features that link it to a particular cultural context, Luwian or otherwise? The remains of Late Bronze Age Troy clearly belong within the broad context of Anatolian architectural traditions, extending back in some of its aspects to the very beginning of the Bronze Age. But since we do not at present have any way of determining what the distinctive criteria of Luwian architecture were – if there *were* any – we are not in a position to determine whether or to what extent Troy's remains reflect a Luwian architectural tradition.[23]

Similarly, we can make no confident judgement about whether the cults practised in Wilusa-Troy or the gods worshipped there were of Luwian origin. There is, however, one attractive possibility. In the *Iliad* Apollo figures prominently as the Trojans' chief deity. He inflicts havoc upon the Greek forces; he has a temple in the citadel of Troy; and time and again he assists the Trojans in battle – Hector above all, whom he leads against the enemy and rescues from Diomedes. Other sources of information on Apollo give him an Anatolian origin, associating him particularly with the Troad and other western coastal areas. Can we find Apollo in Hittite texts, particularly those that deal with the western Anatolian countries?

In the Alaksandu Treaty, the list of witnesses to the treaty on Wilusa's side begins with the Storm God of the Army, then names a god called '[. . .]appaliuna', followed by groups of male deities, then female deities, then mountains, rivers and springs. [. . .]appaliuna is clearly very prominent amongst Wilusa's divine patrons.[24] Is his name the Anatolian equivalent of Apollo? That possibility certainly cannot be ruled out and, though a number of scholars remain doubtful,[25] it is just conceivable that we have here one of our most promising links between historical Wilusa-Troy and Homeric tradition. Unfortunately, though [. . .]appaliuna may well have been one of Wilusa's chief deities, we have no way of knowing whether he was specifically or exclusively of Luwian origin.

So we have not yet found a firm answer to our question of whether or not the Trojans of the Late Bronze Age were Luwians. But the question may be too narrowly focused. Even when we have more information at our disposal, it is often extremely difficult to come up with reliable criteria for determining the ethnic composition of an ancient community. That applies very much to Bronze Age Anatolia. There was almost certainly a high degree of ethnic mix in its kingdoms and cities – as also in many other parts of the Near Eastern world. The Hittite capital at the height of its power and influence contained a very broad cross section of many ethnic groups – including but by no means confined to those of indigenous Hattian,

Indo-European, Hurrian, Babylonian and Syrian origin. Nesite (what we call Hittite) was the Hittite kingdom's official language; Akkadian was used for written communications with the kingdom's Syrian vassals and royal peers; hieroglyphic Luwian was used on seals and in monumental inscriptions. The first of these languages may reflect to a greater or lesser degree the ethnic origins of the kingdom's royal dynasty, but it may not have been the language of the great majority of the population of the capital, or of the Hittite homeland. It was certainly not the majority language of the empire at large.

So, too, Luwian may well have been the language spoken by the political and social elite of the Arzawan states and perhaps also by a significant part of the general populations of these states. Hittite had apparently been adopted as the official language of communication with the Arzawan kingdoms. But no doubt there was a range of other languages spoken in these kingdoms as well, in some cases representing population groups dating back to the days before the arrival of the Luwian-speaking peoples, and in other cases reflecting other population movements in the general region. The coastal areas in particular provided homes or at least temporary residences for a number of persons of Aegean origin. Greek would have been heard at various places along the coast, including Apasa, the royal capital of the kingdom of Arzawa Minor and later a part of the Arzawan kingdom of Mira, and particularly Milawata, which had become substantially Mycenaeanized by the late fourteenth century.

So who were the Trojans? To begin with, the doubts about whether or not Wilusa-Troy was inhabited by a Luwian-speaking people have probably been overstated. That Wilusa is not consistently referred to as an Arzawan kingdom does not mean that it was not considered a regular member of the Arzawan complex or make it any less likely that it had a significant Luwian element in its population. The term Arzawa is by no means invariably used when the texts refer to other states whose membership of the Arzawa lands is never doubted. And while none of the other pointers to a possible Luwian population of Wilusa-Troy are anywhere near conclusive, even when considered collectively, no evidence has yet been produced that negates the likelihood of a Luwian element in the city. That said, Troy's population may well have been a very mixed one.

A possible scenario is that a Luwian-speaking population group became politically dominant in the Troad from 1700 (if not much earlier), just as other Luwian groups became dominant in other parts of the region covered by the term Luwiya. Luwians may then have been responsible for the building of Troy VI, which showed a marked break with predecessor levels on the site. Luwian was the language, we may suppose, of Wilusa's elite ruling class. Perhaps as in other Arzawan states, scribes in Wilusa were also well versed in Hittite, which became the medium of communication with the Hittite royal court. But the site had already been occupied for 1,300 years or more, and through five major levels, before the Late Bronze Age city was built. And though the physical and cultural character of Troy markedly changed then, along with a major change in its ethnic configuration, there may still have been substantial residual elements of the previous populations who continued to inhabit the city, or at least those parts of it that lay outside the citadel. (Of course we cannot rule out the possibility that there was a greater or lesser Luwian component in Troy's population for many decades or even centuries prior to the sixth city.) Further, there is little doubt that Troy was an integral part of the international sea-trade network. This, too, may have impacted upon the composition of its population, for as in other cities of the Near Eastern world, merchants from foreign lands may well have set up trading quarters here.

In accordance with our scenario, the kingdom of Wilusa-Troy was the creation of a dynasty of Luwian ethnic origin that established its authority in the region at the beginning of the Late Bronze Age. The kingdom's seat of power was the citadel on the mound now called Hisarlık which was extensively redeveloped by the new dynasty. It featured a royal palace surrounded by spacious residences, all enclosed within massive fortifications. Under its kings, who ruled over a population made up of a range of ethnic groups, Wilusa became one of the five major western Anatolian kingdoms of the Late Bronze Age known as the Arzawa Lands. In terms of its political and military significance, Wilusa was probably overshadowed by the other Arzawan kingdoms. But, like them, it became a subject state of the Hittite empire, and Hittite kings considered it important enough to protect it with expeditionary forces and even, perhaps, to go to war with the kingdom of Ahhiyawa to keep it within the Hittite fold.

Though located on the periphery of the Near Eastern world, it was probably one of the more significant regional cities of this world, and one of the most prosperous. To what was its prosperity due? Do Troy's commercial activities provide the answer?

TROY'S ROLE IN THE WORLD OF TRADE

Legendary tradition depicts Greeks and Trojans as arch enemies. But the actual relations between them generally appear to have been of a peaceful nature. Archaeological finds give us clear indications of trading contacts between the Greek world and Troy, probably beginning in the early centuries of the second millennium (and therefore predating both Troy VI and the Mycenaean civilization). But the most substantial evidence for these contacts is provided by the quantities of Mycenaean pottery found in Troy VI, dating from *c.*1600 onwards.[26] In addition to the common ceramic ware imported from Mycenaean Greece, luxury items of Mycenaean manufacture also found a market in Troy VI, such as boxes of ivory, silver pins, carnelian and ivory beads. It is possible that Troy imported a number of Mycenaean craftsmen as well as their products. Many items of apparent Mycenaean origin may in fact have been produced locally by such craftsmen, or by locals working under their tutelage. There is, however, no sign of Mycenaean settlement at Troy in this period, and we should stress that the Mycenaean pottery unearthed there represents only a tiny fraction of the total ceramic ware found on the site, the overwhelming quantity of which is of local style.[27]

Overall, the Mycenaean finds at Troy suggest regular but not intensive trade between the Troad and the Mycenaean world.[28] We should also allow for the possibility that much of the Mycenaean material may not in fact reflect direct trade between Mycenaeans and Trojans. Many of the goods in question may simply have been picked up at Mycenaean ports by vessels on the international trading circuit and discharged at Troy along with trade items from other parts of the Near Eastern and Mediterranean worlds. Apart from Greece, Troy had access to a wide range of products from many sources of supply, including amber from the Baltic region, luxury items from Mesopotamia and Syria, tin from perhaps as far afield as central Asia and ceramic ware and copper from Cyprus.

Troy's commercial contacts with the Aegean and Near Eastern worlds must have been due in large measure to its inclusion within a sea-trading network. The discovery of two sunken ships dating to the Late Bronze Age off Turkey's south-west coast has provided us with much important information about sea trade in this period. One, the Uluburun wreck, discovered 8 kilometres offshore from Kaş, dates to c.1300 BC; the other found off Cape Gelidonya dates to c.1200.[29] The ships' origins are uncertain. They may have been Syrian vessels (or perhaps Cypriot in the case of the Gelidonya wreck), but with crews and cargoes from many places of origin. The Uluburun vessel appears to have carried several high-ranking Mycenaeans – merchants or royal officials sent to escort home a particular order that their master had placed rather than run-of-the-mill crew members.[30] During the sailing season, the ships constantly travelled a course, apparently in an anticlockwise direction, which took them to all the major ports of the Aegean and eastern Mediterranean coastlands.[31] From the ports of the Syro-Palestinian coast they proceeded to Cyprus, then westwards along the southern coast of Anatolia, from there northwards along Anatolia's western coast, subsequently crossing the Aegean to mainland Greece, and from there south to Crete, Egypt, and back to the Syro-Palestinian ports. Almost certainly, Troy was included in the loop.

From the substantial quantities of copper and tin ingots found in the Gelidonya and Uluburun wrecks, we conclude that consignments of these metals were the largest and most regular components of the cargoes conveyed by the ships of the period. Both metals were in constant high demand in the Late Bronze Age kingdoms and communities. The Uluburun wreck alone contained 10 tons of copper ingots (around 500 ingots) and 1 ton of tin – precisely the ratio in which copper and tin were mixed for the production of bronze. Shipments of tin were probably taken on board at redistribution centres along the Syro-Palestinian coast, to which they had been transported overland by merchant caravans. The caravan routes began in central Asia and then continued westwards via Mesopotamia to the ports on the eastern Mediterranean. Cyprus was a major source of the copper exported by ship to Mediterranean and Aegean ports. These basic cargoes were supplemented by other items, some from the Syro-Palestinian emporia, others acquired when goods taken on at one port were unloaded at other ports of call and new goods loaded in their place. Apart from the main consignments of commodity metals, a ship's total cargo might be made up of gold, silver, ebony and cedar logs, elephant and hippopotamus ivory, faience, glass, amber, ostrich eggshells, spices, jars of frankincense, terebinth resin, orpiment, fig medicine, cylinder seals and a range of domestic utensils, tools and agricultural implements.

Troy's inclusion in the loop of international sea trade gave it access to the wide variety of goods conveyed from port to port by merchant ships that plied the eastern Mediterranean and Aegean sea routes.[32] What did it have to exchange in return for the goods it imported? While undoubtedly Troy continued, as in earlier periods, to produce its own pottery for various overseas markets, its main items of export may have left no trace in the archaeological record. At least, no direct trace. Numerous spindle whorls indicate a flourishing textile industry at Troy, and woven goods of Trojan manufacture may well have found their way into various Aegean and Near Eastern markets. We are reminded of the textile trade that served as one of the important sources of income for the Assyrian merchants in their commercial dealings with the eastern Anatolian kingdoms during the so-called Assyrian Colony period. Horses may also have provided the Trojans with an important export market. In Homeric tradition, the Trojans were noted as breeders of horses. This may well reflect a horse-breeding tradition that goes back to the Late Bronze Age phase of Troy's existence.

To what extent did Troy derive its wealth from its commercial activities? If we believe that Troy VI was the centre of a prosperous kingdom with a thriving, affluent population, at least at its higher levels, what were the main sources of its wealth? We have no evidence that it accumulated riches through war booty or plundering expeditions. (But of course we cannot rule out this possibility.) Nor is there any indication that its exports were of such quality or produced in sufficient abundance to account for its prosperity. Indeed we have no evidence that the Trojans themselves, like the Assyrians, or the Venetian merchant princes of a later age, actively engaged in merchant enterprises beyond their own kingdom. As far as we are aware, they relied on others to do their importing and exporting for them. So where did their wealth come from? Could it have had something to do with their city's strategic location?

This is the line taken by a number of scholars. Troy's harbour provided the last safe haven for ships from the Aegean entering the

Hellespont and then the Propontis (Sea of Marmara) en route to the Black Sea. The passage was no easy one, given the contrary winds and counter-currents of the waterway between the Black Sea and the Aegean,[33] particularly in the centuries before the art of sailing against the wind had been mastered. Even if Bronze Age merchant vessels were capable of effecting passage through the Hellespont and Bosporus to the Black Sea,[34] adverse weather conditions would often have caused lengthy delays to ships attempting to proceed up the Hellespont to the Black Sea, forcing them to accept anchorage in the sheltered harbour of Beşik Bay that lay just 8 kilometres to the south-west of Troy and was possibly the city's main harbour.[35] The Trojans would no doubt have taken full advantage of their location by imposing heavy tolls upon sea traffic using the Hellespont and substantial port fees upon vessels forced to seek anchorage in their bay. Korfmann comments that Troy could have offered a range of services, including provision of food and water and a pilotage facility to enable visiting ships to find and use the right counter-currents through the straits.[36] Troy's wealth has been seen as directly linked with its control of access to the Black Sea. 'So long as Troy was able to exploit its geographical advantage', J. C. Wright comments, 'it could maintain itself as a powerful and wealthy settlement.'[37]

These statements and conclusions beg a fundamental question. Did Late Bronze Age trading activity conducted in the eastern Mediterranean and Near Eastern worlds extend to the Black Sea region? If not, that would significantly undercut any suggestion that Troy's importance and wealth were due to its commercially strategic location. Of course there must have been some sea traffic between the Aegean and the Black Sea coastal regions during the Bronze Age, and A. G. and E. S. Sherratt have suggested that Troy's foundation at the dawn of the Bronze Age marks the beginning of a linkage between Aegean trading networks and these regions.[38] Yet as they go on to say, extensive trade using the waterway between the Aegean and the Black Sea is a much later development, and during the Bronze Age it is unlikely that large trading vessels ever entered the Black Sea; any goods that were transported along this route were probably conveyed by very much smaller vessels, perhaps even canoes.

At present, we have no clear evidence that trade was conducted on a regular basis between Mediterranean and Black Sea ports during the Bronze Age. It is possible that every so often a consignment of goods was conveyed via the Black Sea to its final destination. That might have applied to the consignment of Mycenaean pottery discovered at Maşat (Hittite Tapikka) in north-central Anatolia. But this one isolated find falls well short of providing evidence of regular trading activity along a Black Sea route.[39] There may also have been some access via the Hellespont to the regions of the Danube. If so, Troy would have acted as a point of entry to these parts as well. But, again, we do not know whether the traffic between them and Aegean and Near Eastern markets at this time was any more than small and sporadic.

My position on the above is purely an agnostic one. There is no doubt that Troy was one of the most impressive cities of western Anatolia in the Late Bronze Age. And there is no doubt that it was excellently situated to make substantial profits out of sea traffic passing from the Aegean Sea through the Hellespont to the ports of the Black Sea and the Danube. This, conceivably, was one of the chief sources – if not the chief source – of its wealth. But we have neither archaeological nor written evidence to indicate that in the Late Bronze Age trade with these regions via the Hellespont was conducted regularly enough or on a scale large enough to bring great prosperity to the city that had the means of controlling it. At present, any claim that the Black Sea and Danube regions were important parts of the trading network in the Late Bronze Age is purely speculative.[40] We have yet to answer satisfactorily the question of the source or sources of Troy's wealth. Whether its prosperity can be attributed to its strategically valuable location, to its trading activities, to its region's natural resources, or to a range of these and other factors, is a matter still to be determined.

By the end of the Bronze Age, Troy had already passed the end of its most illustrious era. Yet its life had run but half its course. Others would resettle the site, completely transforming it from what it had been in the Bronze Age. At least in a material sense they would. To all outward appearances, Troy VIII and Troy IX were very much products of the Graeco-Roman age. But the spirit of Bronze Age Troy lived on until well into the Roman period, through the preservation of the stories associated with it in Greek bardic tradition. The city's legendary past would secure its future for many centuries to come.

6

TROY'S ALLIES

THE TROJAN CATALOGUE

In my time I have gone into many battles among men,
yet never have I seen a host like this, not one so numerous.
These look terribly like leaves, or the sands of the sea-
    shore,
as they advance across the plain to fight by the city.[1]

Iris, goddess of the rainbow and messenger of all the gods, has
brought the Trojans grim news: the Achaeans are now advancing
across Troy's plain, primed for battle. Never before has she seen so
vast an army. She urges Hector to issue a call to arms to the leaders
of the allied forces. A muster roll follows. This is the so-called Trojan
Catalogue. It lists all those who have rallied to the defence of Troy,
beginning with the Trojans themselves, under Hector's leadership,
and ending with Sarpedon's Lycians in the far south. Troy's allies
are a motley assortment, coming from many countries and speaking
many tongues. They are arranged in five geographical groups. Starting with the contingents from the Troad, the catalogue then radiates
outwards, in four directions, to the homelands of the allies from
other regions:[2]

- Group 1 from the Troad, including Trojans, Dardans, Zeleians
  and Pelasgians;
- Group 2 across the Hellespont, from Thrace westwards,
  including Thracians, Ciconians and Paeonians;

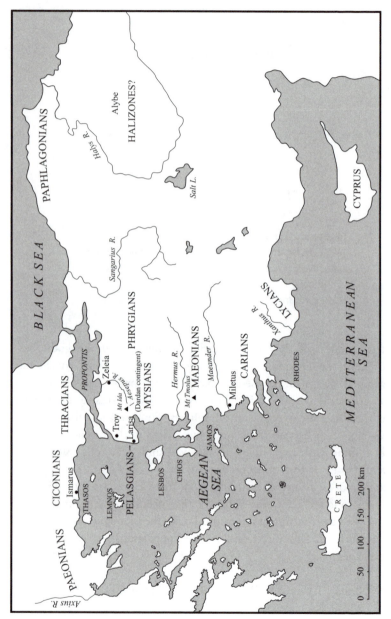

Map 6.1 Troy's Homeric allies.

128

- Group 3 from regions south of the Black Sea, including Paphlagonians and Halizones;
- Group 4 from regions south-east of the Troad, including Mysians and Phrygians;
- Group 5 from south-western Anatolia, including Maeonians, Carians and Lycians.

Each of these groups fights under the command of its own leaders, for reasons of practical necessity as well as morale, given the multi-ethnic, multilingual composition of the alliance.[3]

We can attribute very little historical credibility to the catalogue that closes the second book of the *Iliad*. The list of allies is clearly a poetic contrivance, necessary within the context of the poem to provide a counterpart to the more detailed Achaean Catalogue of Ships. It is undoubtedly a post-Bronze Age compilation, and very little of it has any basis in Late Bronze Age geography. What it does reflect, in some measure, is the emerging geopolitical scene of parts of western and central Anatolia during the late second and early first millennia, in the wake of the collapse of the Bronze Age civilizations.

But in terms of what it is fundamentally all about – the formation of a confederacy of Anatolian states united against an external aggressor – the catalogue does have a Bronze Age ring about it. In Chapter 5, we drew attention to the so-called Assuwan Confederacy, a military alliance of western Anatolian states established early in the fourteenth century. The list of twenty-two countries making up the alliance begins with the country of Lukka,[4] which was located in south-western Anatolia and included the region where first-millennium Lycia lay, and ends with Wilusiya and Taruisa, which we have identified with Ilios/Troy. Interestingly, the Trojan Catalogue in the *Iliad* begins and ends with the same places, but in the reverse order. It starts with Troy and ends with Lycia. Otherwise, the correspondence between the two lists of allies is very slight. We really have no basis for assuming that the Assuwan alliance served as a kind of historical prototype for the Trojan catalogue. On the other hand, there is no doubt that coalitions of the kind indicated by the catalogue were formed in the Late Bronze Age – primarily, it seems, for rebellion or aggression against the Hittites. That raises an intriguing question.

WHERE ARE THE HITTITES?

The Hittites are very conspicuous throughout the *Iliad* – by their absence from it! There is not one single identifiable reference to them – a remarkable omission, given that (a) they were the dominant power in Anatolia throughout the period of Troy VI, (b) they were actively involved in western Anatolian affairs in this period, and (c) Troy, if correctly identified with Wilusa, was one of their vassal states. If the *Iliad* really does have an historical basis, why do the Hittites fail to rate a single mention in it? Of course at the time of its composition in the eighth century, the Anatolian-based Hittite empire had long since disappeared. But we should not too readily assume that Homer knew nothing of the Hittites, particularly since he picked up and preserved many authentic relics of the Bronze Age past in his poems. We should also bear in mind that, while the Hittite kingdom in central Anatolia did not survive the end of the Bronze Age, collateral branches of its royal family did survive, along with a modified form of Hittite culture, in the so-called neo-Hittite kingdoms of Syria, until well into the first millennium. Even if the Bronze Age Hittites had disappeared from western Anatolian tradition, Homer would almost certainly have known of the neo-Hittite kingdoms, and probably also of the traditions that these kingdoms must have preserved of the great Bronze Age kingdom of Hatti once ruled by their ancestors.

The Hittites ought to be somewhere in the Homeric epic, but under another name. At least that is what the above considerations have prompted some scholars to believe. Perhaps they are to be identified with a people known as the Keteioi. This obscure, insignificant group from the region in western Anatolia called Mysia in the first millennium[5] receives a passing mention in the *Odyssey*. Here the Keteioi appear as the subjects of the ill-fated Eurypylus, son of Telephus, who was slain by Achilles' son Neoptolemus.[6] But they make no appearance at all in the *Iliad*, let alone have a place in the catalogue of Troy's allies. Attempts to link them with the Hittite land called Hatti (sometimes transcribed as Khatti) on the basis of a vague name resemblance[7] can only be described as *kling–klang* etymology (based purely on similar-sounding names) at its worst.

A rather more imaginative suggestion is that the Hittites appear in the *Iliad* under the guise of the Amazons. In Greek tradition, the

Amazons are a race of female warriors whose homeland lay in a remote region on the southern shores of the Black Sea. Popular etymology assigned to their name the meaning 'without breast', in the belief that they cut off their right breasts to enable them to take surer aim with their bows and javelins. They were a much favoured subject in Greek art, which almost always depicted them as fully endowed – probably for the sake of balance and symmetry rather than out of ignorance of the alleged meaning of their name. They make two appearances in the *Iliad*. Priam refers to an episode in his youth when they attacked a Phrygian encampment on the Sangarius River. He was in the camp at the time as an ally of the Phrygians. Their second appearance occurs in the context of the tasks imposed by the king of Lycia[8] upon Bellerophon, who came originally from Argos in southern Greece. The Amazons in this case were one of the three enemies of Lycia (the other two were the monster Chimaera, referred to below, and a local hostile population called the Solymians), who had been terrorizing the country's inhabitants. Bellerophon's task was to eradicate all three. With the assistance of his winged horse Pegasus, he succeeded in this task, slaughtering the Amazons along with Lycia's other enemies.

Though their homeland may have been located in a remote, far-off region, the Amazons pop up in legendary tradition in many places in western Anatolia, as founders of cities, such as Priene, Ephesus and Smyrna, and also in Greece – for example, in Chalcis and Athens, where cults were established in their honour. In the *Iliad*, they take no part in the Trojan War. However, in one of the compositions of the epic cycle, the *Aethiopis*, attributed to the poet Arctinus of Miletus, the Thracian queen of the Amazons Penthesilea comes to the support of the Trojans but is killed by Achilles. As he was on the point of dispatching her, the story goes, he gazed into her eyes and fell passionately in love with her. (But he slew her nonetheless.)

What is the basis for the suggested identification between Amazons and Hittites? Initially, it may have had something to do with the notion that there was a matriarchal element in very early Hittite society, as reflected in the powerful position of the Hittite reigning queen, and in (wrongly held) assumptions about royal succession through the female line. There is also an early Hittite tale, the so-called Zalpa legend, which contains the story of a city called Kanesh ruled by a queen, who rears her female babies but exposes her male ones (she has an enormous brood of both).[9] Could any of this have contributed to the creation of legend's matriarchal society *par excellence*? Decidedly not! Hittite society was, from its beginnings, emphatically patriarchal – despite the prominence and influence of a number of royal consorts and the evidence that some Hittite marriages were *matrilocal*. As for the bizarre Zalpa tale, we have no grounds for assuming that it was in any way connected with the Amazons. Though the tale has some suggestive features, the idea that it gave rise to the Amazon tradition should be firmly relegated to the realm of scholarly fantasy.

So too should attempts to find Amazons in visual representations of the Hittites. Charles Texier, in his 1834 visit to the famous Hittite rock sanctuary, today called Yazılıkaya, believed that the converging processions of male and female Hittite deities carved on the rock face represented the Amazons' meeting with the Paphlagonians. Of course, at the time of his visit, no one knew that Yazılıkaya was a Hittite sanctuary or that the Hittites, then known only from biblical references, had anything to do with the central Anatolian region where it was located. Many decades were to pass before this region was identified as the heartland of the Hittite world.

Attempts were then made to find an Amazon–Hittite link in other representations. For example in the famous two-metre high sculpture on the so-called 'King's Gate' in the Hittite capital Hattusa. The figure, almost certainly a Hittite god, is equipped as a warrior. He wears a helmet, with long plume and cheek flaps, and a kilt, and carries a battle axe in his right hand and a curved sword in his left. His hair is long, his cheeks are smooth and unbearded, and his chest has soft, round contours. Could those who saw this figure, long after the Hittite empire had fallen, have interpreted it as a female warrior? Was this the origin of the Amazon tradition? Again, an interesting theory, but several scholars have pointed out an apparently incontestable objection to it: though the contours of the figure's upper torso may on their own have been mistaken for those of a female, the chest itself is endowed with a flourishing crop of hair. Even the most casual observer can hardly fail to notice this.

We must conclude that the Hittites, the most powerful people in Anatolia during the Late Bronze Age, are given no place in the

Figure 6.1 (a) Warrior God (?) at Hattusa.

Figure 6.1 (b) Detail showing Warrior God's chest.

Iliad. As we have already remarked, it is difficult to believe that Homer knew nothing about them, let alone that they were for a time overlords of Troy, particularly if we allow the possibility that the western Anatolian region in which the poet lived preserved for generations memories of its Bronze Age past in which the Hittites had played a major part. It is, I suppose, possible that Homer relied very largely on bardic traditions from the Greek world for his story of the war. The minstrels and bards of this world probably had extremely limited knowledge of, or interest in, the overall political structure of Bronze Age western Anatolia, and knew little if anything about the Hittites. Could the Hittites' omission from the *Iliad* be due to no more than Greek tradition's ignorance of their existence? Perhaps. Nevertheless, we cannot rule out the possibility that Homer himself knew about the Hittites but deliberately kept them out of his epic, so that they would not diminish the status of his Trojans and consequently that of their opponents and the epic conflict in which they were engaged.

There is a further possible reason for the Hittites' non-appearance in the *Iliad*. If we accept that the epic is to a large extent the product of a post-Bronze Age era – and there is some reason for believing that this may have been the case (see p. 189) – then by that time the Hittites had disappeared entirely from Anatolia and were therefore quite irrelevant to the tale of Troy's final days.

Apart from the Hittites, the *Iliad* contains no reference to a number of peoples and cities we would expect to find in it as Troy's allies. No mention is made, for example, of Ephesus which, under its Late Bronze Age name Apasa, had been an important city throughout the Late Bronze Age and was subsequently refounded by Ionian colonists some generations before Homer's lifetime. Nor is there any mention of Smyrna, again founded by Ionian colonists around 1000 BC, on the site of a Dark Age settlement and one of the favoured candidates for Homer's own birthplace. In fact the whole Aegean coast between the southern Troad and Miletus is missing from the catalogue. Kirk suggests that this may be due to deliberate archaizing.[10] That is to say, the cities and peoples of this region were left out because it was assumed that they played no part in the Bronze Age world. However, Miletus, the most important of all the Ionian colonies on the Aegean coast, does appear in the list of Troy's allies. Was it considered a special case? Called Milawata in Hittite texts, it had provided a base for Ahhiyawan/Mycenaean enterprise in the Late Bronze Age and by the early thirteenth century probably had a substantial Mycenaean population. Perhaps its close association with the Mycenaean world resulted in greater consciousness in Greek tradition of its Bronze Age pedigree. The fact that the catalogue lists it as a city of the Carians is a matter to which we shall return.

ALLIES IN THE TROAD

The Dardans

We have suggested that the poet may have included, or highlighted the roles of, certain peoples and places in his poem in response to the wishes of important families whose patronage he enjoyed. This, perhaps, explains the role assigned to Aeneas and his followers in the *Iliad*. Cousin to Hector and Paris, Aeneas comes from a secondary branch of the Trojan royal family. All the members of the family are descendants of the legendary Dardanus. In the catalogue Aeneas appears second in the list, immediately after Hector, as the leader of the Dardan contingent from Mount Ida, which lies to the southeast of Troy. Poseidon prophesies that he will survive the fall of

Troy and henceforth become the new overlord of the Trojans. According to one tradition, he does so by setting up a ruling dynasty in the Troad itself; according to another, he takes to the sea with a band of refugees and founds a new kingdom in the west. The first of these traditions (we shall return to both of them in Chapter 7) may have been promoted by members of a local Troad family who saw themselves as the descendants of Aeneas and, therefore, the rightful heirs to the kingdom that he allegedly established in the region after the fall of Troy.

What was this kingdom called? Several scholars have suggested that the tradition that refers to it was connected with an actual Anatolian kingdom called Dardania, whose name *may* appear in several Egyptian texts of Bronze Age date. For example, a contingent from a place called Drdnjj, vocalized as 'Dardany', figures amongst the Hittites' allies in Ramesses' account of the battle of Kadesh.[11] The name crops up in earlier Egyptian sources as well. It is clearly a genuine historical name, and Peter Haider has proposed that the Troad region was so called in the Bronze Age.[12] Though Trojans and Dardans are listed consecutively a number of times in the *Iliad*, implying that they are separately identifiable, the Trojans are also referred to as 'Dardanidae' (the children of Dardanus), and, on occasions, 'Trojan' and 'Dardan' appear to be synonymous terms. If Haider is correct, then Wilusa must have lain to the south of the Troad, and its equation with Troy/Ilios could no longer be maintained.

Unfortunately, there is no identifiable reference to Dardania or Dardans in the Hittite texts. One might of course use this as support for the view that Troy lay totally outside Hittite control or interest, and one might argue that it could explain why there is no reference to the Hittites in the *Iliad*. But even if we allow the possibility of a Troad kingdom called Dardania, it would be most surprising if the Hittites had no dealings whatever with it, and saw no reason to refer to it in their records, in spite of their otherwise close and active involvement in western Anatolian affairs. The case for Wilusa as the kingdom that had Troy as its royal seat remains the more likely one. Egyptian records provide the only contemporary historical evidence we have for a place called Dardania. These give no indication of where this land lay, and the name similarity to Homer's Dardans is not on its own a sufficient basis for locating a kingdom called Dardania in the Troad.

The Zeleians

Following the Dardans, the catalogue lists another contingent from the Troad. This one came from Zeleia, a city located on the edge of the foothills of Mount Ida and by the 'dark, still waters' of the Aesepus, a river that empties into the Propontis. Also called Trojans, this band of warriors was led by Pandarus, son of Lycaon. Aeneas states that Pandarus surpasses all others, Trojan and Lycian alike, in his skill with the bow.[13] He had acquired this skill under the tutelage of the greatest of all archers, the god Apollo himself. Pandarus' implied association with the Lycians picks up on an earlier passage in Book 5 of the *Iliad*,[14] where the master archer claims that he came all the way from Lycia, in the far south-west, to take part in the conflict. This is puzzling, since elsewhere Zeleia in the Troad is clearly designated as his homeland,[15] and his role in the *Iliad* is definitely that of the leader of a Trojan not a Lycian contingent. As we shall see, the leaders of the latter were Sarpedon and Glaucus.

How do we account for this inconsistency? Contrary to what the *Iliad* claims, it is likely that Pandarus travelled not from Lycia to Troy, but in the opposite direction – from Troy to Lycia. That is to say, the folklore of a hero Pandarus was transplanted from the Troad to the south-west, reflecting the southward movement of a population group from the north-west during the upheavals at the end of the Bronze Age. The story of a pirate chief called Chimharrus (see p. 149) provides a further link, at least in legend, between Zeleia and Lycia. We might also compare the Pandarus tradition with that of the Leleges (a Troad people according to Homer)[16] and their southward progression down the Aegean coast until their final settlement in the south-west corner of Caria.[17] The apparent anomaly in the *Iliad*, which represents Pandarus both as a Lycian and as a native of the Troad, probably reflects an incomplete synthesis between earlier and later traditions concerning the folk hero. The Lycian connection is almost certainly later than the Trojan one; from other sources we learn of Pandarus' links with first-millennium Lycia, the city of Pinara in particular.[18] The inconsistency in representing him both as a Trojan and a Lycian is a good example of the dynamic process of oral composition, involving the partial updating of a tradition to bring it into line with contemporary beliefs and practices without entirely eliminating an earlier superseded phase of it.

The Pelasgians

The name 'Pelasgian' occurs in various parts of western Anatolia, Crete and mainland Greece and comes to be used as a general term for the pre-Indo-European peoples of the Greek and Aegean worlds. In the *Iliad*, the Pelasgians are a specific population group listed among the allies of the Trojans and are said to come from the city of Laris(s)a. There are a number of settlements so called.[19] This one has been located either south of Troy, on the western coast of the Troad or in Thrace. The former seems much more likely, for it appears to be the last-mentioned of Troy's allies before the catalogue moves north-westwards across the Hellespont to Thrace.

TROY'S EUROPEAN ALLIES

Thracians, Ciconians and Paeonians

Troy's European allies, Thracians, Ciconians and Paeonians, are a curious inclusion in the catalogue. As far as we are aware, their appearance here finds no echo in later sources. The Thracians, led by Acamas and Peirous, are the most easterly of these allies. The Ciconians, probably also from Thrace, subsequently appear in the *Odyssey*, where they are the first people encountered by Odysseus on his voyage home from Troy. Odysseus begins the tale he tells (to the Phaeacian king Alcinous) of his adventures after leaving Troy by relating his sack of the Ciconian city Ismarus,[20] probably to be located on the coast of Thrace. In typical heroic fashion, Odysseus followed up his destruction of the city by plundering it, slaughtering its menfolk and abducting its women. Then, after sharing out the spoils of conquest, he warned his men to depart with all possible speed. But, instead of heeding the warning, the victors fell to drinking and feasting on the site of their victory. This gave the Ciconians time to summon reinforcements and to stage a counter-attack. In the fighting that ensued, Odysseus' men suffered a defeat and heavy casualties before managing to escape.

The Paeonians were the most westerly group of Troy's European allies. They hailed from Amydon on the Axius River, and can thus be located north of the Chalcidice peninsula, close by the region where the later kingdom of Macedonia arose.

THE NORTH–CENTRAL ALLIES

The Halizones

The Halizones, 'from far-off Alybe', were the easternmost of Troy's allies. Homer refers to their land as 'the birthplace of silver'.[21] Where was this land? For several scholars, the names Halizones and Alybe call to mind the Halys River and a people called the Chalybes. In a tradition recorded by Strabo,[22] Alybe is in fact directly linked with Chalybe, the land of the Chalybes, who were famous in legend as workers of iron. In this tradition, their home seems to have been located on the southern coast of the Black Sea, but probably to the east of the Halys River, and perhaps in the mountains south of Trapezus (modern Trabzon).[23]

If, however, we allow the possibility of a connection between the Halizones, Alybe and the Halys River, then once more we appear to be heading back into Hittite territory. We recall that the Halys, known as the Marassantiya in Hittite times, defined the boundary of the Hittite homeland. Does Homer's reference to the Halizones' land as the birthplace of silver have any bearing on this? Silver deposits have in fact been found within the Halys region, but we are unable to determine whether or not these were worked in the Late Bronze Age.[24] (Interestingly, though probably irrelevantly, the logographic version of the name of the Hittite capital Hattusa is KÙ.BABBAR, which means 'silver'.) In any case, there are over two dozen important deposits of silver distributed throughout Anatolia,[25] and even if those in the Halys basin were exploited during the Hittite period, it is most unlikely that the region was a major producer of the metal. Unfortunately the claim made by Professor Kirk that the Hittites were major suppliers of silver to the Greek world is not consistent with what we know of the sporadic and very indirect commercial contacts between Hittites and Mycenaeans.[26] The suggested silver link between Halizones and Hittites is no more than a red herring. The best we can do for the Halizones is to concede that if there is any hint at all of the Hittites in Homer's account of the Trojan War, they probably have the strongest claim to represent them. But, unlike the Hittites, they are (like the Keteioi) an obscure, insignificant people. By indulging in speculations of this kind, we are getting ourselves well and truly into straw-clutching territory.

The Paphlagonians

The Paphlagonians, who appear in the catalogue immediately before the Halizones, have a much firmer historical foundation. They occupied the mountainous coastal region lying between Bithynia and the Black Sea called Pala (combined with Tummanna) in the second millennium. The language spoken by its inhabitants, Palaic, was one of the three Indo-European languages (along with Nesite and Luwian) introduced into Anatolia probably during the course of the third millennium. Lying to the north-west of the Hittite homeland, the Palaians became attached to the Hittite kingdom as a vassal state. Pala occupied an important strategic location from the Hittite point of view, near the Kaska zone and serving as a kind of north-western buffer zone for the Hittite homeland. We hear of attacks upon it by the Kaska mountain tribes, and also of an occasional anti-Hittite uprising by one of its own cities. The traveller proceeding westwards from Pala through northern Anatolia would eventually have reached the kingdom of Wilusa-Troy. But a distance of some 600 kilometres separated Pala from Wilusa. The intervening region seems never to have been under Hittite control.

THE ALLIES SOUTH-EAST OF THE TROAD

The Mysians

Following the Halizones, the catalogue lists a people called the Mysians, led by Chromis. Their country lay in the north-west sector of Anatolia and extended to the Aegean coast south of the Troad. It probably covered much of the territory occupied in the Late Bronze Age by the Arzawan kingdom called the Seha River Land; the river itself was very likely the Classical Caicus or Hermus. In Greek tradition, Mysia was close enough to Troy for the Greeks to land on its coast and begin plundering it, in the mistaken belief that they had actually reached Troy itself. Telephus, heir of the Mysian king Teuthras, succeeded in killing many of the invaders before he was finally driven into flight by Achilles.

The Phrygians

The Phrygians are a genuine historical people who figure on six occasions in the *Iliad*, although their arrival in Anatolia almost certainly dates to the last years of the Bronze Age. By the end of the second millennium they had become firmly established in central Anatolia, particularly within the region enclosed by the Halys River – that is, the old Hittite homeland. They were, in effect, the territorial heirs of the Hittites, building a new settlement upon the ruins of the Hittite capital Hattusa. Towards the end of the eighth century they amalgamated with a people called the Mushki. The amalgamation was almost certainly due to the Mushki king Mita, better known by his Greek name Midas. During his reign, Phrygia became a highly prosperous state and a major political power in Anatolia. Midas' fabled 'golden touch' may well be a reflection of the high level of prosperity that his kingdom attained. From his capital at Gordion, *c.*100 kilometres west of modern Ankara, Midas ruled a kingdom that extended eastwards towards the Euphrates River, southwards into the region later known as Cappadocia, and westwards as far as the Aegean Sea. He was also in contact with mainland Greece, where he made offerings to the god Apollo at Delphi.

Around 695 his kingdom fell victim to a group called the Cimmerians, who invaded Anatolia from the north and occupied almost the entire region. The united Phrygian empire was at an end. But a number of Phrygian settlements recovered from the Cimmerian onslaught and, after the invaders finally withdrew from Anatolia, they regained much of their former prosperity in the first half of the sixth century as small principalities subject to the kings of Lydia.

Midas appears to have been an almost exact contemporary of Homer, and no doubt the poet was fully aware of the great power Phrygia was becoming, or had become, at the time he composed his epics. It was also becoming well known for the excellence of its material civilization. Crafts and trades flourished, and Gordion in particular has yielded a fine range of artefacts of bronze, iron, wood, ivory and a wide assortment of ceramic ware. Phrygia's cultivation of the arts very likely put it in the market for the acquisition of art treasures from other lands. We may see an anachronistic reflection of this in Hector's lament that his own kingdom has been forced to sell off its art treasures to Phrygia and Maeonia in order to pay the costs involved in maintaining the war effort.[27] It made good sense for Homer to give this wealthy powerful nation some role in the *Iliad*, though this role amounts to no more than an alliance with

Priam in the early days of his reign and a token appearance in the catalogue. There is no suggestion that Phrygians took any part in the conflict itself – beyond helping to finance the Trojan conduct of the war by buying up Troy's art treasures. The insertion of this particular piece of information in the *Iliad* leads one to wonder whether the Phrygians might actually have boasted that in their collection of art they still had the items allegedly acquired from Troy. A couple of lines by Homer referring to such an acquisition could have helped 'authenticate' the claim made by its current owners. Dependent as he probably was on the patronage of the wealthy and influential, the poet was no doubt all too willing to oblige his patrons in ways such as this, particularly if he could expect some tangible benefit from doing so.

In the art and literature of fifth-century Athens, Trojans and Phrygians were closely linked, to the point where their names became virtually interchangeable. This was in no way a compliment to the Trojans, for by now the name Phrygia had become a byword for luxury and decadence.

THE ALLIES OF SOUTH-WESTERN ANATOLIA

The Maeonians (= Lydians?)

The western Anatolian kingdom of Lydia, bordering on Phrygia in the east and the Ionian colonies in the west, appeared in the wake of the destruction of Midas' empire, with the rise of a ruling family known as the Mermnad dynasty around 685. It was founded by a king called Gyges. From its capital, Sardis, Lydia went on to become the dominant power in Anatolia, subjugating in the process the Ionian Greek colonies along the Aegean coast, with the exception of Miletus. Some 140 years later, under its last ruler Croesus (*c*.560–546), Lydia succumbed to the Persian empire.

The Lydians make no appearance in the Trojan Catalogue or anywhere else in the Homeric poems. This is understandable, since the foundation of their kingdom almost certainly post-dates Homer's lifetime by a generation or so. On the other hand, in a tradition recorded by Herodotus,[28] the Mermnad dynasty was preceded by an earlier Heraclid dynasty, whose members were allegedly descendants of Heracles; this dynasty ruled for twenty-two generations, or 505 years, roughly from the period of the Trojan War to the early seventh century. Apparently Homer knew nothing of the tradition, for it would otherwise be most strange that he should include no reference to these early Lydians, given the inclusion of far more remote peoples in the catalogue and the *Iliad* in general. They may, however, appear in the catalogue under a different name. Immediately after the Phrygians, the catalogue lists a people called the Maeonians, whose homeland lay under Mount Tmolus (modern Boz Dağı) in the region of ancient Lydia. According to Herodotus, the Lydians were originally known as the Maeonians, but subsequently called themselves Lydians in commemoration of a legendary king Lydus who ruled the region before the Heraclid dynasty.[29]

It is possible that these Maeonians, or early Lydians, do reflect an actual Late Bronze Age people, the people of a country called Masa in Hittite texts. Masa appears several times in the texts alongside another country called Karkisa. Both were located somewhere in western Anatolia and both apparently remained independent of Hittite rule throughout the Late Bronze Age. Maeonia has been etymologically linked with Masa and Karkisa with Caria.[30] In each case the assumed name link is uncertain, but it cannot be ruled out.

The Carians

The next group listed in the catalogue are the Carians, 'men from Miletus'. Herodotus records a tradition about their alleged Aegean origins. According to this tradition, which supposedly came from Crete, the Carians were immigrants to western Anatolia from the Aegean islands, displaced from their original homelands by Ionian and Dorian Greeks.[31] On this basis, the Carians could be included in the general migratory movements to the coastlands of western Anatolia in the late second millennium. However, the Carians themselves, as Herodotus points out, claimed that they were native Anatolians, and that they had always been called Carians. This claim would of course be compatible with the proposed etymological link between Caria and the Bronze Age Anatolian name Karkisa. Significantly, the Trojan Catalogue describes the Carians as 'speakers of a barbarian language'[32] – which clearly distinguishes them from immigrant Greeks, whether the latter came in the Late Bronze Age or during the upheavals that followed it.

In Hittite texts, Masa and Karkisa appear to have been governed by councils of chiefs rather than by kings, an indication that they never had the status of politically coherent kingdoms like those of the Arzawa Lands. Much the same seems to have applied to the Carian tribal groups of the first millennium, each of whom was subject to its own ruling dynasty. Masa and Karkisa both had sporadic contacts with the Hittites, sometimes collaborating with them, sometimes in conflict with them. In the treaty that the Hittite king Muwattalli drew up with Alaksandu, King of Wilusa, Masa and Karkisa are mentioned together as possible starting points for a Hittite campaign, which Alaksandu might be called upon to support. In his account of the battle of Kadesh, Ramesses lists both Masa and Karkisa in the ranks of the massive army that the Hittites raised for the conflict. They were there almost certainly in a mercenary capacity, consistent with Ramesses' derogatory comment that his Hittite opponent had to strip his land of silver in order to pay the troops mustered beneath his banner.

It is quite impossible to fix precise or even approximate locations for Masa and Karkisa in western Anatolia and, even if we could, the likelihood is that their post-Bronze Age descendants shifted to new areas during the population upheavals of the late second millennium. But the Hittite texts make clear that they were militarily active in Late Bronze Age coalitions, and it is possible that an echo of their Bronze Age role occurs in the listing of Maeonians and Carians in the Trojan Catalogue.

The Lycians

That brings us to the final entry in the catalogue: the contingent from far-off Lycia, which came to the support of Troy under the leadership of Sarpedon and his cousin Glaucus. The brief, two-line reference to the Lycians at the end of the list does scant justice to the role that they and especially their commander-in-chief, Sarpedon, played in the war. They were indisputably the most important of Troy's allies. And their participation in the conflict may bring us as close as we can get to a genuine, historically based tradition.

We have already noted that Lycia in south-western Anatolia formed part of the region that constituted the homeland of the Lukka people in the Late Bronze Age. Indeed, the name similarity is sufficient in itself to suggest this. But 'Lycia' is not the name used by the Lycians themselves. In their own language, they called their country 'Trm̃misa' and themselves 'Trm̃mili', represented in Greek as 'Termilae'. 'Lycia', or more strictly 'Lykia', is the later Greek name for the country. Unwittingly, the Greeks may have preserved a genuine Bronze Age name for the people, though they assigned to it a false Greek etymology. There are several explanations for the name in Greek tradition, the most attractive being that recorded by Antoninus Liberalis: the country was called Lycia by the goddess Leto, in honour of the wolves ('lykoi') who had guided her to the Xanthus River in her flight with her baby children Apollo and Artemis from the wrath of the goddess Hera.[33]

This river, the main waterway of the country, is frequently linked with the name Lycia in the *Iliad*. Indeed, it is clear that, for Homer, the country Lycia and the Xanthus River valley were virtually identical. Within this valley, he located the fertile, deep-soiled domain of Sarpedon, rich in crops and orchards.[34] On the Xanthus River Lycia's chief city lay, also called Xanthus by the Greeks. Its native name was Arñna, a derivative of the Late Bronze Age Awarna. So too Pinara, Tlawa (the Lycian name for Tlos) and Pttara (Patara in Greek), all names of settlements in the Xanthus valley, are derivatives of the Bronze Age names Pina(li), T/Dalawa, and Patar(a) respectively. But none of these individual city-names appear in the *Iliad*.

So far, substantial material evidence for settlement in Lycia goes back no earlier than the late eighth century to remains of buildings on the acropolis of Xanthus. These belong to the period of Homer's own lifetime. But there can no be no doubt from textual evidence that Lycia was inhabited at least from the Late Bronze Age onwards. Almost certainly too, Homer took over an existing tradition of Lycian participation in the Trojan War and did not simply make it up. He was conscious of how far Lycia was from Troy and of the apparent lack of motive for Lycia's involvement in the conflict. But instead of seeing this as a problem, he turned it to dramatic advantage in the scene where Sarpedon utters his splendid rallying call to Hector. Sarpedon contrasts the Trojans' lack of spirit in battle with the Lycians' own full-blooded commitment to the conflict — a commitment all the more noteworthy because they have come from so far away and have not the least stake in the conflict's outcome.[35]

One of the most graphic and poignant passages in the *Iliad* relates Sarpedon's death at the hands of Patroclus, followed by the furious battle over his corpse, the stripping of his armour and weapons by the Greeks and his final journey back to Lycia for burial in the arms of the twin brothers Sleep and Death.[36] Sarpedon's death marks a pivotal point in the conflict, for it leads to the revenge killing of Patroclus by Hector and, in turn, to the revenge killing of Hector by Achilles, the act that ultimately seals Troy's fate.

The overall picture we have of the Lycians is of a fiercely warlike people who have come from a far-off country to fight on the Trojan side, without apparent motive or incentive. We have already suggested that in the roles he assigns to some of the participants in the conflict, the *Iliad*'s composer may have been influenced by wealthy aristocratic patrons of his own day. Could this account for the prominence he gives to the Lycians? Homer was a poet of the east Greek Ionian world, and Herodotus tells us that some of the Greeks of this world were subject to the authority of Lycian rulers – descendants of Glaucus, the second-in-command of the Lycian contingent at Troy.[37] If there is any truth in this, then it may be that local rulers who claimed a Lycian ancestry influenced Homer into assigning a high profile to their alleged ancestors. Peter Frei put forward an alternative suggestion: that Homer's knowledge of the Lycians was based on an epic about Lycia composed by a Greek poet for a Lycian prince, perhaps the ruler of Xanthus, some time before the end of the eighth century.[38]

Figure 6.2 The death of Sarpedon (scene from the Euphronius Crater, Metropolitan Museum of Art, New York).[39]

A further link between Lycia and the Ionian region of western Anatolia is provided by the Greek tradition that associates Sarpedon with a group of Cretan immigrants to Anatolia called Termilae. As we have noted, 'Termilae' is the Hellenized form of the name that the Lycians called themselves. In yet another tradition preserved for us by Herodotus, Sarpedon was a Cretan prince forced to flee his country after a dispute with his brother Minos.[40] The dispute, Apollodoros informs us,[41] was over a boy called Miletus, who favoured Sarpedon. Minos emerged victorious from the hostilities that followed, and Sarpedon, Miletus and their supporters were driven from their island home. Miletus took refuge in Caria where he founded the city that was named after him, Sarpedon in Cilicia where he was received by his uncle Cilix and subsequently established as king of Lycia. In a slightly different tradition, Sarpedon himself founded the city of Miletus, naming it after the Cretan city of his origin.[42]

We thus have two basic traditions in which Sarpedon features. One of them makes him the leader of a band of refugees from Crete called Termilae, the other the leader of the Lycian contingent at Troy. A number of ancient commentators sought to reconcile the two traditions, either by making Sarpedon live for three generations after becoming king of Lycia, or by making the Lycian leader at Troy the grandson of the migrant from Crete.[43] Either way, the tradition that Lycia was settled by emigrants from Crete or their descendants gains some credibility from the fact that the name of these emigrants, Termilae, is clearly reflected in the Lycians' indigenous name Trm̃mili. And the legendary association between Crete and settlement at Miletus could be seen as a reflection of Minoan colonization of Miletus, c.1600, in the Middle Minoan IIIb period. All in all, it is possible that first-millennium Lycia had within its population an ethnic group who had links with Miletus and whose ancestral roots lay in Crete.

But there is no doubt that the Lycians spoke a language closely related to Bronze Age Luwian and retained a number of features of Bronze Age Luwian culture. The latter is indicated by the names of a number of Lycian deities, most notable amongst whom is the female deity called *ēni mahanahi*, 'mother of the gods', a direct descendant of the Bronze Age Luwian mother goddess. The Lycian language survives primarily in the form of approximately 180 inscriptions carved on stone. The great majority of these are sepulchral inscriptions appearing on the Lycians' rock-cut tombs. They contain instructions for interment and often a list of relatives and other family connections eligible for burial in a particular tomb. Unfortunately, much of the Lycian language is still largely unintelligible. Most challenging is a long inscription, some 255 lines in length, containing two forms of the language and a twelve-line Greek epigram. The text appears on a stele in the agora or marketplace of Lycia's chief city, Xanthus – the so-called Inscribed Pillar. With the exception of the Greek epigram, and a few phrases and the odd sentence here and there, the inscription still defies decipherment.

We can be sure that Lukka people inhabited Lycia during the Late Bronze Age, and we have from various Hittite texts a range of information about the Lycians' Bronze Age Anatolian ancestors. As we have noted, Lukka appears first in the list of western Anatolian states forming a coalition that we have called the Assuwan Confederacy, and that may well have extended from Lycia in the south to the Troad in the north. The Lukka people seem also to have had a reputation as sea pirates, carrying out raids on the coastal cities of Alasiya (Cyprus) and Egypt. The pharaoh Akhenaten in fact

Figure 6.3 Rock cut tombs, Lycia.

complained to the Alasiyan king about their raids, accusing him of complicity in them. It is just possible that a reflection of their role as pirates occurs in a tradition preserved by Plutarch, who wrote in the first–second centuries AD. In referring to the legend of the Chimaera, the fire-breathing monster, part lion, part serpent, part goat, who terrorized the country of Lycia, Plutarch records several suggestions as to the monster's origins.[44] One of these is that the Chimaera tradition originated with a pirate chief called Chimarrhus, who commanded a pirate fleet from a 'Lycian colony' in the vicinity of Zeleia in the Troad; Chimarrhus' flagship had a lion as its figurehead and a serpent at its stern, and his fleet travelled south to Lycia where it terrorized the populations of the coastal cities and made the sea unsafe to travel. As we have noted, the tradition, admittedly a very late-attested one, provides an additional link between Zeleia, whence came Pandarus, and Lycia, where a cult of Pandarus was later established. It could be that it represents a genuine southward sea migration by a group of marauders from the north who initially plundered the Lycian coast and then subsequently settled there – Lycia's own version of the Sea Peoples.

Later Greek tradition aside, the Lukka people appear elsewhere as fractious and aggressive, sometimes subject to Hittite authority, sometimes rebelling against it. But they seem to have been associated with a number of locations, which probably indicates that while their homeland lay in the south-west, they were also widely distributed throughout western Anatolia, perhaps in many cases leading a nomadic or semi-nomadic existence. We never hear of a kingdom called Lukka, or of treaties drawn up with rulers of Lukka. As far as we can judge, they had to be dealt with on a community by community or tribe by tribe basis. Their apparent lack of a firm stable kingdom might go some way towards explaining our failure to find any material evidence of their existence in Lycia, or indeed anywhere in southern Anatolia, during the Bronze Age.

On the other hand, it is also possible that the name 'Lukka' was not only used of a relatively specific region of south-western Anatolia in the Late Bronze Age, but also sometimes referred in a generic sense to all Luwian-speaking peoples of western Anatolia.[45] In any case, the theme of Lycian participation in the Trojan War could have come to Homer from traditions associated with the ancestors – whether in a specific or in a broad sense – of the first-millennium

Lycians, and preserved through the generations that bridged the gap between the end of the Bronze Age and the early centuries of the first millennium. These traditions were given their fullest artistic expression in the *Iliad*. Perhaps the Lycians' involvement in the Trojan War had, more than that of any other allies of Troy, some historical basis – in so far as it can be seen as a reflection of their Bronze Age Lukka ancestors' participation in a series of conflicts in western Anatolia, sometimes on the side of a foreign power such as Hatti or Ahhiyawa, sometimes as part of a coalition fighting against such a power.

The Lycians' reputation in the *Iliad* for courage and ferocity in battle finds echoes in later ages. One incident in particular serves to illustrate this. During the campaign of conquest conducted by the Persian general Harpagus through south-western Anatolia around 540, the Lycians were the only people to make a stand against the might of the Persian army. Herodotus tells the story of the courageous and ultimately futile resistance mounted by a small force of Lycians on the plain outside the city of Xanthus:

> When Harpagus marched his army into the plain of Xanthus, the Lycians came forth and fought with much courage, though few against many. But they were defeated and driven back into their city. Thereupon they herded their wives, their children, their property, and their slaves into the acropolis, which they set ablaze and burnt to the ground. Having done this the Xanthians swore terrible oaths, and sallying forth once more for battle, they perished to the last man.[46]

They were indeed worthy descendants of Sarpedon, the greatest Lycian of them all!

7

THE NEW CITY
(LEVELS VIII TO IX)

A FRESH LEASE OF LIFE

Aeolian Greeks had become the proud possessors of the all but derelict site where they believed great heroes had once dwelt, where once King Priam had ruled. Before its walls mighty warriors had fought, slaughtered and died, their exploits celebrated in a succession of bardic songs spanning many centuries and culminating finally in the tale told by Homer, the greatest bard of them all. His was the creative genius that would ensure immortality for this setting and the story that allegedly took place within it.

But the great days of the city were now long past. There would be no glorious new era for Troy, now called Ilion. The new age Trojans went about their daily activities in relatively comfortable obscurity. In practical terms the city had lost its essential *raison d'être*. Whether or not it had served as the gateway to regular trading contacts with the Black Sea and regions beyond in the Bronze Age, its close sea access had undoubtedly been a key to its prosperity and to the attractions it offered to those with whom it came into contact, whether in peace or in war. Its location on the north-western flank of the Hittite empire had made it a strategically valuable asset to the empire in a region that was prone to insurrectionist activity and unwelcome intervention from across the Aegean. But changes in the topography of Troy's coastal areas, which were imposing increasing limitations on its sea access, removed any major practical incentive for its redevelopment on a large commercial scale. Further, the political reshaping of the western Anatolian region deprived it of the strategic importance it had enjoyed in the days of the Great Kingdom of Hatti.

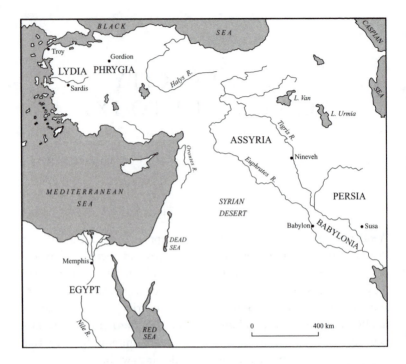

Map 7.1 Homelands of the Near Eastern kingdoms, first half of first
millennium BC.

Ilion was left largely undisturbed by the dramatic changes that
were taking place in the Near Eastern world during the first half
of the first millennium. Five great empires rose and four of them
fell in this period. The first of these was the so-called Neo-Assyrian
empire. From his northern Mesopotamian homeland, the Assyrian
king Adad-nirari II (*c.*911–891) embarked upon a programme of
aggressive territorial expansion that reached its peak in the reign
of Sargon (*c.*721–705), around the time Aeolian settlers were occupying the site of Troy. A century later, the Assyrian kingdom fell to
a coalition formed between the Chaldean rulers of Babylonia and
the newly emerging kingdom of the Medes east of the Tigris. The
Chaldeans now became the new overlords of Mesopotamia. But the
empire that they built was one of the briefest in the history of

the Near East. After peaking in the reign of the biblically infamous Nebuchadnezzar (c.605–562), it was destroyed in 539 by the newly emerging Persian empire founded by Cyrus the Great. Already Cyrus had conquered the Lydian empire of western Anatolia, which had arisen after the collapse of the kingdom of Phrygia; the latter, whose royal seat lay at Gordion in central Anatolia, had been founded in the eighth century by King Mita (Greek Midas). Cyrus comprehensively defeated the Lydian king Croesus in a battle outside the Lydian capital Sardis in 546, and thereupon incorporated his kingdom into the Persian empire, which now extended to the Ionian cities along the Aegean coast, formerly subjects of the Lydian king.

This constant reconfiguring of the map of the Near East appears to have had minimal effect on the backwater settlement in the Troad. The present little township on the site, which lacked even the status of a *polis*, was but a pale shadow of the royal capital that had once been there. But Ilion was not destined to sink into oblivion. On the contrary, current developments in the Greek world ensured that its name would become ever more widely known. The great Greek diaspora (c.800–500 BC) commonly called the colonization movement did much to facilitate the spread of Homer's tales to many parts of the expanding Greek world. And in sixth-century Athens, during the regime of the tyrant Pisistratus, performances of the Homeric epics were incorporated into the newly reorganized Panathenaic festival. Perhaps now for the first time they gained permanent form in writing.[1]

Athens' official adoption of the epics could hardly have been prompted by the role that Homer assigned its warriors in the Achaean Confederacy. The part the Athenian contingent played in the conflict was a minor one and produced no Athenian heroes worthy of note. Rather, under Pisistratus' leadership Athens was inspired by a panhellenic vision in which it saw itself as the cultural as well as the commercial centre of the Greek world. The ambitious new building programmes, the city's vigorous commercial development and the revamping of its religious festivals were all explicit statements of its self-assumed role as the leading state in Greece. By embedding the Homeric poems within their city's most important religious and cultural festival, the Athenians were in effect closely identifying the city with the greatest and most widely known literary masterpieces of the Greek world. Henceforth Athens would become the cultural and spiritual home of these masterpieces. Their adoption was an explicit statement of the city's role as the focus of panhellenic culture.

It was also the expression of an outlook that drew no distinction between those who fought on the Greek side and those who fought on the Trojan. Though both sides slaughtered each other mercilessly on the plains of Troy, Homeric tradition united them in a common culture, with shared beliefs and customs, and adherence to a common set of ideals and values. So too, Pisistratid Athens embraced all its Homeric heroes without distinction. And the incorporation of the epics in Athens' most important festival no doubt spawned generations of little Hectors and Priams and Andromaches alongside many an infant Achilles, Agamemnon and Helen.

But any affinity or empathy the Classical Greeks may have felt with the legendary inhabitants of Troy was soon to give way to feelings of a quite different kind – in the context of the rise of Persia and its relentless advance westwards.

THE PERSIAN FACTOR

After the fall of the Lydian empire, the Greek states along Anatolia's Aegean coast were also forced to acknowledge the conqueror Cyrus as their sovereign. For most practical purposes, they were merely exchanging one overlord for another. But they fiercely resented their subjection to the Persian despot. For almost fifty years the resentment simmered. Finally, in the reign of the emperor Darius, the Greek states joined forces in an heroic and ultimately futile rebellion against Persian rule (499). Athens responded to an appeal for assistance by dispatching to their Ionian kinsfolk a small fleet of twenty ships. But defeat was inevitable. Darius ruthlessly crushed the rebellion and then turned his attention to the Greek mainland. He was furious at Athens for its support of the rebels. This, allegedly, was one of the reasons for his abortive invasion of mainland Greece in 490 – which was followed by a much more ambitious and determined invasion by his son and successor Xerxes ten years later.

Troy once more comes to our attention in the course of Xerxes' preparations for leading his vast army from Asia into Europe. On reaching the Scamander River and before crossing the Hellespont, Xerxes ascended the citadel of Troy, where he was told the whole story of the place. Thereupon, he sacrificed 1,000 oxen to the goddess Athena of Ilion and ordered his priests to offer libations to the heroes of the Trojan War.[2]

According to Herodotus, the Persians dated their hostility to Greece right back to the time of Troy's fall. And it is possible that Xerxes sought to represent himself as the avenger of Troy's defeat – the avenger arising from the bones of King Priam. His arrival at Troy was a critical point in his campaign against Greece. For he was now on the very spot of the Greek triumph celebrated in legend. It was the last stopping point on his expedition before the crossing of the Hellespont and, with this crossing, the die would be cast. The Persian onslaught upon the Greek world would now begin in earnest. A spectacular gesture like a mass animal sacrifice was a fitting means of marking the occasion.

Of course it was all very propagandistic. The notion that this upstart power that had arisen east of the Tigris but a few decades earlier was the inheritor of a vendetta extending back seven centuries in a place thousands of kilometres to the west is patently absurd. There is not the slightest indication that a desire to avenge the destruction of Troy figured amongst the reasons for Xerxes' campaign against the Greek world, let alone provided a fundamental cause for it. Indeed there is nothing to suggest that Xerxes showed much interest at all in Troy before his arrival there, and it has even been suggested that alleged Persian resentment over Troy was a fiction arising out of later representations of Persians in Greek art and literature as latter-day Trojans.

None the less, Xerxes was probably well aware of the Trojan War tradition long before he set out on his campaign and, upon reaching the famous site of Troy, would hardly have missed exploiting the propaganda opportunity that his presence there provided. It was calculated propaganda with a practical and a political purpose. The conversion of 1,000 livestock on the hoof to meat on the table might have reduced significantly the logistical problems involved in crossing the Hellespont – which was no small undertaking for a massive army and its commissariat, as Xerxes was soon to find out. And it could be done within the context of a great public sacrifice to the goddess of Ilion and a grand celebratory feast for the king's troops. Furthermore, a lavish sacrifice and feast might have helped integrate local Greeks into the Great King's army.[3]

Xerxes' visit to Troy[4] was probably one of the factors that led to a rekindling of interest in the site itself, to a new stage in its post-Bronze Age history. But in the years following the repulse of the Persians, its image in the Greek world appears by and large to have been a negative one. According to Herodotus, the Persians explicitly identified themselves with the Greeks' opponents at Troy. They established a clear divide between Europe and the Greeks on the one side, and Asia and the non-Greeks on the other.[5] This may have had some bearing on the image that Troy conjured up in the Greek world after Persia's defeat by the allied Greek states. Henceforth Persians and Trojans became closely linked in Greek, especially Athenian, literary and artistic tradition: the Persian court wallowed in decadence, luxury and ostentatious display; the Persian world was ruled by a king who epitomized all these qualities – the very essence of barbarism. So too, by association, these were the qualities now associated with the court of King Priam. For the Athenian playwrights, Troy was a world of degenerate opulence, presided over by a despot in what was allegedly the Persian manner. To emphasize the Persian connection, Trojans in Greek theatre were endowed with Persian-style titles and decked out on stage in Persian-style costumes. They were also sometimes called Phrygians, a name with an authentic historical pedigree, extending back at least to the time of Homer, but now increasingly a byword for luxury and decadence.

Once again, the image is highly propagandistic and very decidedly an Athenian-promoted one. After the repulse of Persia, Athens took on the role of champion of panhellenic interests, seeking to develop a strong unity throughout the Greek world against any future threat that Persia might pose to this world. Hence the so-called Delian League came into being,[6] effectively under Athenian leadership. Athens sought to promote and to maintain both the image and the practice of panhellenic unity in a number of ways. Propaganda, as expressed through art and literature, created a sharp division between the Greek and non-Greek worlds, by establishing an uncompromising contrast between all the noble qualities that allegedly characterized the former and all the base qualities of extravagance, decadence and self-indulgence that were inherent in the latter. Troy was now represented as an integral part of the non-Greek world, with all that that implied.

Was there not scope for using the *Iliad* to kindle afresh the panhellenic spirit, for ensuring that the Greeks remained united against the enemy across the sea, inspired by the great triumph won by their ancestors in the heroic past? We have no indication that the *Iliad* was ever used in propaganda directed against non-Greeks. In fact, it was largely ignored by fifth-century Athenian writers, as well as by vase painters and other visual artists of the period.[7] Almost certainly we cannot explain this as due simply to the accident of survival. Rather, it is a reflection of the fact that the *Iliad* was totally unsuitable for fifth-century Athenian propaganda. The tale it tells ends not with a Greek triumph, but with an eloquent statement of shared human grief and suffering, cutting across international boundaries. Hardly the stuff for rallying the troops against the enemy! Greeks and Trojans share the same values and ideals, their customs and beliefs have much in common, their characters are equally a mixture of good and bad. All this is totally out of keeping with the propaganda that merged the image of the Trojan with that of the Persian. Both were now symbols of oriental decadence, far removed from the heroic image shared by Greek and Trojan in the Homeric poems.

We do not know to what extent the depiction of Trojans on stage and in the visual arts reflected or influenced popular opinion in Athens. Athenian society's attitude towards the Trojans may have been an ambivalent one, as Professor Erskine suggests:

> The new image and the old one sat uncomfortably together. The pre-Persian War attitude could not just be abandoned. Men born before the war had been named after Trojan heroes, their houses contained pre-war vases that emphasized the heroic qualities of the Trojans. So within the house Athenians may have been surrounded by a different set of signs from those apparent in the public sphere.[8]

We hear little about Ilion itself in the century and a half that followed Xerxes' visit to the site. There are but a few scattered pieces of information. For example, it was a tribute-paying member of the Athenian empire in the 420s,[9] it came under the authority of the Phrygian satrap Pharnabazus in 413, and in 386 its subjection to Persia was confirmed by the ignominious agreement called the

'King's Peace', in accordance with whose terms all the Greek cities in Asia were ceded to the Persian king.

Fifty years after this agreement, Ilion's fortunes were to change dramatically.

THE IMPACT OF ALEXANDER

In the year 334, Alexander the Great landed his fleet on Anatolia's north-west coast, not far from Ilion, in preparation for his campaign against the Persian empire. This was his first point of contact with Asia, and he made sure he was the first of all the Greeks to leap upon the beach. In so doing, he was tempting providence, for it was prophesied in legendary tradition that the first Greek warrior to disembark on Troy's shore would immediately be killed. That had happened in the past. When the Thessalian prince Protesilaus jumped ashore ahead of the rest of Agamemnon's forces, he was promptly slaughtered by Hector. Fortunately for Alexander, history, or rather tradition, did not repeat itself, and once his feet touched dry ground he proceeded directly to the place about which Homer, his constant guide and companion, had sung so eloquently.

What he saw was hardly a sight to capture the imagination. Ilion was an insignificant little settlement, the most outstanding feature of which was its 'small and cheap' temple of Athena.[10] But conscious of the city's past glories, Alexander made sacrifice to the goddess, just as Xerxes had done some 150 years earlier. His act of homage was in a sense a symbolic political statement, a response to Xerxes' gesture all those years before. The Persian Emperor had sacrificed here in preparation for his attack upon the Greek mainland. Alexander was now paying his own respects to the goddess, in preparation for his conquest of the Persian empire. He also emulated Xerxes' action in giving homage to the heroes of the Trojan War, honouring Greek and Trojan alike in the true Homeric spirit. On the Trojan side, he made sacrifice to Priam at the altar of Zeus, seeking peace with the Trojan king who had been slaughtered by Neoptolemus.[11] This was an act of personal reconciliation, for Neoptolemus was allegedly a member of the ancestral family to which Alexander himself belonged.[12] On the Greek side, Alexander paid due homage to Neoptolemus' father, the great Achilles, by running naked up his funeral mound and laying a wreath there.

Figure 7.1 Alexander the Great, date uncertain, in the National Archaeological Museum of Athens.

Figure 7.2 Troy VIII, sanctuary.

His visit to Ilion had a lasting impact, for it marked the beginning of an upsurge in the city's fortunes that was to continue through the following decades. Alexander gave orders that Ilion was to be accorded special status. But not because of practical or strategic considerations. Conferral of this status was due primarily, if not entirely, to the city's famous legendary associations. In acknowledgement of these, its illustrious visitor declared it exempt from tribute and elevated it to the status of a *polis*. He also promised that its most important institution, the temple of Athena, would be rebuilt – a promise which his general Lysimachus eventually fulfilled. Lysimachus erected a new marble temple to Athena some time after the battle of Ipsus, fought in 301.[13] His victory in this battle resulted in his becoming overlord of the Anatolian region north of the Taurus. The goddess's new abode became the religious focus of a league of cities that had been established in the Troad in 306, with Ilion as its capital. Adopting the image of a new Athens in the east, Ilion instituted Panathenaic games – no doubt making sure that an honoured place in the festival programme was reserved for the recitation of its famous eponymous epic.

Ilion was now a part of the Hellenistic world that emerged in the wake of Alexander's conquests. 'Hellenistic' is a modern label applied to the civilization that developed and flourished in the period from Alexander's death in 323 until the late first century BC. The period saw a wide diffusion of many elements of Greek culture in the lands conquered by Alexander on his eastern campaigns, from Anatolia through Syria, Egypt, Mesopotamia, Persia and India. The many cities called Alexandria that sprang up throughout the eastern world in this period are in themselves testimony to the extent of Alexander's legacy. But an important feature of the new age was the fusion of Greek and non-Greek cultures. This was part of Alexander's vision – a blending of east and west, incorporating the best elements of each. Cultural, ethnic and political divides would henceforth disappear. Networks of roads would provide safe travel and link all the great centres of civilization in this new world. Trade and

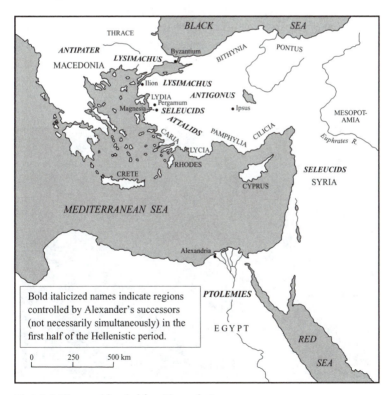

Map 7.2 The world ruled by Alexander's successors.

commerce would henceforth flourish on an international scale as never before.

New cities were founded in large numbers, often at strategic locations on trade routes. Many were excellent examples of town-planning and became highly prosperous through thriving commercial activity. Relatively small towns could boast many of the facilities of the large cities. Trade and exploration as far as the North Sea and the Atlantic Ocean helped expand the boundaries of knowledge. There were important advances in the various scientific fields, such as physics, astronomy, mathematics, mechanics and anatomy. Great libraries were established, most notably in the new city of Alexandria in Egypt and in Pergamum on Anatolia's Aegean coast, not far south of Ilion. Pergamum developed into one of the most important cities of Hellenistic Anatolia and a showpiece of town-planning and engineering achievement, built as it was on a series of terraces up a steep mountainside. It was also renowned for its promotion of the arts – associations of authors, actors and musicians were formed here – and, in the second century, it became the centre of the production and export of parchment, as indicated by the Greek name *pergamena*, from which 'parchment' derives.

Figure 7.3 Pergamum.

Despite the high level of material prosperity of the age and the great advances in culture and learning, the Hellenistic world was a divided and volatile one. There were dramatic fluctuations in the fortunes of the kingdoms that sprang up in the wake of Alexander's conquests. The empire that he had built so rapidly, in little more than a decade, fragmented even more rapidly after his death as his successors squabbled over his legacy. In the west, his general Antipater became ruler of Macedon, Alexander's homeland. In Thrace and the north-west of Anatolia, Lysimachus established his control. The rest of Anatolia, along with the eastern parts of Alexander's empire, fell to Seleucus. In western Anatolia, Philetaerus, who ruled Pergamum under Seleucus' overlordship, founded the Attalid dynasty, which, in the third century, made Pergamum the centre of a powerful independent kingdom extending down to Anatolia's southern coast, where the city Attaleia (modern Antalya) was founded. South across the Mediterranean, Ptolemy I became master of Egypt.

Ilion was on the periphery of all these developments. Though it became the centre of a league of cities in the Troad, it was in no way comparable with any of the major cities of the day. And in contrast to its impressively fortified Late Bronze Age ancestor, its redevelopment in the early Hellenistic period apparently included no fortifications – in spite of Strabo's claim that Lysimachus built a wall around the city.[14] We know that such a wall was eventually built, but not until after Ilion had been occupied in 278, apparently with little or no resistance, by Gallic mercenaries in the pay of a king of Bithynia called Nicomedes. The Gauls had been looking for a stronghold after their arrival from Europe, but because of Ilion's lack of defences they had no desire to settle there and immediately abandoned the city.[15] A wall was eventually built, probably in the 230s, either by Attalus, king of Pergamum, or by his opponent Antiochus Hierax ('the Hawk'), during their struggle for the domination of Anatolia.[16] Clearly, Ilion held some interest for the Hellenistic powers who competed for supremacy in Anatolia. Suggested reasons for this include a desire to emulate Alexander and so assert their claim to rule, the importance of respecting the traditions of a strategically significant region, the wish to associate themselves with the heroes of the Trojan War, and the value of winning the favour of the goddess Athena.[17]

Understandably, Ilion sought to extract the maximum possible advantage from its famous legendary associations that had attracted to it, and would long continue to attract, a number of distinguished visitors and patrons. By and large it did well out of them. The Hellenistic warlords who fought for supremacy in the region generally respected the privileges Alexander had conferred upon the city, sometimes perhaps after initiatives taken by the inhabitants themselves in the form of a declaration of support for one of two rival powers. Of course such declarations involved a calculated gamble – that the Ilians would correctly predict who their eventual overlord would be. Generally they were successful. Thus they wisely declared their allegiance to the Seleucid king Antiochus I in 275 during his campaigns in the region, setting up a statue and holding a festival in his honour and appointing a priest to administer his cult. Antiochus responded by reconfirming the freedom of the city, which now became his staunch ally.

Ilion was also courted by the man who was to become Rome's bitter enemy, Antiochus III (223–187), known as 'the Great', the most powerful of all the Seleucid kings. After an earlier promise to preserve Ilion's ancestral privileges, Antiochus visited the city and paid his respects to the goddess Athena Ilias by making sacrifice to her.[18] Ilion may well have derived a number of benefits from Seleucid patronage. But the days of this patronage were now fast drawing to a close. Inevitably, Antiochus' domination of the Near Eastern world and, more particularly, a foolhardy and disastrous expedition he made into Greece, brought him into head-on conflict with Rome. The final showdown between the greatest powers of the age took place in the battle of Magnesia (190 BC), a Lydian city that lay in the Hermus Valley near Anatolia's central Aegean coast. Antiochus was comprehensively defeated and his army destroyed. This outcome marked a turning point in Rome's relations with the Near Eastern world. In accordance with the treaty drawn up with Antiochus (the Peace of Apamea, 188), Rome now became ruler of the whole of Anatolia north of the Taurus range. As far as Ilion was concerned, the new overlords were apparently no less ready than their predecessors to respect and acknowledge the city's ancestral traditions. Already before Magnesia the consul Lucius Cornelius Scipio, a member of one of Rome's most illustrious families and Commander-in-Chief of the Roman forces at Magnesia, camped beneath Ilion's walls and made sacrifice to Athena Ilias before moving on to his decisive contest with Antiochus.[19] And after Rome's victory at Magnesia, Ilion had its privileges confirmed and, indeed, extended by the addition of two nearby settlements to it.[20]

Our sources subsequently have little to say about Ilion until a notorious event occurred in 85 BC, the year that is generally seen as marking the end of Level VIII on the site and the beginning of Level IX. It was the most traumatic episode in the city's history since its alleged destruction by Agamemnon's Greeks 1,200 years earlier. As told by Strabo, the story runs thus: the Roman quaestor Fimbria had mutinied against and slain his military commander Valerius Flaccus, who had been sent to Asia to conduct military operations against Mithridates, King of Pontus (a region on the southern shores of the Black Sea). Taking over the command of Flaccus' army, Fimbria had led his troops to the walls of Ilion and demanded entry into the city. When the Ilians refused, he placed the city under siege, capturing it on the eleventh day.[21] According to the Greek historian Appian, he then set about slaughtering the population and razed the city to the ground. Not one house, temple or statue was left standing.[22] Fimbria was fully aware of Ilion's famous legendary associations and its alleged traditional links with Rome (see pp. 166–70). But far from deterring his attack upon the city, this simply made him all the more boastful about his achievement. Agamemnon, he declared, had taken ten years to capture Ilion, and even then had needed the support of 1,000 ships and the entire Greek world to do it. He himself had achieved the same result in only ten days. 'Yes,' responded one of the Ilians, 'but that's because we had no Hector to fight for us!'[23]

There is a major difficulty with this episode. We have no clear archaeological corroboration for it. If the devastation of the city was as thorough as Appian indicates, it should certainly have left its mark in the archaeological record. At best, the evidence is equivocal,[24] leaving us to suspect that Appian's account of the destruction, which he recorded some 250 years after it supposedly happened, is grossly exaggerated – for reasons unknown. Perhaps, as Erskine suggests, it was simply a case of trying to equate Fimbria's assault upon Ilion with Agamemnon's sack of Troy. But there may well have been other reasons of a political nature for misrepresenting or falsifying Fimbria's action.[25]

TROY AND ROMAN TRADITION

In the reign of the emperor Augustus, which effectively began with the defeat of Antony and Cleopatra in the battle of Actium in 31 BC,[26] the city now called Ilium Novum (New Ilium) had come to occupy an extremely important place in Roman imperial propaganda. No longer was it respected merely for its own ancestral traditions. It was now an integral part of Roman tradition. How and why did this integration occur?

In attempting to answer this question, we must begin with the role that the *Iliad* assigns to the Trojan warrior Aeneas. Our warrior is of royal blood, a descendant, like Priam, Hector and Paris, of Dardanus, ancestor of the Trojan royal family. But, as we learn from the *Iliad* and other sources, Aeneas is from a secondary branch of this family, through his father Anchises who is a cousin of Priam.[27] He figures in a number of the *Iliad*'s battle scenes, rallying his comrades-in-arms,[28] and distinguishing himself by his ferocity, his courage, his military prowess and his physical strength. He fights, and survives, duels with two of the Greeks' most formidable champions, Achilles and Diomedes. He is the leader of the Dardanians, who dwell in the region of Mount Ida, lying to the south-east of Troy. On more than one occasion he is rescued from death at the last minute by the intervention of Apollo, the Trojans' chief divine protector, and by his mother Aphrodite. Indeed destiny has decreed that he must survive the war to ensure that the line of Dardanus will not perish, that the Trojan race will survive under him; he and his descendants will be the Trojans' new overlords. Thus Poseidon informs the other gods:

> It is destined that he shall be the survivor, that the generation of Dardanus shall not die, without seed obliterated, since Dardanus was dearest to Cronides of all his sons that have been born to him from mortal women. For Cronus' son has cursed the generation of Priam, and now the might of Aeneas shall be lord over the Trojans, and his sons' sons, and those who are born of their seed thereafter.[29]

So, too, in one of the so-called Homeric hymns, composed in the seventh century BC, Aphrodite prophesies to Anchises that Aeneas, their son, will rule over the Trojans and establish a dynasty that will last for all time.[30]

The prophecy is fulfilled. Aeneas survives the fall of Troy and becomes the new overlord of the Trojan people. But where? There was a strong tradition that he and his followers remained in the Troad, and that it was there that the new Trojan ruling dynasty established itself. Strabo maintains that the prophecy in the *Iliad* clearly indicates that the dynasty ruled in Troy itself, contrary to all claims that Aeneas set sail with his band of refugees and founded a new home in Greece or Italy.[31] Not surprisingly, Ilion's own occupants staunchly defended this tradition, declaring that their city had never been abandoned and that the great temple of Athena, where the maidens of Locris were regularly sent,[32] dated right back to the time of the Trojan War. In Chapter 6, we raised the possibility that in Homer's time the members of a local dynasty in the Troad sought to claim kinship with Aeneas, and to represent themselves as the true heirs to the kingdom of Priam. If Homer's services were those of a court poet, he may have been induced by one of his patron families to give some legitimacy to their claims by inserting the prophecy in the *Iliad*.[33]

But the *Iliad*'s version of the prophecy makes no pronouncement on *where* Aeneas is to re-establish the royal dynasty of Troy. It does not in itself preclude the possibility that Aeneas will seek a new home for his people in the west. This is the view espoused by (amongst others) Dionysius of Halicarnassus,[34] a Greek writer who lived in Rome during the reign of Augustus. Unfortunately, we have no historical or archaeological evidence to indicate either (a) the survival and resurgence of a Late Bronze Age population in the Troad during the early centuries of the first millennium, or (b) the reappearance of such a group in the western Mediterranean in the same period. It is possible, however, that during the dispersal of the western Anatolian populations at the end of the Bronze Age, some groups travelled westwards, resettling in places like Italy, Sicily and Sardinia. Herodotus attributes a western Anatolian ('Lydian') origin to the Etruscan civilization that emerged in western Italy early in the first millennium.[35] And it has often been suggested that Sardinia and Sicily owe their names to eastern groups called (respectively) the Sherden and Shekelesh in Egyptian accounts of the so-called Sea Peoples.[36] During the great diaspora that followed the collapse of the Bronze Age civilizations, some of these peoples may well have sought new homes in the west. In such a setting, the westward movement of a refugee people from the Troad at the end of the Bronze Age is not altogether implausible.

Does this provide a historical context for the post-Trojan War story of Aeneas and his followers – and Troy's alleged role in the foundation of Rome? The tradition linking Troy with refugee settlements in the west appears in a number of Greek writers, beginning with the fifth-century historian and mythographer Hellanicus, a native of the island of Lesbos. His lost work *Troica* told of Aeneas' flight from Troy to northern Greece; thus Dionysius of Halicarnassus informs us.[37] In another account, Aeneas resettled in Arcadia in southern Greece, and yet other accounts took him to Italy, where he became embedded in Roman folklore.[38] There were in fact many legendary traditions circulating in the Greek world in the fifth and fourth centuries about Rome's origins, but the Aeneas story probably held pride of place amongst them. By the beginning of the third century, Aeneas had been accepted into Roman tradition. His Trojans had now become the founders of the Roman nation. Was it possible to reconcile this Trojan foundation tradition, which originated in the Greek world, with native Italian tradition?

From our Roman sources, we learn of a school of native ballad poetry in Rome's early days when it was the custom for guests at banquets to compose and perform songs, to flute accompaniment, about the splendid deeds of their famous predecessors.[39] We are reminded of the ballads that minstrels and bards sang in honour of great heroes at the courts of Homer's kings and noblemen. Rome's legendary founder Romulus appears to have figured prominently in early Roman ballads, which no doubt told of his origins, his growth to manhood and his founding of the city of which he became the first king.

The native Italian tradition, to which his story belongs, contains the following elements: there was a Latin king called Numitor, ruler of Alba Longa, a precursor settlement of Rome. Numitor lost his throne in a coup to his wicked brother Amulius, who promptly made Numitor's daughter Ilia (Rhea Silvia) a Vestal Virgin. This was to prevent her from marrying and bearing children, for Amulius had heard a prophecy that offspring of hers would one day overthrow him. But his precautions were in vain. Ilia was seduced or raped by the god Mars and became by him the mother of the twins Romulus and Remus. Still seeking to thwart destiny, Amulius had the infants cast into the Tiber. But they were washed ashore, suckled by a she-wolf and brought up by a shepherd. On reaching manhood, they overthrew Amulius. The prophecy was fulfilled! Thereupon they decided to found a new settlement where the Tiber had deposited them. The omens that they took indicated that Romulus was to be king of this new settlement, called Rome. He built his city on the Palatine Hill, and settled it with refugees from the surrounding areas.

With the acceptance of Aeneas into Roman tradition, there was an obvious need to reconcile the two conflicting versions of Rome's foundation, one of Greek, one of Italian origin. The Roman poet Ennius (239–169) illustrates part of the reconciliation process in a composition called the *Annals*. This, his best-known work, purports to be a history of Rome, written in hexameters and beginning with an account of the city's legendary origins. Unfortunately, only fragments of the *Annals* now remain. In one of these, from an early part of the composition, Greek and Italian traditions are linked by making Ilia the daughter of Aeneas, who thus becomes the grandfather of Romulus and Remus.

But this caused a fresh problem. Only two generations now separated Aeneas and Romulus, though Greek tradition set the fall of Troy many centuries before Rome's traditional foundation date of 753. The reconciliation process needed more work. And as a result, the tradition was modified: while Aeneas laid the foundations of the Roman nation, he died long before the birth of the city that was to become its capital. The most dramatic expression of this piece of chronological rationalization appears in Virgil's *Aeneid*, where the dying Dido pronounces a curse upon Aeneas and expresses the wish that he too may die before his time and never have enjoyment of the kingdom he was sent to found.[40] So it came to pass. Aeneas departed this world generations before the foundation of Rome. His son Ascanius became the first of a dynasty established at Alba Longa. The second last of the line he established was Numitor, father of Ilia/Rhea Silvia, still a descendant of Aeneas but not his daughter. Thus Romulus, founder of Rome, was also a descendant of Aeneas, though many generations removed.

While we cannot rule out the possibility that emigrants from the Troad resettled somewhere in the western Mediterranean, the tradition that gives Rome a Trojan ancestry is clearly a spurious one. But that did not stop it from taking root in Roman tradition, where it reached maturity in Virgil's *Aeneid* in the age of the first Roman emperor Augustus.

TROY IN ROMAN PROPAGANDA

In the aftermath of the Fimbrian episode, Ilium (we shall henceforth call the city by its Roman name) grew and flourished, eventually attaining a size greater than at any other time in its history. The Roman dictator Sulla had apparently provided some funds for rebuilding the city after its alleged destruction by Fimbria. But most of the credit for its redevelopment must go to Julius Caesar and his great-nephew Octavian, later to be called Augustus. The prominence Troy achieved in this last phase of its existence is closely connected with the rising fortunes of the Julian clan, of whom Julius Caesar and Augustus were the most illustrious members. The alleged links between Troy and Rome date back at least to the fifth century in Greek tradition and had become embedded in Roman tradition no later than the third century. But the impact that this made on Roman consciousness before the tradition was embraced by the Julian clan in the first century BC was probably very limited, even though a succession of Republican Roman authors like Q. Fabius Pictor, Cato the Elder, Naevius and, as mentioned above, Ennius dealt with or at least referred to it.

According to Lucan, an epic poet of the first century AD, Julius Caesar visited the site after his victory over Pompey the Great at Pharsalus in Thessaly on 29 June 48 BC.[41] Surprisingly, none of the more historically reliable writers like Plutarch, Strabo or Caesar himself make any mention of such a visit, which must cast considerable doubt on its authenticity.[42] There is, however, no doubt that Caesar became a benefactor of the site, as Strabo tells us, and it was certainly due to him, initially, that Troy rose to high prominence in the Roman world. Indeed, it appears that he even considered re-establishing his capital there, as the Emperor Constantine the Great was to contemplate doing some four centuries later.

Caesar saw the political benefits of closely identifying himself with Troy – above all by linking his family with the family of Aeneas. Aeneas' son Ascanius, the legendary founder of Alba Longa, was also known as 'Iulus'. We do not know when Ascanius was first called Iulus, but in Virgil's *Aeneid*, both names are used interchangeably and with approximately the same frequency. As Professor Austin comments: 'Whatever the origin of the equation Ascanius–Iulus, Virgil's use of the name Iulus plainly reflects his wish to connect the *gens Iulia* and the imperial house of Rome with its Trojan past.'[43] Without doubt, Virgil was also reflecting the wishes of his emperor.[44] For the equation provided the Julian clan with what they saw as sufficient justification for claiming Iulus Ascanius, and therefore Aeneas, as their ancestors. Thus Caesar traced his family roots back to the very founder of the Roman nation, and Troy had been the ancestral home of this founder. For a man whose ambitions went far beyond that of a mere republican magistracy, despite any claims he had made to the contrary, and for a man who but recently had been declared an enemy of the state by the Roman senate, there was obviously political capital to be made out of his alleged descent from his country's founder.

Yet Caesar had little opportunity to benefit from his supposed ancestral roots before his assassins cut him down. It was left to his great-nephew and de-facto successor Octavian to exploit the full political potential of the link he had claimed with Aeneas and son. Literature provided one of the vehicles for doing this. Hence the commission bestowed, or rather imposed, upon the poet Virgil. In 31 BC, shortly before Virgil began work on the *Aeneid*, Octavian had triumphed over the forces of Antony and Cleopatra in the battle of Actium, the naval engagement fought off the western coast of Greece. This battle brought to a conclusive end the Roman republic, which had come into existence almost 500 years earlier with the expulsion of the last king of Rome, and also established Octavian as the undisputed master of the Roman world.

It was a world that had been torn apart by a century of faction strife and civil war. The Republican institutions had collapsed, after repeated failures to give order and stability to this world. Yet Caesar's fate had but recently demonstrated his countrymen's abhorrence of one-man rule and their deep-seated mistrust of anyone suspected of harbouring monarchical ambitions. This was the

Figure 7.4 The young Octavian, replica of the Roman original.

challenge confronting Octavian who, as Augustus, became the first emperor of Rome, with the bland title *princeps*, 'first man', in the year 27 BC. There was now more ready acceptance of his position than there would have been a few years earlier, in the period before his chief rivals and opponents had been eliminated – first his great-uncle's assassins, then his former comrade-in-arms Antony. And Augustus himself declared that he would hold the office of *princeps* only until the republic could be restored. But doubtless there were many who had misgivings about his extraordinary status. To them, in particular, he sought to present himself as the great peace-maker and reconciler, the restorer of old traditions and values, the legitimate and direct successor of his country's founder and the one whose coming had been foretold back in the days of Aeneas himself.

These images of Rome's first emperor were to be incorporated in the great project entrusted to the poet Virgil – the composition of a national epic about the Roman nation's founding hero. Virgil originally had a different topic in mind. In Book 3 of his *Georgics*, written in the late 40s and early 30s, he writes *mox tamen ardentes accingar dicere pugnas Caesaris*: 'soon I shall gird my loins to tell of the blazing battles of Caesar' (i.e. Octavian). That is to say, he was intending to write a poem about Octavian's military triumphs. But he abandoned the idea before embarking upon it – understandably so, and perhaps at the insistence of Octavian himself, for a laudatory account of Octavian's battle achievements would have been contrary to the spirit of reconciliation that the new age called for and would run the risk of opening up old wounds. The story of Aeneas was a much more appropriate choice.

Virgil's version of it begins with the Trojan prince's flight from the blazing city, accompanied by a band of refugees, with his paralysed father Anchises on his back and his son Iulus Ascanius by his side. The refugees put to sea in a small fleet, which encounters great perils as it sails westwards in search of the promised land Hesperia. A violent storm blows it off course and destroys all but seven of its vessels. Exhausted and much depleted in numbers, the survivors eventually find anchorage on the coast of north Africa, where they are hospitably received by Queen Dido, ruler of Carthage. A banquet is held in their honour. In the midst of the festivities, their royal hostess bids Aeneas recount the tale of Troy's fall. He agrees to do so, but with great reluctance – for the memories are painful. Taking up the narrative at the point where the *Iliad* leaves off, he describes the city's destruction in graphic detail. His tale begins in Book 2 with an account of the Trojan horse, a ruse hit upon by the wily Ulysses (Odysseus in Greek) as a means of penetrating Troy's impregnable defences.

But the *Aeneid* has much more to do with what is to come than with what is past. In Book 6, with his stay in Carthage and its tragic consequences already dim memories, Aeneas visits the ghost of his father in the underworld. Here, a vision of Rome's future unfolds before him. Anchises leads him to a mound and points out all the souls that, clothed in human flesh, will become famous in Roman history. These are Aeneas' own descendants, stretching through many generations down to Virgil's own time. And here we see the ultimate purpose of the epic, the reason for the emphasis on destiny. All that has gone before is by way of preparation for the reign of Augustus:

> This is the man, this is the one whom you have so often heard promised to you, Augustus Caesar, son of a god, the founder once more of a golden age in Latium, throughout the lands where Saturn once ruled.[45]

There is another passage where Augustus also appears as the one foretold by destiny, at the climax of Rome's progress through the ages. In Book 8, Aeneas receives from his mother Venus a shield fashioned by the god Vulcan (we are reminded of the shield which Hephaestus presents to Achilles in Book 18 of the *Iliad*). Its surface provides a canvas for all the great events that are to occur in Rome's history. The climactic scenes depict Augustus' victory in the battle of Actium, his triumphal procession through the streets of Rome and the image of the victor seated on the threshold of Apollo's temple, inspecting the peoples and gifts of conquered nations.[46]

Both passages reveal much about the poem's overall purpose, conveyed to us via a Trojan-flavoured *mélange* of Roman history, legend and folklore, heavily laced with Augustan propaganda.

Aeneas' experiences and reactions in Troy's final hours tell us something more about the poem's intentions. A critical turning point in the story occurs in Book 2 when Aeneas witnesses the slaughter of Priam and his family. The scene is set in the palace of

Troy. The Greeks have occupied the city and are putting it to the torch. Aeneas is on the palace roof. He watches helplessly as the Greek warrior Pyrrhus, son of Achilles, contemptuously thrusts aside the spear Priam has cast at him and drags the old man to the altar, slithering in his son's blood. He entwines his left hand in Priam's hair, hoists him up and sinks his sword into his ribs. Recoiling in horror at this fresh atrocity, Aeneas suddenly catches sight of Helen – the cause of all Troy's sufferings – cowering by the threshold of the goddess Vesta. Consumed with a burning desire for revenge, he is on the point of leaping down and killing her. But Venus intervenes. She gently rebukes her son for his useless outburst of fury. It is fated that Troy should fall. It is the gods, not Helen, or even Paris, who should be blamed for this. She urges him to give thought to his family – father, wife and son – and to escape while there is yet time. He has a higher purpose to fulfil. This purpose becomes clear when he plunges back into the blazing city, searching desperately for his wife Creusa who has gone missing, unaware that she is now beyond mortal help. It is her ghost that now suddenly appears and lays before him the mission for which he is intended – to travel to Hesperia and establish there a new kingdom for his people.

By the end of Book 2 the divine plan for Aeneas has been revealed, and he has submitted to the gods' will. The loss of the heroic code by which Aeneas acted in Book 2 is replaced by another code, the code of Roman *pietas*. *Pietas* becomes Aeneas' defining quality. It is a quality which requires the subordination of all personal desires and emotions to one's duty to others – to one's friends, family, gods and to one's country. Adherence to a code in which the defence of personal honour and the pursuit of personal vendettas, as embodied in the conduct of a Homeric Achilles, is no longer appropriate in an age in which reconciliation and reconstruction are of paramount importance. Herein lies Virgil's most important message for the Roman of the Augustan era.

THE LAST PHASE

Troy is where it all began, and in Augustus' reign the city took on a new significance. The *Aeneid*'s story and potent symbolism no doubt helped ensure that what was now touted as the birthplace of the Roman nation became a popular destination for pilgrims and tourists. Like many other cities of Asia Minor, it derived substantial benefit from the romanization of the region. Some of these cities had, like Troy, a distinguished pedigree extending back to the Bronze Age. Ephesus and Miletus were notable examples. We recall that both had been important centres in the Late Bronze Age, the former the royal seat of an Arzawan kingdom, the latter the base of operations of the king of Ahhiyawa on the Anatolian mainland. But in the Roman period Troy, or New Ilium, differed from them in a very important respect. They continued to flourish for a number of important practical reasons, which had to do with their valuable strategic locations and their close involvement in the political and commercial activities of their region. Troy was an artificially propped-up city. It survived and flourished in the present because of what it had been in the past. No doubt its famous legendary associations would have been sufficient in themselves to ensure a continuing flow of privileges to it in the Roman period as in earlier times, such as the granting of special status, tax exemptions and at least token hegemony over the other cities in the region. But the new emphasis that Julius Caesar and Augustus gave to the link between Troy and the foundation of Rome – because of their alleged descent from their country's legendary Trojan founder – promised even greater benefits and privileges for the city once ruled by Priam.

In this last phase of its existence, Troy developed into an impressive showplace city, in the same period as a little town called Bethlehem in Judaea became the birthplace of the founder of Christianity. Its walls encompassed, with lower city and citadel combined, an area larger than any of its predecessors, including the great Troy VI. Augustus himself, who visited the site, made provision for major new building works. Athena's temple, built several hundred years earlier by Alexander's general Lysimachus, was now extensively restored. The work involved major levelling and terracing of the citadel's surface, destroying much of what still remained of the earlier levels. Other constructions during Augustus' reign included a Roman bath with fine mosaics and, subsequently, a concert theatre and council chamber (*bouleuterion*). Aqueducts were built to pipe water to what was now becoming a thoroughly Roman city.

Troy had experienced a modest flow of visitors, including some of considerable distinction, throughout much of its first-millennium history. But the flow now turned into a steady, ever-increasing

Figure 7.5 Troy IX, theatre.

stream of pilgrims and tourists. For them, Troy was not merely a place of antiquarian interest, but the ancestral homeland of the Roman nation, whence came the direct lineal ancestor of their emperor. Conditions for tourist travel were now much better than they had ever been before. Roman rule now extended, since Asia became a Roman province in 133, through the region where Troy lay, and Augustus' reign had resulted in a *pax romana* which made travel much safer for both commercial as well as recreational purposes. For Romans visiting the Greek world, Troy was conveniently located on a tourist route that took in islands like Rhodes, Samos and Chios, and that lay only a short boat trip from Lesbos.[47]

Of course visitors to New Ilium no longer saw the city as it was in the time of the alleged Trojan War. But local guides could still point out many monuments allegedly from that period, such as the tombs of Hector, Achilles, Patroclus and Ajax. And there were plenty of souvenirs of local manufacture to be had. The inhabitants of Troy were fully aware of the attractions of their city and left no opportunity untapped for exploiting them. In 188, after the Peace of Apamea was concluded, they began producing coins featuring the goddess Athena Ilias, aware that this was the city's most potent symbol, the most important object of veneration by visitors to the site. But in a departure from this motif, Julius Caesar issued a coin called a denarius with Aphrodite-Venus, mother of Aeneas, on the obverse and Aeneas' flight from Troy on the reverse. The *Iliad* prophesies that Aeneas will survive the sack of Troy, but his actual flight from the burning city belongs to other traditions. Caesar's coin was one of the most widely circulated of his issues and a worldwide affirmation of his claimed Trojan ancestry.[48] The Trojans themselves took advantage of this. From the reign of Augustus onwards, the motif became a regularly recurring feature of their own coinage.

Troy's future was secure, so long as it remained under the emperors' patronage. Its inhabitants, fully conscious of how much their fate depended on their benefactors, were always careful to cultivate imperial goodwill, though there was an occasional lapse. It seems that they were slow in sending a delegation to Tiberius, Augustus' successor, to express their condolences at the death of his son Drusus. Tiberius contemptuously dismissed the delegation's expressions of sympathy with a pointedly sarcastic reference to their late arrival: 'Let me too express my condolences to you, on the death of your most distinguished fellow-citizen Hector.'[49] Tiberius' nephew and adopted son Germanicus visited Ilium in the year 18 AD,[50] and composed there an epigram for Hector's tomb.[51] Thirty-five years later, a sixteen-year-old Nero, stepson of the emperor Claudius and already a highly accomplished orator, spoke so eloquently on Ilium's behalf, highlighting its special status as the birthplace of the Roman nation, that the city was granted permanent exemption from all taxes.[52]

After the demise of the Julio-Claudian dynasty, Ilium continued to enjoy the privileges that the members of this dynasty had conferred or reconferred upon it,[53] and to play host to a number of distinguished visitors. In 124, the emperor Hadrian graced it with his presence. And ninety years later, Caracalla stopped at Troy on his expedition to the east against the Parthians. Picturing himself as a latter-day Alexander, Caracalla made sacrifice at Achilles' tomb, erected a statue in his honour and, in imitation of Achilles' burial rites for Patroclus, cremated on a large funeral pyre his favourite but now deceased freedman Festus.[54] Some fifty years later, around 267, the city came close to a violent end when the Goths plundered it during the reign of the emperor Gallienus. But Roman troops stationed at Byzantium succeeded in driving them off before the city was utterly razed. Indeed there were prospects of its entering into a splendid new era when Constantine the Great considered making it or the nearby site of Sigeum his new capital. Apparently, Constantine had actually started building walls and a major new harbour before deciding to develop the immensely more suitable site of Byzantium.[55] Had he proceeded with the Troad site, one wonders whether his New Rome would ever have become the capital of an empire that was to last 1,000 years, or whether indeed there would ever have been such an empire. Troy's greatest days had long since gone and would never return. Any attempt to establish a new imperial capital here would almost certainly have ended in failure.

Even after the institution of Christianity as the offical religion of the new empire, Troy continued to flourish for a time – as a tourist theme park. And the old pagan traditions continued. As Vermeule notes, when the apostate emperor Julian visited the site in 355 he was amazed and gratified to find the altars still burning before the tomb of Hector and the hero's statue still being anointed.[56] He also saw the tomb of Achilles still undamaged. The persistence of these pagan practices was probably due at least as much to hard-nosed mercenary considerations on the part of its citizens as to any lasting veneration for the city's legendary past. Once the links with Homeric tradition were severed, Ilium would no longer have any reason for its existence. At the very least the tourist trade would dry up. But in the Byzantine period the city sank slowly into obscurity, the empress Eudoxia, wife of Theodosius II (421–44), remarking that in her day it was a complete ruin, with not even its foundations remaining. It did not entirely disappear, however, and even in the tenth century the Byzantine emperor Constantine VII Porphyrogenitus mentions a bishop of Ilium.[57]

Troy had one last illustrious visitor: the Ottoman sultan Mehmet II, conqueror of Constantinople in 1453. Ten years after his conquest, Mehmet visited the site and 'gloried in the fact that he had defeated the descendants of those who had destroyed the city. They had, at last, he declared, paid the debt they owed the people of Asia.'[58]

8

THE FINAL WORD?

I once attended a conference on Troy at which some forty papers were presented, many of them addressing one or more of three fundamental questions: Was there an actual poet called Homer? Did Troy exist? Was there really a Trojan War? The line-up of speakers constituted a kind of *Who's Who* of Homeric scholarship and Bronze Age archaeology. A number of new theories and discoveries were presented, and there was much stimulating discussion. But by the end of it all, most participants admitted that they were even further from providing answers to the questions posed than they had been before the conference began.

That is an occupational hazard for anyone who ventures into the realms of scholarship on Homer and Troy. But it has never been a deterrent. The historical authenticity of the war and its participants, and the poet most famously associated with it, continues to be widely debated. At one end of the spectrum of opinion is the conviction that there was indeed such a war and that it was pretty much as the poet described it. From that we pass through varying degrees of scepticism and agnosticism to the other end of the spectrum where the tradition is consigned wholly to the realm of fantasy: fictitious events whose participants lived in an imaginary society and spoke a contrived, artificial kind of Greek, with the whole thing cobbled together not by a person but by some sort of editorial process. In other words, the *Iliad* is a story about a war that never took place, fought between peoples who never lived, who used a form of Greek that no one ever spoke and belonged to a society that was no more than a figment of the imagination of a poet who never existed.

The challenge to prove or disprove the fundamental truth of the Trojan War tradition has been taken up repeatedly since the time of the ancient Greeks themselves, and most recently in a number of books and articles, as well as by a spate of producers for television and cinema. Hence we have a succession of titles that are all variations on the same basic theme: 'In Search of the Trojan War', 'The Search for Troy', 'The Truth of Troy', 'The Trojan War: Myth or Reality?', 'Was There a Trojan War?', 'The Trojan War: Is There Truth Behind the Legend?', 'Has the Trojan War Been Found?', 'Is Homer Historical?', 'Why Troy is Troy and the Trojan War is Real'.

I do not believe for one moment that I can put the whole matter to rest with a few final comments and reflections. That would be unduly presumptuous. The title of this chapter is merely a piece of wishful thinking. But let us at least take stock of some of the fundamental facts and assumptions associated with a belief in the basic historicity of the Trojan War tradition. Most scholars currently believe that the *Iliad* was, by and large, the composition of a poet called Homer, an Ionian Greek of western Anatolia who lived in the second half of the eighth century. The setting for his epic was the mound now called Hisarlık and the plain adjacent to it on the southern shore of the Hellespont. After its final destruction in the late second millennium, the site at Hisarlık was reoccupied in the late eighth century by Aeolian Greeks and called Ilion. With a few notable exceptions, the ancient Greeks believed that this was the location of Priam's city. Homer himself called it by two alternative names: Troia and Ilios.

Of course the fact that Homer, who composed his epics some hundreds of years after the alleged conflict, did locate the Trojan War here need not necessarily mean that it was in fact the site of such a war. We should keep two questions separate. Did the site at Hisarlık provide Homer with the setting for his tale? Was this tale based on historical fact? The Arthurian cycle of legends presents two similar questions: Did Geoffey of Monmouth use Cadbury Castle as his setting for his tale of Camelot? Were his stories about King Arthur, composed, like the *Iliad*, centuries after the period to which they allegedly belonged, based on historical fact?

The great majority of scholars now believe that the Late Bronze Age settlement at Hisarlık was indeed the setting for Homer's tale.

And many scholars have also come round to the view that Hisarlık/ Troy was the centre of the kingdom that in Late Bronze Age Hittite texts is called Wilusa. This view is based on an assumption: that references to Wilusa in the Hittite texts, reinforced by a hieroglyphic inscription near Anatolia's central Aegean coast (the Karabel inscription), point to a location for Wilusa in the north-west of Anatolia. The assumption is very likely a correct one. But the evidence in support of it, both archaeological and textual, is purely circumstantial, and we cannot make an unqalified identification until we have clear, tangible proof of it – proof of the kind that established beyond doubt the identification of the Hittite provincial city Sapinuwa in central Anatolia, from information contained in tablets found on the site (modern Ortaköy). Similarly we have strong – some would say overwhelming – circumstantial evidence for the identification of the kingdom of Ahhiyawa with a mainland Mycenaean kingdom. But here too the equation must remain an assumption until unequivocal proof for it turns up, such as cuneiform tablets containing the name Ahhiyawa in a Mycenaean palace centre.

HISTORICAL EVIDENCE FOR A TROJAN WAR?

If we accept the above assumptions – that Wilusa = Ilios/Troy and Ahhiyawa = a Mycenaean kingdom – can we go a step further and find historical references to a war between these kingdoms? Three texts, to which we have already referred, may be of relevance. All are letters and all date to the thirteenth century, the period most favoured for the alleged Trojan War. Let us remind ourselves of their contents:

Letter 1 (early thirteenth century):   from Manapa-Tarhunda, ruler of Wilusa's southern neighbour the Seha River Land, to his Hittite overlord Muwattalli. A fragmentary passage in the letter contains information about troubles in Wilusa, perhaps caused by a renegade Hittite subject called Piyamaradu, who may have occupied Wilusa with his forces. Muwattalli dispatched a Hittite expeditionary force to the kingdom to restore Hittite authority over it.

Letter 2 (mid-thirteenth century): the so-called Tawagalawa letter, from the Hittite king Hattusili III, brother and second successor of Muwattalli, to the king of Ahhiyawa. From this letter, we learn that Piyamaradu was a protégé of the letter's addressee and may well have acted as his agent for the expansion of Ahhiyawan/Mycenaean influence and authority in western Anatolia. Hattusili recalls that he and his Ahhiyawan 'Brother' had previously been at enmity over Wilusa. This is the only text in which Ahhiyawa, Wilusa and a conflict are all mentioned together.

Letter 3 (later thirteenth century): the so-called Milawata letter, from the Hittite king Tudhaliya IV, son and successor of Hattusili, to the man apparently appointed by Tudhaliya as a kind of regional overlord in western Anatolia. He is perhaps to be identified with Tarkasnawa, king of Mira, the largest of Hatti's vassal states in the region. From a text join to the letter, we learn that the Wilusan king Walmu had been deposed from his throne and that Tudhaliya was in the process of restoring him to it, with the cooperation of the letter's addressee who was apparently Walmu's regional superior. Ahhiyawa nowhere appears in the letter (or what remains of it), and by this time may have ceased to have any presence or influence in the region.

In sum, the highly fragmentary information these letters present is of a north-western Anatolian state Wilusa that (a) *may* once have been occupied, with or without its inhabitants' consent, by an anti-Hittite rebel leader known to have links with Ahhiyawa, (b) was later involved in a confrontation between a Hittite king and his Ahhiyawan counterpart, and (c) later again saw its own king deposed and driven into exile. Greek tradition tells us that Troy/Ilios was attacked, occupied and destroyed by the Greeks and the members of its royal family killed or driven into exile. Do the isolated scraps of information we have about Wilusa in the thirteenth century provide us with the makings of a Trojan War tradition? At least they would not be inconsistent with such a theory. But we should be careful not to take too blinkered a view of the evidence – as those who believe that known events in Wilusa's history provide a genuine historical kernel of Homeric tradition are inclined to do.

The extremely meagre material available to us is capable of more than one interpretation.

Let us look in a little more detail at the texts we have dealt with above, beginning with the passage from the Manapa-Tarhunda letter. The passage is a very fragmentary one, and it needs to be heavily restored if we are to make much sense of it. This is what we actually have, with restorations and translation by Professor Houwink ten Cate (the square brackets indicate the restorations):

> [Gassus (the Hittite commander) . . .,] arrived and brought
> along the Hittite troops. [And whe]n [they . . .] set out
> again(?) to the country of Wilusa in order to attack (it) (or:
> [they] set out to the country of Wilusa in order to attack
> (it) again), [I, howe]ver, became ill. I am seriously ill, illness
> holds me [pro]strated.
> **paragraph divider occurs here**
> When [Piyam]aradus had humiliated me, he set Atpa
> [again]st me(?) (lit. he brought Atpa [u]p [before] me) . . .[1]

A common interpretation of this passage is that Piyamaradu had attacked and occupied Wilusa, that Manapa-Tarhunda had tried to dislodge him from it, suffering a humiliating defeat in the process, and that the Hittites were now obliged to do the job he had failed to do, with Manapa-Tarhunda pleading illness as an excuse for not joining them. But we really cannot be sure that the passage actually says this. Much depends on how it is restored. There is no doubt that Hittite troops had arrived in the area. But it is quite unclear whether they had come to Wilusa to liberate it from Piyamaradu's control or whether they were there to restore order in a vassal kingdom that had rebelled against Hittite authority, perhaps by overthrowing their Hittite-appointed ruler. Piyamaradu may well have had some part in such a rebellion – typical of what we know from other sources of his insurrectionist activities. And the reference to Atpa, who was Piyamaradu's father-in-law and who governed Milawata on behalf of the Ahhiyawan king, may provide an indirect link between this passage and Ahhiyawa; Piyamaradu may have been operating in the region of Wilusa as the agent of the Ahhiyawan king. But the notorious troublemaker is not clearly linked with Wilusa in the text. The lines that deal with him come after a paragraph divider, which might well indicate that the author of the text has now finished with Wilusa and is now moving on to a different subject. The reference to Piyamaradu's activities may not be relevant to events in Wilusa. Overall, the letter is of very dubious value in terms of any possible bearing it may have on the Trojan War tradition.

At first sight, the passage from the Tawagalawa letter that mentions Wilusa appears to provide stronger support for a Wilusa–Trojan War link. As we have mentioned, its author Hattusili indicates that there had been enmity between the Ahhiyawan king and himself over Wilusa: 'Now as we have reached agreement on the matter of Wilusa over which we fought . . .'. Güterbock says this '*may* indicate that it was only a diplomatic confrontation, but the possibility of actual war is not ruled out.'[2] There was a danger that the conflict would flare up again because of the activities of Piyamaradu, who now clearly appears in the role of the Ahhiyawan king's protégé. We might reconstruct events thus: the Ahhiyawan king had attacked Wilusa, a Hittite vassal state, and the Hittites had involved themselves in the conflict by coming to its rescue. But the passage could be differently interpreted. There is no indication that Wilusa itself took part in an actual war between Ahhiyawa and Hatti. There may well have been a conflict over the sovereignty of Wilusa – just as Hatti and Egypt disputed control over the Syro-Palestinian states of Kadesh and Amurru – without Wilusa itself becoming a participant in or victim of the conflict. Nevertheless we cannot entirely rule out the possibility that the Tawagalawa letter indicates an attack on Wilusa by Mycenaean Greek forces or by Mycenaean-sponsored local forces and that, in accordance with the normal treaty obligations, the Hittites sent an expedition to the support of its vassal and thus came into direct confrontation with its attackers. But even if this were so, we are left far short of anything resembling a conflict of the nature or on the scale of Homer's narrative. And Troy was certainly not abandoned at this time.

The passage from the Milawata letter indicates that a king of Wilusa actually lost his throne and was probably driven from his kingdom. This may well have been the result of Ahhiyawan or Ahhiyawan-sponsored activity. But again we do not know this. There is nothing to indicate whether his overthrow was the outcome of an external attack upon Wilusa or the result of an uprising by the Wilusan king's own subjects. It was certainly not unknown for a vassal king, particularly one loyal to the Hittites, to lose his throne in a coup and subsequently regain it with Hittite backing. That was the happy outcome for the Wilusan king. We have no prototype here of an aged Priam slithering in his son's blood and dying horribly on the blade of Neoptolemus as his city goes up in flames around him. This last known episode in Wilusa's history could also be totally irrelevant to the Trojan War question.

The truth is that we have too little information about Wilusa's history to be of any use in a search for possible historical origins of the Trojan War tradition. Of course the less material one has, the more easily it can be manipulated to fit whatever conclusion one wishes to come up with. To be sure, the tiny scraps of information about Wilusa seem to indicate that it suffered from political upheavals and quite possibly external aggression. But the same could be said of many parts of the Near Eastern world for much of their Late Bronze Age history.

THE TRADITION IN ITS HISTORICAL CONTEXT

This was an era in which warfare and rebellion were endemic, in which peace, not war, was an aberration from the norm. As far as western Anatolia is concerned, that is very clearly borne out by the texts themselves, particularly those dealing with the Arzawa Lands. In these lands, there were frequent uprisings, conflicts between states, rebellions and resistance to foreign aggression. Wilusa's history probably differed very little from that of other lands of the region, particularly those with coastal territories that were vulnerable to Ahhiyawan penetration. It could well be argued that episodes from the history of any of these lands might have contributed to the source material from which the Homeric epic finally emerged. That is to say, the Trojan War story was the outcome of a whole raft of traditions reflecting conflicts spread over a number of centuries and finally distilled into a single ten-year episode.

From the storyteller's point of view this distillation of centuries of conflict into a ten-year war is quite understandable. Hollywood has gone much further and compressed the whole thing into just a few days. Indeed in this respect it probably comes a good deal closer to historical reality than Homer does. While military conflicts between hostile forces sometimes extended, on and off, over many years, the possibility of a single conflict involving a ten-year siege is quite out of the question. Protracted siege warfare was certainly not unknown in the Late Bronze Age world, particularly when the Hittites were involved who were not very good at it, but the longest known siege lasted no more than a few months. Our Anatolian written sources provide no evidence for a single, major, extended assault by invading Greeks upon an Anatolian kingdom that led to the eventual destruction of that kingdom. Rather, the pattern is one of a number of limited attacks carried out over several centuries and, perhaps, an occasional temporary occupation of a beleaguered kingdom. A ten-year encampment on enemy territory and an accompanying siege of the same duration belong to the realm of poetic hyperbole. So too does the notion of an armada of 1,186 ships, many times greater than the largest known fleet in *any* period of the ancient world. Indeed in the days when Priam's father Laomedon ruled Troy, we are told of a *first* Trojan War, but on a much smaller scale. In Trojan War I, Heracles captured and sacked Troy with just six shiploads of men. Compared with this, Agamemnon's armada really does look like a case of overkill.

As for the reasons for the assaults upon Troy: Heracles' sack of the city was by way of punishing Laomedon for cheating the gods of a payment of horses he had agreed to give them; Agamemnon's motive was revenge for the abduction of his brother's wife. It was not of course her fabled beauty that led to the expedition. Rather, it was the betrayal of a host's hospitality and the gross insult done to all Greeks that had to be avenged. Even so, this is a motive about which some ancient commentators were sceptical, and most modern scholars dismiss it out of hand. Helen may have been a historical figure or, at least, may have had a historical prototype. But far from the abduction of a beautiful Greek queen providing the *casus belli*, the war must have been fought over something much more practical and sensible, such as disputed fishing rights in the Hellespont. That is what many modern scholars would argue. But let us not be too sceptical. Bronze Age kings sometimes had no hesitation in going to war over the abduction of their subjects, let alone a member of their own family, and Suppiluliuma declared war on Egypt for the murder of his son Zannanza, on his way to Egypt to marry Tutankhamun's widow. A gross insult to a kingdom's honour might well provoke retaliation on a massive scale. On the other hand, ambition and power-lust were likely to be much stronger motives for war, even if revenge for an injustice done was used as a pretext for it. Troy was an attractive target. Its wealth in itself made it worthy of plunder. But possession of it would give its conquerors a strategically valuable prize in an area rich in natural resources and endowed with excellent harbour facilities. These may well have provided strong enough incentives for a Mycenaean attack upon Troy, particularly by a king intent on expanding his territorial holdings along the western Anatolian seaboard.

But there are problems with this line of reasoning. We have yet to find convincing evidence that the archaeological Troy that most closely fits Priam's city was in fact destroyed by enemy action rather than by environmental forces, such as an earthquake. The small number of arrowheads and other weapons of war that have so far come to light in Troy VI go nowhere near providing sufficient evidence to indicate that the city fell to enemy attack, let alone withstood a ten-year siege. As we noted in Chapter 3, those who wish to hedge their bets on this question suggest a compromise, which allows for destruction of the site by *both* human and environmental forces. Maybe the citadel's fortifications were seriously weakened by earthquake to the point where they became vulnerable to enemy conquest; it was a combination of both factors that brought about the citadel's destruction.[3] Like many compromises, this leaves us with neither one thing nor the other.

Of particular significance is the fact that neither archaeological nor textual evidence for the period of Troy VI supports the Greek tradition that the city was *abandoned* after its destruction. Troy VIIa rose up shortly after the destruction of VI, and with the same population group, though the new city was a meaner, humbler settlement than its predecessor. Moreover, if we identify Wilusa with Troy, the surviving references to the former make it clear that whatever damage was inflicted upon it by external aggressors or internal uprisings, order was restored and the old regime reinstated. There is one other important point. If power and ambition for territorial expansion were motives for an attack upon Troy, and if Troy did fall to its attackers, why is there no evidence of their presence on the site in the wake of its destruction? Why did they not themselves occupy and rebuild it, instead, apparently, of simply withdrawing?

Of course, as Michael Wood has pointed out, the Homeric warrior does not destroy to increase political power or to open up trade routes; he sacks cities simply to get booty, treasure, horses, cattle, gold, silver, fine armour and weapons – and women.[4] But this may well be a case where Homeric and historical scenarios are at odds. To be sure, plunder was often one of the immediate benefits of a Late Bronze Age king's military campaigns, but such campaigns were often prompted by the prospect of more enduring benefits and often served as a prelude to the imposition of a more lasting authority over the conquered region, whether for political, commercial or military reasons. The Homeric scenario fits better within the context of a more anarchical world, perhaps in the period after the collapse of the Late Bronze Age Great Kingdoms.

THE FINAL ACT

There did eventually come a time when Troy was destroyed and apparently abandoned by its population. This occurred at the end of Level VIIb (which was but a pale shadow of its Late Bronze Age predecessors), some time between 1050 and 1000, in the aftermath of the great upheavals throughout the Near East and Greece at the end of the Bronze Age. Its destruction was very likely due to marauders like those about whom we hear from Egyptian records – the so-called Sea Peoples. Almost certainly remnant population groups from the Mycenaean world were included amongst the marauders. Memories of these latter-day Mycenaeans may well have become embedded in Homeric tradition as the perpetrators of the final destruction of Troy – some time after the Anatolian-based Hittite empire had been consigned to oblivion. Very likely this was the period when the traditions from which the *Iliad* evolved began taking their final shape. A visitor to Troy in the early centuries of the first millennium may well have been captivated by the still imposing ruins of what was obviously once a great and powerful city. And before the Aeolian settlement, there may well have been a small number of inhabitants on the site who preserved memories of what the city had been in the days of its greatness, memories passed down through the generations. Out of all this Homer's *Iliad* was born.

Undoubtedly there are scraps of truth and authentic relics of history here and there in the story of the Trojan War. But is any real purpose served by speculating inconclusively and endlessly on this? What in fact are the reasons for the never-ending compulsion to prove or disprove whether Homer's story is based on historical fact? It needs to be emphasized repeatedly that Homer wrote not as an historian but as a creative poet. And he himself may well have been amused, or bemused, at how much scholarly ink and breath have been expended on the search for the truth behind his tales.

Of course, he tried to convince his listeners of the reality of the events and the characters that figure in his tale. But that is all part and parcel of being a good storyteller – to persuade one's audience that the people in one's stories actually lived, that the events described in them actually took place. The storyteller does this for the sake of art, not historical truth. This is the essence of those magical words 'Once upon a time' which begin fairy stories told to young children today. We use these words for the sake of the story, because our listeners will more readily be captivated if they believe that there really was once a handsome prince who rescued a beautiful princess from a wicked witch and then lived happily ever after with her. So with Homer the story was the thing, and the skill to tell it in such a way that he could convince his listeners that it all did happen 'once upon a time'.

One of the reasons for attempting to show that Homer's tale is based on historical fact may be the fond belief that the poet's reputation would be all the greater if we could only prove that this was so. Indeed, scholars who believe that they have proved the 'reality' of Homer's Trojan War have declared triumphantly: 'Homer can now be taken seriously!' What an unfortunate misrepresentation of what Homer is all about! It's as if to say the great creative artist cannot be taken seriously unless we can prove that he cribbed his story from history. But surely the opposite is true. Let us suppose that the *Iliad* is entirely a work of imagination, that, despite this, Homer has told his story so well that he has convinced almost all his readers and listeners that his characters were based on real people who participated in events that really did happen. Surely this above all else would demonstrate the full extent of his genius.

But throughout the ages there has been another reason, quite apart from any misplaced desire to do Homer a favour, for insisting upon the basic historical truth of his tale. It can be summed up in two words: *vested interest.* Ever since Troy was resettled by Aeolian Greeks in the late eighth century, the inhabitants of the site were fully aware of the advantages to be gained by exploiting the belief that this was indeed the city of Priam – for example, by nurturing the legend of the Locrian maidens' attendance upon the temple of Athena whose foundations allegedly dated back to the war itself. The city thrived on its past associations, reaping the benefits, financial and otherwise, bestowed upon it by a wide range of visitors, including distinguished patrons such as Alexander the Great. Alexander's own veneration for Homer was based on an implicit belief in the truth of his story and, therefore, in the authenticity of Ilion as the setting for this story. For this reason too Alexander's successors bestowed favours upon the site. And the privileges that Julius Caesar and Augustus accorded it as the home of the founder of the Roman nation – their own lineal ancestor – ensured that New Ilium would continue to survive and flourish for generations to come. Of course it was very much in Augustus' own interests to endorse the historical truth of the tale of Troy, and consequently the story of Aeneas, for the latter provided useful propaganda in justifying the position Rome's leading citizen had now assumed at the head of the Roman empire.

Vested interest in matters to do with Troy and the Trojan War continues to flourish today. Troy is one of the the world's great tourist attractions, as far as archaeological sites go, but its popularity rests entirely on the belief that it is the site of one of the most famous wars of the ancient world. Tourist guides will point out the Scaean Gate, before which Hector and Achilles duelled to the death, and also where Hector bade his wife Andromache and baby Astyanax farewell, the coastal area where the Greeks beached their ships, the mounds where Achilles and Patroclus and Hector are buried. These are not scenes out of a fairy story. The events associated with them really happened, so the visitor is told. And just to be sure we're in no doubt about this, an enormous modern wooden horse towering over the souvenir shops reinforces the Trojan War theme (though the horse has no part in the *Iliad*), besides providing visitors with the site's only really prominent feature.

For, as I said in the Introduction, Troy is unprepossessing – from the visitors' point of view, little more than a jumble of mudbrick,

Figure 8.1 A modern version of the Trojan Horse, at Troy.

stone, earth and weeds. It is kept alive by its legendary associations. Without these, there would be no steady stream of visitors. For all the skill of the current excavators of the site, and for all that they have achieved, the ongoing fame and popularity of Troy depend essentially on Homer's story. Vested interest must insist that this story is based on real events and is not a figment of poetic imagination. This is not simply a case of attracting the tourists. Substantial funds are necessary to finance what is one of the most expensive excavations in the Near Eastern world (more than 350 scholars, scientists and technicians from nearly twenty countries have been collaborating on the excavations). One must ask whether this flow of funds would continue if it were proved that there was either no Trojan War or it was fought on a completely different location.

Vested interest in an historical Trojan War has other aspects as well. We have referred to the succession of books and television programmes that have embarked on a search for the war. Anyone who undertakes such a search cannot be entirely free of vested interest in its outcome. After all, there are readers, publishers and viewers to satisfy, and satisfaction will only be achieved if the searchers come up with something to justify their efforts, generally in the form of 'new evidence' that there really is an historical basis for Homer's tale. We will continue to look for truth behind the legend, and, by so doing, ensure that the Trojan War industry remains alive and well. I must say too, as a Hittitologist, that this industry has given a higher public profile to Hittite studies. For the Hittites, who long remained an obscure people in popular perceptions of the ancient world, have featured now in numerous books and television programmes about Troy, ever since it became apparent that the archives of the Hittite capital contained information that could be relevant to Troy's history. The Hittites too have benefited from having room made for them on the Trojan War bandwagon.

There is another reason for the enduring interest in the quest for an historical Troy. Sheer curiosity. In a way, it is the same sort of curiosity that has inspired a whole army of scholars and enthusiastic amateurs to engage in the much more quixotic enterprise of seeking out the 'truth' behind one of the most brilliant and most enduring of all hoaxes: the lost civilization of Atlantis. Certainly the search for the historical Troy of the Trojan War has a much more credible basis. And we may well have established some truth about Troy's Late Bronze Age history, if we have succeeded in linking the kingdom of Wilusa known from Hittite texts with the site at Hisarlık.

But does this truth tell us something that we really want to hear? For by establishing it, what we have really done is to demystify and degrade the image of Troy. We have reduced this splendid city of legend with its dazzling opulence and its great heroes to the status of an outpost vassal state of the Hittite empire, peopled not by great warriors but by merchants and traders and craftsmen, creatures of a much lower order of humanity in Homeric society. Far from holding out for ten years against the combined might of the Mycenaean world, this little kingdom fell victim on more than one occasion to its neighbours and needed its Hittite overlord to come to its rescue. That, if anything, is the real truth about Homer's Troy.

Above the entrance to its Arts and Law building, the University of Queensland has inscribed the words: *GREAT IS TRUTH AND MIGHTY ABOVE ALL THINGS*. Noble though this sentiment undoubtedly is, it must be said that the truth sometimes leads us into places we would prefer not to go. Far better to abandon our search for a historical Troy and let Homer have the last word. For he has provided a story of human courage and endurance, of human frailty and human sorrow that needs no enquiries into its literal historical truth to confirm it as one of the most enduring and most eloquent expressions of the triumphs and tragedies of the human condition.

NOTES

INTRODUCTION

1 Throughout this book, the term 'city' is used in a very broad sense to refer to Troy, on the understanding that in several phases of its existence the settlement at Hisarlık was little more than a stronghold or the preserve of an elite class. This will become clear when we come to discuss each phase of the settlement's history.

2 In the representation of Greek names, I have adopted the transcriptions used in the *Oxford Classical Dictionary*.

1 THE POET AND THE TRADITION

1 The other five are Rhodes, Colophon, Salamis (in Cyprus), Argos and Athens.

2 West (1995) argues for a slightly later date, between 670 and 640.

3 *Hymn to Apollo*, 169–73.

4 The Phaeacian bard Demodocus who, in the *Odyssey* (8.44–5, 62–4), performs at the court of Alcinous though the Muse had deprived him of his sight, served as a kind of archetypal image of the blind bard.

5 Vermeule (1986: 86). Xenophanes was highly critical of both Homer's and Hesiod's conception of a divine society to whose gods they assigned all the failings and vices of humankind.

6 Josephus, *Against Apion*, 1.2.12.

7 See Latacz (2004: 262).

8 On Homer's use of epithets, see also Latacz (2004: 254–9).

9 *Iliad* 6.168–9.

10 Some scholars have argued that even here the reference is merely to symbols or signs (*sēmata*) and not to genuine writing, for which the Greek word *grammata* would normally be used.

11 According to a somewhat garbled statement by Cicero (*De oratore* 3.137), it was at this time that the 'books' of Homer were first put into a fixed order. Socrates allegedly stated that Pisistratus' son Hipparchus was the first to bring the poems of Homer into Athens (pseudo-Plato,

Hipparchus 228 B). There is no clear or reliable information in any of our literary sources as to whether texts of the Homeric poems, or at least complete texts, existed prior to the Pisistratid era.

12 See, for example, Latacz (1996: 65).

13 Though according to Cicero (n. 11 above), written copies of the individual 'books' of the poems already existed, but were not put in a fixed order until the Pisistratid period.

14 Cf. Högemann's discussion (2000).

15 *Odyssey* 9.5–11.

16 The question of Aegean colonization movements from the end of the Bronze Age until the eighth century BC has been discussed by A. Yasur-Landau in his paper 'Two Centuries of Staying (mainly) at Home?', presented at the conference *Lighten our Darkness: Cultural Transformations at the Beginning of the First Millennium BC – From the Alps to Anatolia*, Birmingham University, 6–9/1/2000.

17 Herodotus, *Histories* 1.146 and 147 respectively.

18 Within the context of the revolutionary changes taking place in the Ionian world, Latacz (1996: 65; 2004: 185–7) sees the *Iliad* as reflecting the need of an eighth-century aristocracy to redefine and justify itself, in terms of its fundamental values and ideals.

19 See, for example, Bryce (2002: 185).

20 However, Mee (1998: 138–9) notes that a number of instances of cremation are also found on some of the islands of the eastern Aegean, along with several instances at Müskebi.

21 *Iliad* 23.233–61.

22 See, for example, Bryce (2002: 261–8).

23 Lucian, *Verae historiae* 2.20.

24 Plato, *Ion* 530b.

25 As Latacz (1996: 67) notes (citing the sixth-century Xenophanes' indignant remark that 'from the beginning, all have learned in accord with Homer'), school requirements may well have played a part in the early dissemination of the Homeric epics.

26 Similarly from the late second century onwards, 'the Homeric poems were seen as the embodiment of all the spiritual and religious truths embodied in the human soul. This was especially true of the approach of Porphyry and the Neoplatonists.' Sage (2000: 215).

27 *Iliad* 2.484–760.

28 The Greek historian Thucydides (*Histories* 1.11) attempts to explain the vast Greek force's inability to seize Troy by claiming that only a fraction of the Greeks were actually engaged in the fighting at Troy while the rest devoted themselves to plundering expeditions and cultivating the land.

29 However, Anderson (1995: 184) makes the point that, while it is established fact that many sites ceased to be inhabited at the end of the Bronze Age, it is often just conjecture that they had in the Bronze Age the ancient names assigned to them by modern scholars.

30 This summarizes the proposal by Anderson (1995: 188–9). See also Powell (2004: 30) who suggests that Homer himself worked in Boeotia. *Contra* the assumption that the Catalogue was an early first-millennium composition compiled by a single bard, or even by several bards, during travels through Greece, see most recently the lengthy discussion of Latacz (2004: 219–49), who concludes (2004: 248) that the compilation of place names, from which the Catalogue of Ships derives, can only have been made in Mycenaean times.

31 Herodotus *Histories* 2.112–18.

32 The Thucydidean references are to *Histories* 1.3, 1.10 and 2.41 respectively. The passage cited is translated by R. Warner.

2 THE EARLY CITIES OF TROY
(LEVELS I TO V)

1 See the recent investigation of Kraft et al. (2003), who conclude, 166 (2003): 'The reality of Homer's description of place, event, and topography correlated with geologic investigation helps show that the *Iliad* is not just a legend, but regularly consistent with palaeographic reconstructions.'

2 For contrasting assessments of Schliemann, see, for example, Traill (1995) and Easton (1997).

3 A travel writer of the second century AD. The reference occurs in Pausanias 2.16.6.

4 Strabo, 13.1.25, 13.1.42. Strabo believed that Ilion was not established until the period of the Lydian king Croesus (reigned *c*.560–46).

5 See Allen (1999) for a detailed discussion of this relationship.

6 See, for example, Robinson (1994, 1995).

7 The letter is cited and discussed by Easton (1994).

8 Blegen (1963: 20).

9 It is still attested in 1463 when the Ottoman sultan Mehmet II, conqueror of Constantinople, visited the site – though at that time, and probably for many years beforehand, it may have been virtually derelict.

10 Gates (2003: 143–4) notes that, in contrast with later Mycenaean megarons, the Troy II examples are free-standing, not embedded inside a larger palace complex.

11 See Lloyd (1967: 16), Mellaart (1971: 371–403).

12 Brief accounts of these are given by Akurgal (1962: 15–25), Lloyd (1967: 20–9).

13 Akurgal (1989) has suggested a later dating, to *c*.2100–2000.

14 See Bryce (2005: 24–6).

15 A new edition of the literary versions of the legend extant in Babylonian sources has been published by Westenholz (1997: 102–31).

16 It was the most distinguished of more than twenty hoards found in this level.

17 See Traill (1995: 114, 116).

18 See, for example, Traill (1995: 120–1). Schliemann has similarly been accused of salting several of the shaft graves at Mycenae with finds taken from elsewhere.

19 The letter, dated 27 December 1873, is cited by Traill (1995: 116–18).

20 See, for example, Wright (1997: 360–3).

21 For a survey of the kingdoms of the late third and early second millennium, see Van De Mieroop (2004: 59–98).

22 In general on the Assyrian merchant operations in Anatolia and the kingdoms with which they dealt, see Bryce (2005: 21–40).

3 THE KINGDOM OF PRIAM
(LEVELS VI TO VII)

1 This is largely conjectural. Note the reservations of Hertel and Kolb (2004: 76).

2 *Iliad* 16.702–11.

3 For general accounts of the so-called lower city, see Korfmann (1995; 1997a; 1997b).

4 See Korfmann et al. (2001: 397, Figs. 23, 26, 77, 462, 465). It is suggested that the first ditch dates to Level VI, the second ditch to Level VIIa.

5 See most recently Hertel and Kolb (2004: 83–4).

6 Korfmann (2004: 38).

7 We might note, by way of comparison, that the total population of the Mycenaean kingdom of Pylos in the western Peloponnese has been estimated at around 50,000; see Chadwick (1976: 68). Some scholars raise the estimate to *c.*100,000.

8 See Easton et al. (2002).

9 Hertel and Kolb (2004).

10 See Mountjoy (1999). It is quite likely that Level VIh continued for a time after production of LH IIIA ware had ceased. The presence of LH IIIB1 pottery in the destruction deposits would seem to support this, despite Mountjoy's claim that the LH IIIB sherds were later intrusions.

11 The dates assigned to it in Greek sources range mostly between the thirteenth and the early twelfth centuries. Herodotus 2.145 proposes a date 'about 800 years before my time' – i.e. mid-thirteenth century.

12 Archaeologists now regard Level VIIa, as identified by Dörpfeld, simply as a later stage of Level VI (VIi), though the original designation is generally retained to avoid confusion. The first of the two stages of Level VIIb also belongs stratigraphically with Level VI.

13 But not necessarily. See Easton (1985: 190–1).

14 Easton (1985: 189) comments that the LH IIIC sherds among deposits of Level VIIa suggest that the destruction took place at a date later than that of the Mycenaean palaces, when Mycenaeans ought not to

have been able to muster a coalition of the sort described by Homer. See also Mee (1978: 147, 1984: 48–50), Mellink (1986: 97), Muhly (1992: 17).

15 For the distinction between it and the Grey Minyan ware of Early Helladic (EH) III Greece, see Mee (1978: 146).

16 To judge from the LH IIIC ceramic ware found on the site, representing the final stages of Mycenaean ceramic ware.

17 See Hawkins and Easton (1996). The seal is further discussed by Alp (2001).

18 In general on the history of the Hittite kingdom, see Bryce (2005).

19 See Bryce (2003a: 131).

20 For a comprehensive treatment of Luwian history, inscriptions, language, religion, art and architecture, see Melchert (2003).

21 See Bryce (2003b: 28–31).

22 The equation between (W)ilios and Wilusa was first made in 1924 by the Indo-European philologist Paul Kretschmer; cited by Latacz (2004: 75).

23 See Bryce (2003a: 169, map).

24 Goetze (1940).

25 Published by Otten (1988).

26 Two inscriptions from the former, five from the latter. See most recently Hawkins (2000: 433–41).

27 For the inscription, see Dinçol (1998), and for the career of Kurunta, Bryce (2005: 269–71, 302–3, 319–21).

28 Thus Hawkins in Easton et al. (2002: 97).

29 KUB (Keilschrifturkunden aus Boghazköi, Berlin) XXI 6a.

30 In general on the Lukka people, see Bryce (2003b: 73–8).

31 On the inscription and its contents, see Hawkins (1995: 66–85).

32 See also the discussion by Mellink (1995).

33 See most recently Hawkins (1998: 1), and in Easton et al. (2002: 97), Niemeier (1999: 142), Büyükkolanci (2000).

34 Thus Hawkins (1998: 24).

35 Herodotus 2.106.

36 Hawkins (1998: 4–10).

37 See Peschlow-Bindokat and Herbordt (2001). Unfortunately the names are only fragmentary.

38 See Houwink ten Cate (1983–4: 48 n. 38), Starke (1997: 451, nn. 40, 41), Hawkins (1998: 23–4), Niemeier (1999: 142).

39 See Gurney (1992: 221), Niemeier (1999: 142–3), Hawkins in Easton et al. (2002: 100).

40 The so-called Manapa-Tarhunda letter, referred to below. The reference to Lazpa occurs in line 8.

41 The letter has been transliterated and translated by Houwink ten Cate (1983–4: 39–40). We shall be discussing it further in Chapters 5 and 8. Lines 3–6 deal with events relating to Wilusa.

4 THE AEGEAN NEIGHBOURS

1 *Odyssey* 19.172–4, after E. V. Rieu. In the *Iliad* 2.649, 100 cities are attributed to Crete.

2 Thus Castleden (1990).

3 The notion of a Minoan thalassocracy goes back at least to the fifth-century BC historian Thucydides, who reports a tradition that King Minos was the first person to organize a navy, enabling him to control the greater part of the Aegean Sea (*Histories* 1.4).

4 See the discussions by Laffineur (1998: 56–60), and W.-D. and B. Niemeier (1998: 78–82, 85–96).

5 See Rehak (1998).

6 Knapp (1995: 1439) also suggests that the name may refer to the Aegean area or to Aegean peoples in general. For the extensive bibliography on the Keftiu, see Rehak (1998: 40 n. 12).

7 See Latacz's discussion (2004: 128–33). Mee (in a forthcoming article 'Mycenaean Greece, the Aegean, and Beyond', to appear in *The Cambridge Companion to the Aegean Bronze Age*) notes that one interpretation of this inscription is that it records the itinerary of an Egyptian embassy, sent by Amenhotep, at a time when Crete was still a political force and Mycenaean Greece had emerged as a rival power.

8 See Mee (1998: 137, with references in n. 1).

9 According to the conventional and most widely accepted chronology. For a 'high' or 'early' chronology, see Manning's chart (1999: Table 1, p. 3).

10 We cannot be sure whether Cnossus too was destroyed at this time.

11 Drews (1988, especially pp. 178–96). *Contra* Drews' proposals, see Dickinson (1999).

12 The Cyclades, however, was a producer of silver.

13 From a list of the international materials found in the shaft graves; see Vermeule (1972: 89–90).

14 Further on the question of the Mycenaean administrative system, see Shelmerdine (1999).

15 Mee (1998: 138) comments that what we see following this collapse is a steady escalation in the level of Mycenaean activity, not a sudden transition from Minoan to Mycenaean.

16 Bass (1998: 186). Mee discusses the question of Mycenaean contacts with Egypt in his forthcoming article referred to in n. 7 above.

17 Guzowska (2002: 506–7) notes evidence that the Mycenaeans used penteconters (50-oared ships) or equally strong ships for maritime ventures towards the end of the Bronze Age.

18 Knapp (1995: 1443).

19 Cf. Knapp (1995: 1435).

20 See Mee (1978: 129–30; 1998: 139).

21 For a comprehensive treatment of the Mycenaean presence in western Anatolia, see W.-D. Niemeier (1998).

22 'Danaan' and 'Argive' were other terms used in Homeric tradition for the Greeks. For an explanation of the alternatives as synonymous metrical variants, see Latacz (2004: 135).

23 The name seems also to occur in a Linear B tablet from Cnossus (though the reference here is problematical) and in an inscription from Egypt, dated to *c.*1200 (references in Latacz 1996: 37).

24 The German scholar F. Starke has recently claimed that one of the 'Ahhiyawa documents' in the Hittite capital's archives is a letter addressed by an Ahhiyawan king to a Hittite king. His proposal has still to be published in detail, enabling it to be subjected to peer scrutiny. Before its validity is fully assessed, it cannot be used for the purposes of historical investigation. The document in question is KUB (Keilschrifturkunden aus Boghazköi, Berlin) 26.91, published by Sommer (1932: 268–77). Starke's proposal is briefly referred to by Latacz (2004: 243–4).

25 Niemeier (1999: 149).

26 For the text itself, see Beckman (1999: 153–60), and for a discussion of it, see Bryce (2005: 129–36).

27 Strabo 8.6.11. These giant labourers are said to come from Lycia which, as we noted in Chapter 3, was the Greek name for part of the region called the Lukka Lands in the Late Bronze Age.

28 Chadwick (1976: 81, 152) (also A.G. and E. S. Sherratt in Easton et al. (2002: 105)) suggests that western Anatolia had a particular expertise and reputation in this craft, and that its products would have been valued even in areas which now supported their own textile industries. See also Wood (1996: 145–7, 150), Parker (1999: 496–7). For references in the Linear B tablets to women of Troy (To-ro-ja), see Zengel (1990: 54). For the kidnapping of women during raiding expeditions, see *Iliad* 1.366–9, 9.328–9, 11.624–7, 20.191–4.

29 Chadwick (1976: 14) believes that for strategic reasons it was impossible that the Argive Plain was divided between Mycenae and Tiryns; the latter, he concludes, must have been a dependency of the former.

30 See Mee (1978: 135).

31 Thebes has also been suggested; see Niemeier (1999: 144) and, especially Latacz (2004: 238–46), the latter drawing support from Starke's still-to-be-assessed proposal referred to in n. 24.

5 TROY'S ROLE AND STATUS IN THE NEAR EASTERN WORLD

1 This topic has also been discussed at some length by Starke (1997).

2 For a translation of the treaty, see Beckman (1999: 87–93).

3 As first proposed by Heinhold-Krahmer (1977: 136–47). See also Bryce (2005: 197).

4 We cannot be sure whether there was one or two early Hittite New Kingdom rulers of this name; see Bryce (2005: 122–3).

5 See Bryce (2005: 145–8).
6 Cf. Latacz's discussion and conclusions (2004: 96–100). He comments (p. 99) that 'Greek Troy poetry could only welcome the availability of two names for the same geographical entity, since both names, with their differing metrical forms, made it easier to work this fabled city into hexameters.'
7 See Hawkins (1997).
8 Ramesses lists Arzawa (probably used in the generic sense) along with other western countries among the states that provided troops for the Hittite army at Kadesh.
9 It is part translated by Gurney in Garstang and Gurney (1959: 111–14).
10 Translated by Gurney.
11 Hoffner (1982). For a translation of the augmented but still fragmentary text, see Beckman (1999: 144–6).
12 The addressee has been plausibly identified by Hawkins (1998: 19) with the then king of Mira, Tarkasnawa, whose name has recently been deciphered on the rock-cut inscription in the Karabel mountain pass near Izmir.
13 See Bryce (2005: 309–10).
14 See Bryce (2005: 304–5).
15 Hertel and Kolb (2004: 71) comment that recent investigations of other sites south of Troy, such as Panaztepe, Ephesus and Miletus, 'promise to put the ruins on the hill of Hisarlık into a more sober perspective – probably as a site of reduced importance.'
16 Hertel and Kolb (2004: 74, 76) suggest that the population may have been no larger than 2,000, or even 1,000.
17 Letter from the El Amarna archives, EA 32, translated by Moran (1992: 103).
18 See Starke (1997: 456).
19 Güterbock (1986: 34–5.).
20 Melchert (2003: 12). Latacz (2004: 117–18) suggests that Alaksandu may have been the son of one of Kukkunni's Greek concubines.
21 See, for example, the comments of Watkins (1986: 56–7), Starke (1997: 458) and Hutter (2003: 266).
22 Neumann (1999: 16–19), cited also by Hutter (2003: 213 n. 3).
23 Cf. Aro (2003: 287).
24 Güterbock (1986: 42) comments that despite the break in the text at the beginning of the name, it is not likely that there were many signs lost before the *ap*, and the context demands a divine name.
25 Cf. Hutter (2003: 267).
26 It was imported from as early as Late Helladic IIA.
27 The quantity of local pottery is 98–9 per cent according to Mee (1978: 146, 1998: 144).
28 Cf. Haider (1997: 122).
29 Both locations lie off the coast of ancient Lycia.
30 See Bass (1998: 188), Pulak (2000: 137).

31 See Cline (1994: xviii), with respect to the circular pattern of the sea-trading routes.

32 Guzowska (2002: 508, with references) sees this reflected in the large amount of imported objects, especially of Mycenaean derivation, found in the cemetery at Beşik Tepe during Troy VI.

33 See, for example, Korfmann (1986: 6–7). Korfmann notes that the daily average speed of the winds is 16.2 kilometres per hour. Guzowska (2002: 506) notes that the current in the Bosporus Strait has an average maximum of 4 to 5 knots (about 2.2 to 2.7 kilometres per hour), which can climb to 7 knots (about 3.8 kilometres per hour).

34 As Guzowska (2002: 506–7) has argued for Mycenaean vessels towards the end of the Bronze Age.

35 As Korfmann has frequently argued (for example, 1986), in support of a long-held theory against the traditional assumption, beginning at least as early as Homer, of a Hellespontine location for the harbour.

36 Korfmann (1995: 182).

37 Wright (1997: 357).

38 Sherratt and Sherratt in Easton et al. (2002: 104).

39 See Mee (1998: 144). Guzowska (2002: 504) notes in particular the very scanty evidence for Mycenaean contacts with the Black Sea, but attributes this (2002: 511–12) to the dominating role of Troy in the Dardanelles area. (That of course is a matter of assumption, not of fact.)

40 See also Hertel and Kolb (2004: 73).

6 TROY'S ALLIES

1 *Iliad* 2.798–801, translated by R. Lattimore.

2 See the detailed discussion of the catalogue by Kirk (1985: 250–63).

3 Inscriptions of the first millennium indicate that a number of the members of the alliance, notably the Phrygians, Maeonians (if they can be identified with the Lydians), Carians and Lycians spoke related Indo-European languages. So, too, the predominant language of Late Bronze Age Troy may have been the Indo-European Luwian language, as discussed in Chapter 5.

4 On the assumption that '[L]ukka' is a correct restoration.

5 See Heubeck and Hoekstra (1989: 108), citing an 'attractive' suggestion which goes back to the philologist Paul Kretschmer and the British politician W. E. Gladstone. See also Raaflaub (1997: 82).

6 *Odyssey* 11.521.

7 Rieu in the Penguin Classics edition of the *Odyssey* went so far as to translate 'Keteioi' as 'Hittite men-at-arms', a translation retained by his son in the revised edition of the translation.

8 Not named in the *Iliad*, but in other sources called Iobates or Amphianax.

9 Published by Otten (1973).

10 Kirk (1985: 263).

11 Kadesh Inscription P40–53.
12 Haider (1997: 117–19).
13 *Iliad* 5.173.
14 *Iliad* 5.105.
15 *Iliad* 4.103 and 121.
16 *Iliad* 20.87; see also Strabo 13.1.49.
17 See Strabo 14.1.3 and 2.18.
18 For example, Strabo 14.3.5.
19 Strabo 9.5.19 lists eleven.
20 *Odyssey* 9.39–61.
21 *Iliad* 2.857.
22 Strabo 12.3.20.
23 See also Strabo 12.3.19 (where they are located opposite Pharnacia, which lies on the coast just west of Trapezus), 14.5.23 (where they are called an unknown people).
24 See de Jesus (1978: 100–1).
25 See Yakar (1976: 118 (map) and 121), together with the comments of de Jesus (1978: 100–1).
26 Kirk (1985: 259).
27 *Iliad* 18.289–92.
28 Herodotus 1.7.
29 Herodotus 7.74. See also Dionysius of Halicarnassus 1.27.1.
30 For example, Košak (1981: 15).
31 Herodotus 1.171.
32 *Iliad* 2.867.
33 Antoninus Liberalis, *Metamorphoses* 35.3, citing Menecrates of Xanthus and Nicander of Colophon as his sources.
34 *Iliad* 12.313–14.
35 *Iliad* 5.471–92.
36 *Iliad* 16.666–75.
37 Herodotus 1.147.
38 Frei (1978).
39 With respect to 1972.11.10 (composite photograph of figured scene in side A) Greek, Attic, ca. 515 B.C.; Archaic, Calyx-krater, Signed by Euxitheos, as potter; Signed by Euphronios, as painter, terracotta, side A: *The Death of Sarpedon*, terracotta; height 18 in. (45.69 cm); **The Metropolitan Museum of Art, Purchase, Bequest of Joseph H. Durkee, Gift of Darius Ogden Mills and Gift of C. Ruxton Love, by exchange, 1972 (1972.11.10) Photograph, all rights reserved. The Metropolitan Museum of Art.**
40 Herodotus 1.173. See also Strabo 12.8.5, 14.3.10.
41 Apollodorus *Bibliotheca* 3.3.1.
42 Strabo 12.8.5, 14.1.6, quoting Ephorus.
43 Respectively, Apollodorus *Bibliotheca* 3.1.2, and Diodorus 5.79.3.
44 Plutarch *De mulierum virtutibus* 247–8.
45 Bryce (2003b: 43–4).
46 Herodotus 1.176.

7 THE NEW CITY (LEVELS VIII TO IX)

1 On the introduction of the Homeric poems into the Panathenaic festival, see (pseudo-)Plato, *Hipparchus* 228B; Cicero, *De oratore* 3.137.
2 Herodotus 7.43.
3 Thus Erskine (2001: 85).
4 I see no reason to doubt, as Erskine does, that such a visit did take place.
5 Herodotus 1.4.
6 An alliance of Greek states formed after the Persian wars for ongoing defence against Persia.
7 Powell (2004: 159) notes that when the playwright Aeschylus said that his plays were 'slices from the banquet of Homer', he meant that he was stealing plots from the cyclic poems, not from the *Iliad* and the *Odyssey* in which Aeschylus had little interest.
8 Erskine (2001: 83).
9 It appears in the Athenian Tribute Lists for the year 425–424 BC, where its tribute is assessed at two talents.
10 Strabo 13.1.26.
11 He is also known as Pyrrhus, as we shall see below, but is not referred to by this name in Homer.
12 On his mother's side.
13 The battle was fought by the combined armies of Seleucus I and Lysimachus against the forces of the aged Antigonus, another of Alexander's so-called *diadochoi* ('heirs'), who had inherited sovereignty over Phrygia following Alexander's death.
14 Strabo 13.1.26.
15 Strabo 13.1.27, citing the Alexandrian scholar Hegesianax.
16 See Tekkök (2000: 86), who favours the latter on the grounds that he appears from numismatic evidence to have had the support of the Troad in his ultimately unsuccessful conflict with Attalus.
17 These reasons have been suggested by Erskine (2001: 233–4).
18 Livy 35.43.3.
19 Livy 37.9.7, 37.37.2.
20 Livy 38.39.10. This was not so much, Livy remarks, a reward for any recent services they had done; rather, it was an acknowledgment of their lineage. According to Livy, the two additional settlements were called Rhoeteum and Gergithus.
21 Strabo 13.1.27.
22 Appian 12.(*The Mithridatic Wars*)53. Appian states that the Ilians opened their gates to Fimbria in the mistaken belief that the protection promised them by Sulla (the most powerful Roman of the time) would keep the city safe from harm.
23 Thus Strabo 13.1.27.
24 See Rose (1992: 44).
25 See Erskine (2001: 241–2).
26 Though it was not until 27 BC that Octavian, Julius Caesar's great-nephew, assumed the name Augustus ('the revered one'), and the title *princeps* ('first man') of the Roman world. Officially, this year marked the beginning of Augustus' reign as Rome's first emperor.

27 For the genealogy of the Trojan royal family, see *Iliad* 20.215–41.
28 *Iliad* 17.333–41.
29 *Iliad* 20.302–8, translated by R. Lattimore.
30 *Hymn to Aphrodite*, 196–7.
31 Strabo 13.1.53.
32 See Strabo 13.1.40, Polybius 12.5.
33 Cf. Willcock (1976: 222–3).
34 Dionysius of Halicarnassus 1.45. Alternative views, referred to by Dionysius (1.53.4), were that after Aeneas arrived in Italy and settled his band of refugees there, he returned to Troy and ruled there, or that it was a different Aeneas altogether who went to Italy.
35 Herodotus 1.94. But most scholars now reject this possibility.
36 For example, Sandars (1985: 198–9).
37 Dionysius of Halicarnassus 1.48.1.
38 Dionysius of Halicarnassus 1.49.1–3.
39 Valerius Maximus, *Facta et dicta memorabilia* 2.1.10. Similarly Cicero, *Tusculanae disputationes* 4.2.3 (citing Cato the Censor), *Brutus* 19.75.
40 Virgil, *Aeneid* 4.618–20.
41 Lucan, *De bello civili* 9.966–99. Lucan records the anecdote that as Caesar walked through a patch of grass, one of the locals called out to him: 'They buried Hector there. Take care not to offend his ghost!'
42 Thus Erskine (2001: 248–50).
43 Austin (1964: 216).
44 Virgil's literary patron was Augustus' close confidant Maecenas.
45 Virgil, *Aeneid* 6.791–4.
46 Virgil, *Aeneid* 8.626–728.
47 See Sage (2000: 214).
48 Thus Vermeule (1995: 471).
49 Suetonius, *Life of Tiberius*, 52.2.
50 Tacitus, *Annals* 2.54.
51 *Anthologia palatina* 9.387, cited by Sage (2000: 213).
52 Tacitus, *Annals* 12.58; Suetonius, *Life of Claudius* 25.3. See also Vermeule (1995: 472, with note 68).
53 Elder Pliny, *Naturalis historia* 5.124.
54 Vermeule (1995: 476, with note 100).
55 See Vermeule (1995: 477), Sage (2000: 217–18).
56 Vermeule (1995: 477). See also Sage (2000: 219).
57 For the above information on Ilium during the Byzantine period, see Vermeule (1995: 477, with references in notes 115, 116).
58 Cited from Vermeule (1995: 477–8, with note 117).

8 THE FINAL WORD

1 Houwink ten Cate (1983–4: 40).
2 Güterbock (1986: 37).
3 See, for example, Easton (1985: 189).
4 Wood (1996: 146).

BIBLIOGRAPHY

Akurgal, E. (1962) *The Art of the Hittites*, London: Thames & Hudson.

—— (1989) 'Are the Ritual Standards of Alacahöyük Royal Symbols of the Hattian or the Hittite Kings?', in K. Emre, B. Hrouda, M. J. Mellink and N. Özgüç (eds) *Anatolia and the Near East (Tahsin Özgüçe Armağan) (Studies in Honour of Tahsin Özgüç)*, Ankara: Türk Tarih Kurumu Basimevi, pp. 1–2.

Allen, S. H. (1999) *Finding the Walls of Troy: Frank Calvert and Heinrich Schliemann at Hisarlık*, Berkeley, Calif. and London: University of California Press.

Alp, S. (2001) 'Das Hieroglyphensiegel von Troja und seine Bedeutung für Westanatolien', in G. Wilhelm (ed.) *Proceedings of the 4th International Congress for Hittitology.* Würzburg, 4–8 October 1999) (*Studien zu den Boğazköy–Texten* 45), Wiesbaden: Harrassowitz, 27–31.

Anderson, J. K. (1995) 'The Geometric Catalogue of Ships', in J. B. Carter and S. P. Morris (eds) *The Ages of Homer. A Tribute to Emily Townsend Vermeule*, Austin, Tex.: University of Texas Press, pp. 181–91.

Aro, S. (2003) 'Art and Architecture', in H. C. Melchert (ed.) *The Luwians*, Leiden: Brill, pp. 281–337.

Austin, R. G. (1964) *P. Vergili Maronis: Aeneidos Liber Secundus*, Oxford: Clarendon Press.

Bass, G. F. (1998) 'Sailing between the Aegean and the Orient', in E. H. Cline and D. Harris-Cline (eds) *The Aegean and the Orient in the Second Millennium.* Proceedings of the 50th Anniversity Symposium, Cincinnati, 18–20 April, 1997, *Aegaeum* 18, Liège: University of Liège and Austin, Tex.: University of Texas Press, pp. 183–9.

Beckman, G. (1999) *Hittite Diplomatic Texts*, Atlanta, Ga.: Scholars Press.

Blegen C. (1963) *Troy and the Trojans*, London: Thames & Hudson.

Bryce T. R. (2005) *The Kingdom of the Hittites*, Oxford: Oxford University Press, new edition.

—— (2002) *Life and Society in the Hittite World*, Oxford: Oxford University Press.

—— (2003a) *Letters of the Great Kings of the Ancient Near East*, London: Routledge.

—— (2003b) 'History' in H. C. Melchert (ed.) *The Luwians*, Leiden: Brill, pp. 27–127.

Büyükkolanci, M. (2000) 'Excavations on Ayasuluk Hill in Selçuk/Turkey. A Contribution to the Early History of Ephesus', in F. Krinzinger (ed.) *Die Ägäis und das Westliche Mittelmeer. Beziehungen and Wechselwirkungen 8. bis 5. Jh. v. Chr.* (*Archäologischen Forschungen* Bd 4), Vienna: Österreichische Akademie der Wissenschaften, pp. 39–43.

Castleden, R. (1990) *The Knossos Labyrinth: A New View of the 'Palace of Minos' at Knossos*, London: Routledge.

Chadwick, J. (1976) *The Mycenaean World*, Cambridge: Cambridge University Press.

Cline, E. H. (1994) *Sailing the Wine-Dark Sea: International Trade and the Late Bronze Age Aegean,* Oxford: BAR International Series 591.

Deger-Jalkotzy, S., Hiller, S., Panagl, O. (eds) (1999), *Floreant Studia Mycenaea*, vol. II (Akten des X. Internationalen Mykenologischen Colloquiums in Salzburg vom 1–5 Mai, 1995), Vienna: Österreichische Akademie der Wissenschaften, 495–502.

Dickinson, O. (1999) 'Robert Drews's Theories about the Nature of Warfare in the Late Bronze Age', in R. Laffineur (ed.) *Polemos: Le Contexte Guerrier en Égée à l'Âge du Bronze* (Actes de la 7è Rencontre égéenne internationale, Université de Liège, 14–17 April, 1998), *Aegaeum* 19, Liège: University of Liège, Austin, Tex.: University of Texas Press, pp. 21–7.

Dinçol, A. M. (1998) 'Die Entdeckung des Felsmonuments in Hatip und ihre Auswirkungen über die historischen und geographischen Fragen des Hethiterreichs', *Türkiye Bilimler Akademisi Arkeoloji Dergisi* 1: 27–34.

Drews, R. (1988) *The Coming of the Greeks*, Princeton, NJ: Princeton University Press.

Easton, D. F. (1985) 'Has the Trojan War Been Found?', review of M. Wood, *In Search of the Trojan War*, London, 1985, *Antiquity* 59: 188–96.

—— (1994) 'Schliemann Did Admit the Mycenaean Date of Troy VI', *Studia Troica* IV: 173–5.

—— (1997) 'Heinrich Schliemann: Hero or Fraud?', in D. Boedecker (ed.) *The World of Homer, Schliemann, and the Treasures of Priam*, Washington, DC: Society for the Preservation of the Greek Heritage, pp. 33–43. Reprinted in *Classical World* May/June 1998: 91/5.

Easton, D. F., Hawkins, J. D., Sherratt, A. G. and Sherratt, E. S. (2002) 'Troy in Recent Perspective', *Anatolian Studies* 52: 75–109.

Erskine, A. (2001) *Troy Between Greece and Rome: Local Tradition and Imperial Power*, Oxford: Oxford University Press.

Frei, P. (1978) 'Die Lykier bei Homer', in E. Akurgal (ed.) *Proceedings of the Xth International Congress of Classical Archaeology: Ankara-Izmir, 1973*, Ankara: Türk Tarih Kurumu Basimevi, pp. 819–27.

Galter, H. D. (ed.) (1997), *Troia: Mythen und Archäologie*, Graz: Grazer Morgenländische Studien 4.

Garstang, J. and Gurney, O. R. (1959) *The Geography of the Hittite Empire*, London: British Institute of Archaeology.

Gates, C. (2003) *Ancient Cities: The Archaeology of Urban Life in the Ancient Near East and Egypt, Greece and Rome*, London: Routledge.

Goetze, A. (1940) *Kizzuwatna and the Problem of Hittite Geography*, New Haven, Conn.: Yale University Press.

Gurney, O. R. (1992) 'Hittite Geography: Thirty Years On', in H. Otten, E. Akurgal, H. Ertem, and A. Süel (eds) *Hittite and Other Anatolian and Near Eastern Studies in Honour of Sedat Alp*, Ankara: Türk Tarih Kurumu Basimevi, pp. 213–21.

Güterbock, H. G. (1986) 'Troy in Hittite Texts? Wilusa, Ahhiyawa, and Hittite History', in M. J. Mellink (ed.) *Troy and the Trojan War: Proceedings of a Symposium held at Bryn Mawr College, October 1984*, Bryn Mawr: Bryn Mawr College, pp. 33–44.

Guzowska, M. (2002) 'The Trojan Connection or Mycenaeans, Penteconters, and the Black Sea', in K. Jones-Bley and D. G. Zdanovich (eds) *Complex Societies of Central Eurasia from the 3rd to the 1st Millennium BC*, Vol. II, *Journal of Indo-European Studies Monograph Series* 46: 504–17.

Haider, P. W. (1997) 'Troia zwischen Hethitern, Mykenern und Mysern. Besitzt der Troianische Krieg einen historischen Hintergrund?', in H. D. Galter (ed.) *Troia: Mythen und Archäologie*, Graz: Grazer Morgenländische Studien 4, pp. 99–140.

Hawkins, J. D. (1995) *The Hieroglyphic Inscription of the Sacred Pool Complex at Hattusa (Südburg)*. Studien zu den Boğazköy–Texten, Beiheft 3, Wiesbaden: Harrassowitz.

—— (1997) 'A Hieroglyphic Luwian Inscription on a Silver Bowl in the Museum of Anatolian Civilizations, Ankara', Ankara: *Anadolu Medeniyetleri Musezi*, 1996 Yilligi.

—— (1998) 'Tarkasnawa King of Mira "Tarkondemos", Boğazköy Sealings and Karabel', *Anatolian Studies* 48: 1–31.

—— (2000) *Corpus of Hieroglyphic Luwian Inscriptions*, Vol. I, *Inscriptions of the Iron Age*. Studies in Indo-European Languages and Culture 8/1, Berlin and New York: de Gruyter.

Hawkins, J. D. and Easton D. F. (1996) 'A Hieroglyphic Seal from Troy', *Studia Troica* VI: 111–18.

Heinhold-Krahmer, S. (1977) *Arzawa, Untersuchungen zu seiner Geschichte nach den hethitischen Quellen*, Heidelberg: Carl Winter.

Hertel, D. and F. Kolb (2004) 'Troy in Clearer Perspective', *Anatolian Studies* 53: 71–88.

Heubeck, A. and Hoekstra, A. (1989) *A Commentary on Homer's Odyssey*, Vol. II, Oxford: Clarendon Press.

Hoffner, H. A. (1982) 'The Milawata Letter Augmented and Reinterpreted', in *Proceedings of the 28th Rencontre Assyriologique Internationale, Vienna, 1981*, Horn: Archiv für Orientforschung, Beiheft 19, pp. 130–7.

Högemann, P. (2000) 'Zur Iliasdichter: Ein Anatolischer Standpunkt', *Studia Troica* 10: 183–98.

Houwink ten Cate, P. H. J. (1983–4) 'Sidelights on the Ahhiyawa Question from Hittite Vassal and Royal Correspondence', *Jaarbericht Ex Oriente Lux* 28: 33–79.

Hutter, M. (2003) 'Aspects of Luwian Religion', in H. C. Melchert (ed.) *The Luwians*, Leiden: Brill, pp. 211–80.

Jesus, P. De (1978) 'Metal Resources in Ancient Anatolia', *Anatolian Studies* 28: 97–102.

Kirk, G. S. (1985) *The Iliad: A Commentary*, Vol. I, Cambridge: Cambridge University Press.

Knapp, A. B. (1995) 'Island Cultures: Crete, Thera, Cyprus, Rhodes, and Sardinia', in J. M. Sasson (ed.) *Civilizations of the Ancient Near East* (4 vols.), New York: Charles Scribner's Sons, pp. 1433–49.

Korfmann, M. (1986) 'Troy, Topography and Navigation', in M. J. Mellink (ed.) *Troy and the Trojan War: Proceedings of a Symposium held at Bryn Mawr College, October 1984*, Bryn Mawr: Bryn Mawr College, pp. 1–16.

—— (1995) 'Troia: A Residential and Trading City at the Dardanelles', in *Politeia: Society and State in the Aegean Bronze Age*, Aegaeum 19, Liège: University of Liège, 173–83.

—— (1997a) 'Das homerische Troia war grösser – Ergebnisse der Grabungen 1988–96', in H. D. Galter (ed.) *Troia: Mythen und Archäologie*, Graz: Grazer Morgenländische Studien 4, pp. 67–95.

—— (1997b) 'Troia, an Ancient Anatolian Palatial and Trading Centre: Archaeological Evidence for the period of Troy VI/VII', in D. Boedeker (ed.) *The World of Homer, Schliemann, and the Treasures of Priam*, Washington, DC: Society for the Preservation of the Greek Heritage, pp. 33–43. Reprinted in *Classical World* May/June 1998: 91/5 pp. 369–85.

—— (2004) 'Was There a Trojan War?' section of joint article with J. Latacz and J. D. Hawkins, *Archaeology* May/June, 37–8, 41.

Korfmann, M. et al. (2001) *Troja: Traum und Wirklichkeit. Begleitband zur Ausstellung 'Troia – Traum und Wirklichkeit'*, Stuttgart: Theiss.

Košak, S. (1981) 'Western Neighbours of the Hittites', *Eretz Israel* 15: 12–16.

Kraft, J. C., Rapp, G., Kayan, I., Luce, J. V. (2003) 'Harbor areas at ancient Troy: Sedimentology and geomorphology complement Homer's *Iliad*', *Geology*: February, 163–6.

Laffineur, R. (1998) 'From West to East: the Aegean and Egypt in the Early Late Bronze Age', in E. H. Cline and D. Harris-Cline (eds) *The Aegean and the Orient in the Second Millennium*. Proceedings of the 50th Anniversary Symposium, Cincinnati, 18–20 April, 1997, *Aegaeum* 18, Liège: University of Liège and Austin, Tex.: University of Texas Press, pp. 53–67.

Latacz, J. (1996) *Homer: His Art and His World*, trans. J. P. Holoka, Ann Arbor, Mich.: University of Michigan Press.

—— (2004) *Troy and Homer: Towards a Solution of an Old Mystery*, trans. K. Windle and R. Ireland, Oxford, Oxford University Press.

Lloyd, S. (1967) *Early Highland Peoples of Anatolia*, London: Thames & Hudson.

Manning, S. W. (1999) *A Test of Time*, Oxford: Oxbow Books.

Mee, C. (1978) 'Aegean Trade and Settlement in Anatolia in the Second Millennium BC', *Anatolian Studies* 28: 121–55.

—— (1984) 'The Mycenaeans and Troy', in L. Foxhall and J. K. Davies (eds) *The Trojan War: Its Historicity and Context* (Papers of the First Greenbank Colloquium, Liverpool, 1981), Bristol: Bristol Classical Press, 45–56.

—— (1998) Anatolia and the Aegean in the Late Bronze Age', in E. H. Cline and D. Harris-Cline (eds) *The Aegean and the Orient in the Second Millennium*. Proceedings of the 50th Anniversary Symposium, Cincinnati, 18–20 April, 1997, *Aegaeum* 18, Liège: University of Liège and Austin, Tex.: University of Texas Press, pp. 137–49.

Melchert, H. C. (ed.) (2003) *The Luwians*, Leiden: Brill.

Mellaart, J. (1971) 'Anatolia c. 4000–2300 BC', *Cambridge Ancient History*, Vol. III, 3rd edn, Cambridge: Cambridge University Press, 363–416.

Mellink, M. J. (ed.) (1986) *Troy and the Trojan War: Proceedings of a Symposium held at Bryn Mawr College, October 1984*, Bryn Mawr: Bryn Mawr College.

—— (1995) 'Homer, Lycia, and Lukka', in J. B. Carter and S. P. Morris (eds) *The Ages of Homer: A Tribute to Emily Townsend Vermeule*, Austin, Tex.: University of Texas Press, pp. 33–42.

Mieroop, Van De M. (2004) *A History of the Ancient Near East ca. 3000–323 BC*, Oxford: Blackwell.

Moran, W. L. (1992) *The Amarna Letters*, Baltimore, Md. and London: Johns Hopkins University Press.

Mountjoy, P. (1999), 'The Destruction of Troy VIh', *Studia Troica* 9: 253–93.

Muhly, J. D. (1992) 'The Crisis Years in the Mediterranean World: Transition or Cultural Disintegration?', in A. W. Ward and M. S. Joukowsky (eds) *The Crisis Years: the 12th Century BC*, Dubuque, Iowa: Kendall/Hunt, 10–26.

Neumann, G. (1999) 'Wie haben die Troer im 13. Jahrhundert gesprochen?', *Würzburger Jahrbücher für die Altertumswissenschaften NF* 23: 15–23.

Niemeier W-D. (1998) 'The Mycenaeans in Western Anatolia and the Problem of the Origins of the Sea Peoples', in S. Gitin, A. Maza, E. Stern (eds) *Mediterranean Peoples in Transition: In Honor of Professor Trude Dothan*, Jerusalem: Israel Exploration Society, pp. 17–65.

—— (1999) 'Mycenaeans and Hittites in War in Western Asia Minor', in R. Laffineur (ed.) *Polemos: Le Contexte Guerrier en Égée à l'Âge du Bronze* (Actes de la 7è Rencontre égéenne internationale, Université de Liège, 14–17 April, 1998), *Aegaeum* 19, Liège: University of Liège, Austin, Tex.: University of Texas Press, pp. 141–55.

Niemeier, W.-D. and B. Niemeier (1998) 'Minoan Frescoes in the Eastern Mediterranean', in E. H. Cline and D. Harris-Cline (eds) *The Aegean and the Orient in the Second Millennium*. Proceedings of the 50th Anniversary Symposium, Cincinnati, 18–20 April, 1997, *Aegaeum* 18, Liège: University of Liège and Austin, Tex.: University of Texas Press, pp. 69–98.

Otten, H. (1973) *Eine althethitische Erzählung um die Stadt Zalpa* (*Studien zu den Boğazköy–Texten* 17), Wiesbaden: Harrassowitz.

—— (1988) *Die Bronzetafel aus Boğazköy: ein Staatsvertrag Tuthalijas IV*, Wiesbaden: Harrassowitz.

Parker, V. (1999) 'Die Aktivitäten der Mykenäer in der Ostägäis im Lichte der Linear B Tafeln', in S. Deger-Jalkotzy, S. Hiller, O. Panagl (eds) *Floreant Studia Mycenaea*, Vol. II, Akten des X. Internationalen Mykenologischen Colloquiums in Salzburg vom 1–5 Mai, 1995. Vienna: Österreichische Akademie der Wissenschaften, pp. 495–502.

Peschlow-Bindokat, A. and S. Herbordt (2001) 'Eine hethitische Gross-prinzeninschrift aus dem Latmos', *Archäologischer Anzeiger*: 363–78.

Powell, B. B. (2004) *Homer*, Oxford: Blackwell.

Pulak, C. (2000) 'The Copper and Tin Ingots from the Late Bronze Age Shipwreck at Uluburun', in *Anatolian Metal I*, Montanhistorische Zeitschrift Der Anschnitt Beiheft 13, U Yalçin (ed.) = Bochum: Veröffentichungen aus dem Deutschen Bergbau-Museum, Nr. 92, 137–57.

Raaflaub, K. (1997) 'Homer, the Trojan War, and History', in D. Boedeker (ed.) *The World of Homer, Schliemann, and the Treasures of Priam*, Washington, DC: Society for the Preservation of the Greek Heritage, pp. 33–43. Reprinted in *Classical World* May/June 1998: 91/5 pp. 76–97.

Rehak, P. (1998) 'Aegean Natives in the Theban Tomb Paintings', in E. H. Cline and D. Harris-Cline (eds) *The Aegean and the Orient in the Second Millennium*. Proceedings of the 50th Anniversary Symposium, Cincinnati, 18–20 April, 1997, *Aegaeum* 18, Liège: University of Liège and Austin, Tex.: University of Texas Press, pp. 39–50.

Robinson, M. (1994) 'Pioneer, Scholar, and Victim: An Appreciation of Frank Calvert', *Anatolian Studies* 44: 153–68.

—— (1995) 'Frank Calvert and the Discovery of Troia', *Studia Troica* V: 323–41.

Rose, C.B. (1992) 'The 1991 Post-Bronze Age Excavations at Troia', *Studia Troica* II: 43–60.

Sage, M. (2000) 'Roman Visitors to Ilium in the Roman Imperial and Late Antique Period: the Symbolic Functions of a Landscape', in *Studia Troica* X: 211–31.

Sandars, N. K. (1985) *The Sea Peoples*, London: Thames & Hudson.

Sasson, J. M. (ed.) (1995), *Civilizations of the Ancient Near East* (4 vols.), New York: Charles Scribner's Sons.

Shelmerdine, C. W. (1999) 'A Comparative Look at Mycenaean Administration(s)', in S. Deger-Jalkotzy, S. Hiller, O. Panagl (eds) *Floreant Studia Mycenaea*, vol. II (Akten des X. Internationalen Mykenologischen Colloquiums in Salzburg vom 1–5 Mai, 1995), Vienna: Österreichische Akademie der Wissenschaften, pp. 555–76.

Sommer, F. (1932) *Die Ahhijavā–Urkunden*, Munich: Bayerischen Akademie der Wissenschaften, repr. Hildesheim, 1975.

Starke, F. (1990) *Untersuchung zur Stammbildung des keilschrift–luwischen Nomens* (*Studien zu den Boğazköy–Texten* 31), Wiesbaden: Harrassowitz.

—— (1997) 'Troia im Kontext des historischen-politischen und sprachlichen Umfeldes Kleinasiens in 2 Jahrtausend', *Studia Troica* VII: 447–87.

Tekkök, B. (2000) 'The City Wall of Ilion: New Evidence for Dating', *Studia Troica* X: 85–95.

Traill, D. A. (1995) *Schliemann of Troy: Treasure and Deceit*, London: Penguin.

Vermeule, E. D. T. (1972) *Greece in the Bronze Age*, Chicago, Ill. and London: University of Chicago Press.

—— (1986) '"Priam's Castle Blazing" A Thousand Years of Trojan Memories', in M. J. Mellink (ed.) *Troy and the Trojan War: Proceedings of a Symposium held at Bryn Mawr College, October 1984*, Bryn Mawr: Bryn Mawr College, pp. 77–92.

Vermeule III, C. C. (1995) 'Neon Ilion and Ilium Novum: Kings, Soldiers, Citizens and Tourists at Classical Troy', in J. B. Carter and S. P. Morris (eds) *The Ages of Homer: A Tribute to Emily Townsend Vermeule*, Austin, Tex.: University of Texas Press, pp. 467–80.

Watkins, C. (1986) 'The Language of the Trojans', in M. J. Mellink (ed.) *Troy and the Trojan War: Proceedings of a Symposium held at Bryn Mawr College, October 1984*, Bryn Mawr: Bryn Mawr College, pp. 45–62.

West, M. L. (1995) 'The Date of the Ilias', *Museum Helveticum* 52: 203–19.

Westenholz, J. G. (1997) *Legends of the Kings of Akkade*, Winona Lake, Ind.: Eisenbrauns.

Willcock, M. W. (1976) *A Companion to the Iliad*, Chicago, Ill. and London: University of Chicago Press.

Wood, M. (1996) *In Search of the Trojan War*, London: British Broadcasting Corporation (revised paperback 1985 edn).

Wright, J. C. (1997) 'The Place of Troy among the Civilizations of the Bronze Age', in D. Boedeker (ed.) *The World of Homer, Schliemann, and the Treasures of Priam*, Washington, DC: Society for the Preservation of the Greek Heritage, pp. 33–43. Reprinted in *Classical World* May/June 1998: 91/5 357–68.

Yakar, J. (1976) 'Hittite Involvement in Western Anatolia', *Anatolian Studies* 26: 117–28.

Zengel, E. (1990) 'Troy', in *Troy, Mycenae, Tiryns, Orchomenos. Heinrich Schliemann: The 100th Anniversary of his Death*, Athens: Greek Ministry of Culture, 51–77.

INDEX

Bold figures indicate main references.

References to Anatolia, Homer, the *Iliad*, Troy and the Trojans occur throughout the book, and citations of them here are confined to select references.

215

INDEX

Amnisus (port of Cnossus) 90
Amulius (Latin king) 168–9
Amurru (Syrian kingdom) 185
Amydon (legendary Paeonian city) 138
'Analysts' school of thought on Homer
10
Anatolia 44–7, 77–86, 161, 163; Early
Bronze Age kingdoms 49; Middle
Bronze Age kingdoms 54–5, 56;
Late Bronze Age kingdoms 77–86
Anatolian Grey Ware *see* under pottery
Anchises (father of Aeneas) 30, 166,
173, 174
Andromache (wife of Hector) 58, 59,
191
Anitta (king of Nesa) 55, 56
Ankara (Turkish capital) 46, 78, 141
Ankuwa (Anatolian city) 46
Annals (of Ennius) 169, 170
Antigonus (one of Alexander's heirs)
205 n. 13
Antiochus I (Seleucid king) 164
Antiochus III (Seleucid king) 164–5
Antiochus Hierax (member of Seleucid
dynasty) 163
Antipater (one of Alexander's heirs)
163
Antoninus Liberalis (Greek
mythographer) 145
Antony, Mark (Roman politician) 166,
171, 173
Apamea, Peace of 164, 177
Apasa (capital of Arzawa 'Minor') 77,
83–4, 114, 120, 132
Aphaea-Artemis, temple of (Aegina) 24
Aphrodite (Greek goddess) 1–2, 19,
166, 178
Apollo (Greek god) 4, 6, 60, 119, 137,
141, 145, 166, 174
Apollodorus (Greek writer) 147
[…]appaliuna (Anatolian deity) 119
Appian (Greek historian) 165
Arcadia (mainland Greek region) 168
Arctinus (Greek poet) 131
Argolid (mainland Greek region) 47,
91, 94, 96, 97, 103
Argos (Greek city) 96
Arinna (Hittite city) 46
Aristarchus (Alexandrian scholar) 28
armada against Troy 2, 25

Arñna (Lycian city = Bronze Age
Awarna, Class. Xanthus) 81–2, 145,
146, 148, 150
arrival of Greeks (in Greek mainland)
92, 93, 94
Artemis (Greek goddess) 2, 145
Arthurian legend cycle 181
Arzawa lands (Anatolian region) 76,
83–6, 107, 108, 109, 116, 117–18,
120, 121, 144
Arzawa 'Minor' (Anatolian kingdom)
76, 83, 84, 104, 108, 113, 120, 176
Ascanius (son of Aeneas) 30, 169, 171,
173
Assur (Assyrian capital) 54
Assuwa (Anatolian region) 108
Assuwan confederacy 108, 109, 118,
148
Assyria (Mesopotamian kingdom) 72,
73, 97, 110, 129
Assyrian merchants and colonies 46,
54–5, 124
Astyanax (son of Hector) 191
Athena (Greek goddess) 1–2, 155, 163,
164, 165, 177–8; temple in
Troy/Ilion 59, 158, 160, 167, 176,
191
Athens (Greek city) 96, 131, 153–4
Atlantic Ocean 162
Atlantis (mythical land) 193
Atpa (governor of Milawata) 184
Attaleia (Hellenistic city) 163
Attalid dynasty 163
Attalus I (king of Pergamum) 163
Attarssiya ('Man of Ahhiy(aw)a') 101–2
Attica (mainland Greek region) 96
audiences (of Homeric epics) **16–21**
Augustus (Roman emperor; earlier,
Octavian) 166, 167, **170–4**, 191
Aulis (mainland Greek city) 2, 25, 26
Avaris (Egyptian city; mod. Tell el-
Dab'a) 70, 89
Awarna *see* Arñna
Axius (river) 138
Ayasuluk (Anatolian site; probably =
Apasa) 84
Azzi-Hayasa (Anatolian kingdom) 80

Babylon (Mesopotamian city) 22, 40,
72, 114

INDEX

Related titles from Routledge

Mycenaeans
Life in Bronze Age Greece

Rodney Castleden

Following on from Castleden's best-selling study Minoans,
this major new contribution to our understanding of the
crucial Mycenaean period clearly and effectively brings
together research and knowledge we have accumulated
since the discovery of the remains of the civilization of
Mycenae in the 1870s.

In lively prose, informed by the latest research and using a full
bibliography and over 100 illustrations, this vivid study delivers
the fundamentals of Mycenaean civilization including its
culture, hierarchy, economy and religion. Castleden introduces
controversial views of the Mycenaean palaces as temples, and
studies their impressive sea empire and their crucial interaction
with the outside Bronze Age world, before discussing the causes
of the end of their civilization.

Providing clear, easy information and understanding, this is a
perfect starting point for the study of the Greek Bronze Age.

Hb: 0–415–24923–6
Pb: 0–415–36336–5

Available at all good bookshops
For ordering and further information please visit:
www.routledge.com